On Thoughts and Aphorisms

THE MOTHER

The Mother

On Thoughts and Aphorisms

Sri Aurobindo Ashram, Pondicherry

First edition 1977
Second edition 1998
Third impression 2012

Rs 220
ISBN 978-81-7058-528-2

© Sri Aurobindo Ashram Trust 1977, 1998
Published by Sri Aurobindo Ashram Publication Department
Pondicherry 605 002
Web http://www.sabda.in

Printed at Sri Aurobindo Ashram Press, Pondicherry
PRINTED IN INDIA

Publisher's Note

The Mother's commentaries on Sri Aurobindo's *Thoughts and Aphorisms* were given over the twelve-year period from 1958 to 1970. The commentaries may be divided into four periods according to date, character and form.

    1. Aphorisms 1–12 (1958). Oral replies to questions submitted beforehand in writing by the students, teachers and sadhaks of the Ashram during the Mother's Wednesday classes at the Ashram Playground.

    2. Aphorisms 13–68 (1960–61). Replies, mostly written, a few oral, to questions written to the Mother by a young instructor of the Ashram's physical education department.

    3. Aphorisms 69–124 (1962–66). Oral replies to a disciple. During this period the Mother digressed more and more from direct commentary on the aphorisms and used the occasions to explain the experiences she was having at the time.

    4. Aphorisms 125–541 (1969–70). Brief written replies to questions asked by the instructor mentioned above.

All the Mother's commentaries were spoken or written in French. She also translated Sri Aurobindo's text into French. Her translations of and commentaries on the first twelve aphorisms were published in 1959 under the title *Pensées et Aphorismes: Traduits et Commentés par la Mère*. The remaining translations and commentaries were serialised in French and English in the quarterly *Bulletin of Sri Aurobindo International Centre of Education* between April 1960 and August 1976. A complete edition of the French text, entitled *Pensées et Aphorismes: Traduits et Commentés par la Mère*, was published in two tomes in 1974 and 1976. The first complete edition in English appeared in 1977 as Volume Ten of the Collected Works of the

Mother. The present edition is a reprint of this volume with a few minor corrections.

Sri Aurobindo's *Thoughts and Aphorisms* was written around 1913 during the early part of his stay in Pondicherry. Never revised or published during his lifetime, the aphorisms were first brought out in 1958 under the three headings established by the author: Jnana (Knowledge), Karma (Works) and Bhakti (Devotion).

When the original manuscript of *Thoughts and Aphorisms* was examined preparatory to the publication of a new edition of the English text in 1977, several erroneous readings were found in the text of the first edition; this was the edition used by the Mother in making her translation and commentaries. These errors, mostly minor, have been corrected in this volume. A note has been given wherever the corrected reading is not in line with the Mother's comment.

Contents

JNANA (Knowledge)
First period of commentaries (1958)

Aphorism

1	Knowledge and Wisdom: allied powers	1
	"The truth seen in a distorted medium"	2
	Truth compared to white light	3
2	Inspiration: a slender river of brightness	3
	Inspiration, reason and the senses	5
	"How to develop the capacity for inspiration?"	6
	Best method to profit from Sri Aurobindo's writings	7
3	Reason trembles before higher truths	7
	Supramental revolution	9
4	Knowledge and work	9
	Silence of perfect receptivity	10
5	Obstacles to realisation	10
	Fear, doubt and scepticism	11
	Nature's way of progressing	12
6	Mind receives shock from aphorisms	14
	Role of reason	14
	Danger of abandoning reason	15
	True wisdom	16
7	What men call knowledge	17
	Appearances and "reversal of consciousness"	18
	"How to have the experience?"	19
8	Intolerance of religions	20
	Mechanism of intolerance	21
	Experience, individual and universal	21
	Relationships are like a mirror	22
	True perfection in oneself	23
9	"How do we know what the soul sees?"	23
	Mind and vital: obstacles to the soul	24
	Hearing the soul	25
10	Only the soul can know the soul	26
	What would make humanity progress most	27

Contents

11	"What is the mental personality?"	27
	What Sri Aurobindo calls Immortality	28
	Conditions for indefinite survival of body	28
	Perfection of psychic personality and body	29
	Physical culture	30
	Sadhana of the body	31
12	You can prove anything with the mind	32
	Supreme has a sense of humour	33
	Best way to learn more	34
	Grace and seeing	35

JNANA (Knowledge)
Second period of commentaries (1960–61)

13	Hallucinations	39
	"The miracles of human reason"	39
14	Hallucination: term of Science	40
	"Coincidence"	40
15	Hallucination and vision	41
16	Planes of the mind	42
17	Identification with Divine	43
	Physical mind and knowledge of God	44
18	Idea of illusion is itself an illusion	44
	World is real; perception of it is false	45
19	Does reason alone see things as ugly?	45
	Relativity of beauty and ugliness	46
20	Beauty of the hideous	46
21	Forgiveness and the Divine	47
22–23	"God gave me a good blow"	47
	Nothing and no one to forgive	48
24	Origin of misfortune	48
25	Wisdom and suffering	49
26	Everything happens by the Grace of the Lord	50
27	"To play with Krishna"	51
	God as Torturer	51
28	War and evolution	52
	Descent of Supermind and war	53
29	Divine and personal will	53
30	Purity of instinct and the mental ego	54

Contents

31	Progress and despair	55
	Experience of a life of failure	56
32	The Atheist is God	57
33	Divine perfection and receiving blows	57
34	The blessing of misfortune	58
35–36	Christ and Krishna	59
	Men cherish suffering and hatred	59
37	Existence of Brindavan and Krishna	60
38	Evolution and the death of Christ	61
	Christ as Avatar	61
39	History and legend	62
40	Four great events in history	62
	"The colloquy at Kurukshetra will yet liberate humanity"	63
41	Role of the Gospels	64
42	Existence of heaven and hell	64
	Hell as a state of consciousness	65
43	Contradiction intensifies aspiration	65
44	Creation of falsehood on the mental plane	66
45	Role of logic and reason	67
46	Sri Aurobindo's experience in prison	68
47	Conquest and transformation of the mind	69
48	"The beauty of the hideous"	69
	Words and experience	70
49	Curing evil and ugliness	70
	True collaboration	72
	Love and transformation	72
	Spreading love	72
	Secret of the divine incarnation	73
	Receptivity of divine love	74
50	Not a single sin that is not our sin	74
	Collective human psychological consciousness	75
	Sin is something not in its right place	76
	Revolt is the feeling of an impotent will	77
	Meaning of omnipotence	77
	Hatred of the virtuous	78
51	Nature of self-deception	79
	Anger is a deformation of vital power	81
	Giving favourable explanations to all movements	81
52	Philanthropy and service of the Divine	82
	Love of Divine and man	82

Contents

53–54		Religions and immortality	83
		Physical immortality	84
	55	Kali and supreme Realisation	84
	56	Knowledge and debate	85
		Proving what one feels to be true	85
	57	The truly natural state for man	86
		Mind and individualisation	87
	58	The Mother's memory of earthly paradise	88
		Symbol of the tree of knowledge	89
		First human forms	90
		Evolution and the fall	91
		Story of the serpent	92
		Jehovah as the supreme Asura	92
		Spoiling of earth's atmosphere	94
	59	Giving a beating to God	94
		Nature of idols	95
		Teaching of Sri Aurobindo and religion	95
	60	Memory of past lives	96
		Development of the individual	97
	61	Experience of the Infinite	97
	62	Folly is distorted mask of Truth	98
		No absolute falsehood	98
		"The destruction of a universe"	98
		Beyond Nirvana and Existence	100
63–65		The weakness of God	100
		Idea of "God the Creator"	102
		Nothing other than God	102
		The Divine Play	103
		Perfection	104
		Ways of approaching the Divine	104
	66	Cruelty as an expression of the Divine	105
		Sadism and tamas	106
		Ananda and cruelty	106
		Pralayas of various universes	106
		Equilibrium and perfection	107
		Supermind puts things in their place	107
67–68		Sin and the ego	108

Contents

JNANA (Knowledge)
Third Period of Commentaries (1962 – 66)

69	Capacity to express the supramental world	111
	Equality and the supramental	112
	Two conditions for supramental realisation	113
	Problem of physical transformation	113
	Will of the Self	114
	Supramental life and the mind	115
	Individualisation	117
	Widening the body	117
	Occult creation of new body	117
70	Role of adverse forces in creation	118
	Offering of the earth consciousness	119
	Consciousness of supreme Love	119
	Origin of Falsehood	120
	Do not try to be among the pure	121
71	Thought and Truth	121
	Seeing the Truth in its entirety	122
	Mind always sees successively	122
72	Premonitory dreams	123
	The subtle physical and the material plane	125
	Seeing others in the subtle physical	125
	Sources of vision	126
	Universal mental vision	126
	Sincerity and the power of prediction	127
	Changing events in the subtle physical	128
	Experiences of extended consciousness	129
	Methods of developing subtle senses	131
	Seeing at a distance	132
73	Wisdom and knowledge	133
74 – 75	Inadequacy of scientific and spiritual approach	134
	Door to the total Knowledge	135
	More than one Avatar needed for supramental realisation	137
	The Mother's vision of physical world	138
	Four dimensional world is superficial	138
76	Destruction of Europe by a child	139
	Aphorism contains true prediction	140
77 – 78	Knowledge by inspiration	141
	Knowledge and transformation	142

Contents

	Transformation of the body	143
	Organs replaced by chakras	144
79–80	There is no error	145
	A thing is and is not at the same time	146
	Play of the Lord	146
	Man makes play tragic	147
	World of the "living" and the "dead"	147
	Worry and the play	148
	Error and infinite possibility	149
	Way to get out of tragedy	150
	Dealing with the old consciousness	151
	Physical presence of the Lord	152
	Vibration that contains everything	153
81–83	God's laughter	154
	God never takes his works seriously	154
	Virtue and perfection	155
	Limitations of taking life seriously	155
	Only way to make life perfect	155
	Dissolving suffering and pain	156
	Avoid people who take life seriously	156
	We must learn how to play	157
84–87	What men call miracles	157
	Sri Aurobindo performed miracles in the mind	159
	What would be a true miracle?	160
	Miracle belongs only to the finite world	161
	Thirst for the marvellous	162
	Miracles and aspiration	163
88–92	Nature of opposites	164
	Opposition and progress	165
	Bringing creation out of inertia	166
	Simplicity	167
93	Pain is the touch of our Mother	168
	Teaching the body to bear pain	169
	Pain and fear	169
94	The Mother's experience of renunciation	170
	Progress and the power of dissolution	171
	Renunciation and self-centred consciousness	172
	Rapture and power	173
	Rapturous state of consciousness is dangerous	173
95	Perfect renunciation and satisfaction of desire	174
	Vibrations of desire and the divine Will	175
	Lack of receptivity and desire	176

Contents

	Difference of vibratory quality	176
	Physical is a field of vibrations	177
	Response of cells to supreme Force	178
	Perception of the totality of vibrations	179
	Action, desire and the vibration of Will	179
96	Scriptures are diminution of experience	180
97	Truth and individual experience	181
98	Revelation is the memory of Truth	181
	Revelation is always personal in form	182
	Experience, idea and words	182
	Explosion of truth-power	183
99–100	Understanding and Scriptures	184
101–102	Sun-consciousness and earth-consciousness	185
	Truth-Consciousness and appearance of world	186
	Only way to change the world	187
	Consciousness of the Lord	187
	Perfect sense of Oneness	189
	"Relation of consciousness"	189
	Intervention of the vibration of harmony	190
	Action of the Truth-Consciousness	191
	Falsehood replaced by Light	192
103–107	Vivekananda and Sannyasa	193
	To be free from all attachment	194
	Fear of being mistaken	195
	Renunciation and elimination	195
	Modern hyper-activity	197
	Why the Ashram was created	197
	Aspiration more intense in the outer world	198
	Man needs extremes	199
	Manifestation of divine Love	199
	Power of *pure* Love	200
	Aspire intensely, but without impatience	200
	Haste in which men live	201
	Sincere realisation	202
108	Narada and Janaka	202
	Gods have no psychic being	202
	Shiva will come with the supramental world	203
	Man alone possesses a psychic being	203
109	Sri Aurobindo is a part of the Lord	204
	Falsehood of the creation	204
110	Wonders of physical science and the soul	205
	Science cannot predict the future	206

Contents

	Power of the soul over Matter	207
	Experience and understanding	208
	Perceiving the new	209
	The refusal to know	210
111–112	Power of silence	211
	Acceptance of the apparent denial of Truth	212
	Demand for the Divine to show his power	213
113–114	Vibration of hate and love are the same	213
	Purity of the central vibration	214
	Morality is a choice between distortions	215
115–116	"There is no end and no beginning"	216
	"Memory of eternity"	217
	Life of the earth	218
	Consciousness and limits	219
	Human mind needs to build a dwelling-place	220
	"Error" of material world was indispensable	221
	There is no manifestation without progress	222
	Consciousness of the dead on earth	223
	Seeing and hearing by consciousness	224
	"Are you ready for anything?"	225
	Consciousness of the body	226
	Perfection of sight and hearing	227
	Action of human will on the Mother's body	228
117–121	An irresistable Power governing everything	228
	Nature of Will from above	230
	Resistance and divine Action	231
	How the Force acts	232
	Stopping the resistance	233
122–124	Nature of opinion	233
	Action and opinion	234
	Conditions for intervening in someone's action	235
	How opinions are formed	236

JNANA (Knowledge)
Fourth Period of Commentaries (1969)

125–126	Overcoming the laws of Nature	241
127	Psychic being and the laws of Nature	241
128–129	"The nature which exceeds the body"	242

Contents

130	The role of human aspiration and effort	242
131–132	Disappearance of all human moral notions	243
133	Titans are stronger than the gods	243
134–136	Suffering and delight	244
137	Pleasure and pain depend on inner attitude	245
138	Relationships and psychic contacts	245
139	Who is the superman?	246
140	Human ego and the superman	246
141	The qualities of the superman	247
142	Qualities needed for growth of being	247
143–144	Art reveals what Nature hides	248
	Photography and modern art	248
145	The secret soul of Nature	248
146–150	Shakespeare, the universalist	249
	Action by contrast and negation	250
151	Proof and coincidence	250
	Refusal to learn	251
152–153	Material, immaterial and supramental consciousness	251
154–156	Mind and creation	252
157–158	Sri Aurobindo: "the last Avatar"	253
159	Worship of gods and goddesses	253
160–161	Knowledge and delight	254
	"Intellectual culture"	254
162	Out of man the superman emerges	254
163–164	Law and freedom	255
165	Self-imposed discipline	256
166	The law of sin and virtue	256
	Law and progress	257
167	Ignorance and the Divine goal	258
168–169	The symbol of the Cross in Yoga	258
170–171	Failure of Christ and Mahomed	259
172	Freedom, desire, ignorance and egoism	259
173–174	The human way of understanding	260
175	Meaning of failure	261
176–177	The perfect cosmic vision	261
178	The prison is the ego	262
179	To live for God	263
180	Experiencing eternity	263
181–182	The less you speak the better	264
183–184	Perfection and harmony	264
185–186	Consciousness beyond good and bad	265

Contents

187–188	Vice and virtue used for evolution	265
189–191	Attitude towards poverty	266
192	Individual classed according to his nature	266
193–196	Poverty and society	267
	Ideal of the Ashram and Auroville	268
197–198	Conditions for happiness	269
199–200	Effective remedy for human egoism	269
201–202	Messages to man	270
203–204	Conditions for greatest progress of humanity	271
205	The first step of the superman	271

KARMA (Works)
Fourth period of commentaries (1969–70)

206	Escape from the consequences of past errors	275
207	Escape from evil and suffering	275
208–209	Ego and beatitude	276
	Self-forgetfulness and self-giving	276
210–211	Anger and vengeance	276
212	Only tragedy: failure to find one's soul	277
213	Tragedy and evolution	277
214–215	Nature of genius	278
216	Inspiration and madness	278
217	Mastering and conquering violence	279
218–221	Unity of mankind	279
222–224	Qualities of a converted Asura	280
225–227	Altruism can kill the soul	280
228–230	God's command to slay	281
231–234	Virtues	281
235–237	Instruments and prisons of the soul	282
238–240	Humanity advances by great and noble failures	283
241–242	Atheism and religion	283
243–247	God and temptation	284
	Giving oneself completely to the Divine	285
248–250	Becoming conscious of the Divine Will	285
251	Only choice to be made	286
252–254	God is circling about	286
255–257	"Blind faith"	287
258–261	Reason, faith and instinct	288

Contents

	Goal of the spiritual life	289
262–264	Perceiving the Divine Command	289
265–269	Motives for action	290
270–271	Persistence in effort	291
272–273	Truth is a difficult conquest	291
274–276	Value of asceticism	292
277–278	Soul and action	292
279	Total consecration to the Divine	293
280–281	Soul and the alleviation of suffering	293
282	Purity and action	294
283–285	Sorrow and evolution	294
286–288	Man's possibility of union with the Supreme	295
289–290	To radiate love in all circumstances	295
291–292	Human judgments	296
293–294	Three varieties of self-deceit	296
295–296	World is capable of manifesting the Divine	297
297–298	Beauty and ugliness	298
299–302	Living according to the Truth	298
303–305	Women and spirituality	299
306	Asceticism and action in the world	300
307	God laughed at Shankara	300
308–310	Essential qualities develop through suffering	300
311–312	Attitude towards transformation	301
313–314	Wisdom lies in the union of opposites	301
315–316	All carry in their souls the divine end	302
317–318	Everything exists from all eternity	302
319	The will of Brahman	303
320–321	Anarchic state: true divine state of man	303
322–324	Successful communism	304
	Vedanta and communism	304
325–326	"Freedom, equality, brotherhood" and the ego	304
327–328	Perfection of the individual and society	305
329–331	Greatness of an action	306
332–334	National and human unity	307
335–336	Sri Aurobindo's work and human unity	307
337–338	Artist: imitator and creator	308
339	The Divine is beyond good and evil	308
340	Reaction perfects and hastens progress	309
341–343	Democracy, Socialism and Anarchism	309
	All human governments are a falsehood	310
344–345	Perfection of soul and outer environment	310
346–348	True saintliness	310

Contents

349–351	Knowing God's will	311
	"The soul that is naked and unashamed"	311
352–356	Truth is above all opposites	312
357	True governor of humanity	312
358–361	Effects of the supramental consciousness	313
362	India and religious conventions	314
363–369	Sincerity: condition for hearing the Lord	315
370–373	Grace leads whatever you do	316
374–376	Death and the ego	317
	"Someone who belongs to the Divine"	318
377–378	Liberation from the ego	318
379–381	Excess in any direction is a violence	319
382	Medicines and natural health	320
383–385	The barbarism of modern humanity	320

Disease and Medical Science

386–389	Disease and the mind	321
	The healing power of Grace	322
390–393	The role of mind and faith in medicine	322
394–399	Divine health and disease	323
400–403	Mental faith in drugs	324
404–407	Medicine and the body	325

BHAKTI (Devotion)
Fourth period of commentaries (1969–70)

408–412	Knowing God as a woman	329
413	To commit adultery with God	330
414–420	The joy of being God's enemy	330
421–424	"The four stages of pain"	332
425–427	Love for only the Divine	333
428	Love for Krishna and Kali	333
429–430	Enjoying Nature with the soul	334
431–434	God and the world	334
	Wisdom: capacity to admit all theories	335
435–438	The love of Krishna	335

Contents

439–444	God as lover	336
445–449	Sri Aurobindo reveals the secret of existence	337
450–455	Curing jealousy	338
456–461	God and Satan	339
462–463	The Divine's way of dealing with virtue	340
464–465	The world will manifest divine joy	340
466–468	The mind and God	341
469–471	Man must accept all as Grace	341
472	Beware of all mental constructions	342
473	The Divine accepts all sincere aspiration	343
474–475	God and hell	343
	Delight may be intolerable for humans	344
476	The seven beatitudes of life	344
477–479	Conditions for the world becoming heaven	344
480–481	Falsehood of ordinary human consciousness	345
482–483	Krishna stealing the robes of the Gopis	345
484	Krishna and sin	346
485–489	Realising true Unity	346
490–492	Keeping the Divine contact in all circumstances	347
493–494	Ways of seeing God	348
495–496	Value of suffering and pain	349
497–499	Pain: the training of delight	349
	One true wisdom	350
500–503	Role of suffering and pain	350
504	Divine Love needed in our sorrowful age	351
505	Science, the God-lover and God-knower	351
506	To be able to laugh at this world	351
507	Human science and occultism	352
508	The Mother's experience concerning transformation of the body	352
509–512	True way to understand the Scriptures	353
513–514	Service to the Divine	353
515–516	Doing good to human beings	354
	Liberation from all conventional morality	354
517–518	Weakness and the Divine	355
519	The Titan's four strides to immortality	355
520	Understanding the universe	356
521	Perceiving the Divine	356
522–523	Suffering and bliss	356
524	The soul, mind and pain	357
525–526	Compassion and the Divine Consciousness	357
527–528	Love and pity	358

Contents

529–530	Compassion and pity	358
531–533	Constancy in effort and faith	358
534	Love, human and divine	359
535	"Divine mind"	360
536–537	One drop of true knowledge can create a revolution	360
538	The essence and potency of Maya	361
539–540	Seeing God in Huxley and Haeckel	361
541	Seeing God in the torturer and the slayer	362

Jnana

(Knowledge)

First Period of Commentaries

(1958)

Jnana (Knowledge)

It is no use reading books of guidance if one is not determined to live what they teach.

Blessings
The Mother

1 – There are two allied powers in man: knowledge and Wisdom. Knowledge is so much of the truth, seen in a distorted medium, as the mind arrives at by groping; Wisdom what the eye of divine vision sees in the spirit.

Someone has asked me, "Why are the powers allied?"

I suppose that we are so used to seeing all the elements in man quarrelling among themselves that the idea of their being "allied" causes astonishment. But these quarrels are only apparent. All the powers which come from the higher regions are in fact necessarily allied — they are united, they have agreed to fight the Ignorance. And Sri Aurobindo says clearly enough — for those who understand — that one of these powers belongs to the mind and that the other belongs to the Spirit. This is precisely the profound truth that Sri Aurobindo wants to reveal in his aphorism: if the mind tries to obtain the second power, it is unable to do so, since it is a power that belongs to the Spirit and arises in the human being together with the spiritual consciousness.

Knowledge is something that the mind can obtain through much effort, although this is not the true knowledge, but only a mental aspect of knowledge; whereas Wisdom does not at all belong to the mind, which is altogether incapable of obtaining it, because, in fact, it doesn't even know what it is. I repeat, Wisdom is essentially a power of the Spirit and it can arise only with the spiritual consciousness.

It would have been interesting to ask what Sri Aurobindo

means when he speaks of "the truth seen in a distorted medium". First of all, what is this "distorted medium", and what does the truth become in a "distorted medium"?

As always, what Sri Aurobindo says can have several levels of meaning — one is more specific, the other more general. In the most specific sense, the distorted medium is the mental medium which works in ignorance and which is therefore unable to express truth in its purity. But since life as a whole is lived in ignorance, the distorted medium is also the earth-atmosphere which, in its entirety, distorts the truth seeking to express itself through it.

And here lies the most subtle point of this aphorism. What can the mind arrive at by groping? We know that it is always groping, seeking to know, erring, returning upon its previous attempts and trying again... Its progress is very, very halting. But what can it grasp of the truth? Is it a fragment, a piece, something which is still the truth, but only partially, incompletely, or is it something which is no longer the truth? That is the interesting point.

We are used to being told — perhaps we have also repeated many times — that one can only have partial, incomplete, fragmentary knowledge which therefore cannot be true knowledge. This point of view is rather trite: one need only to have studied a little in life to be aware of it. However, what Sri Aurobindo means by "the truth seen in a distorted medium" is far more interesting than that.

Truth itself takes on another aspect; in this medium it is no longer the truth, but a distortion of the truth. Consequently, what can be seized of it is not a fragment which would be true, but an aspect, the false appearance of a truth which has itself melted away.

I am going to give you an image to try to make myself understood; it is nothing more than an image, do not take it literally.

If we compare the essential truth to a sphere of immaculate, dazzling white light, we can say that in the mental medium, in the mental atmosphere, this integral white light is transformed into thousands and thousands of shades, each of which has its own distinct colour, because they are all separated from one another. The medium distorts the white light and makes it appear as innumerable different colours: red, green, yellow, blue, etc., which are sometimes very discordant. And the mind seizes, not a little fragment of the white light of the white sphere, but a larger or smaller number of little lights of various colours, with which it cannot even reconstitute the white light. Therefore it cannot reach the truth. It does not possess fragments of truth, but a truth that is broken up. It is a state of decomposition.

The truth is a whole and everything is necessary. The distorted medium through which you see, the mental atmosphere, is unsuited for the manifestation or the expression or even the perception of all the elements — and one can say that the better part is lost. So it can no longer be called the truth, but rather something which in essence is true, and yet no longer so at all in the mental atmosphere — it is an ignorance.

So, to summarise, I shall say that knowledge, as it can be grasped by the human mind, is necessarily knowledge in ignorance, one could almost say an ignorant knowledge.

Wisdom is the vision of truth in its essence and of its application in the manifestation.

12 September 1958

2 – Inspiration is a slender river of brightness leaping from a vast and eternal knowledge; it exceeds reason more perfectly than reason exceeds the knowledge of the senses.

A certain number of the questions you have asked are alike: "Why did Sri Aurobindo say it like this?" — one thing or another.

On Thoughts and Aphorisms

I could reply, "He said it like this because he saw it like this." But, to begin with, one thing should be understood; these are definitions given by Sri Aurobindo, definitions which he gives mostly in a paradoxical form to compel us to think.

There are dictionary definitions, which are the ordinary explanations of words as they are commonly understood. These do not make you think. What Sri Aurobindo says, however, is said in order to break up the usual conception, to bring you in touch with a deeper truth. In this way a whole lot of questions are eliminated.

The effort one must make is to try to find the deeper knowledge, the deeper truth that Sri Aurobindo has expressed in this way, which is not the usual way of defining a word.

I shall select some questions: the first one, which interested me because it comes from a thoughtful person, concerns the word "knowledge" and compares the way Sri Aurobindo has used the word in this aphorism with the way he used it in the aphorism we read last week.

When, in last week's aphorism, Sri Aurobindo opposed — as one might say — "knowledge" to "Wisdom", he was speaking of knowledge as it is lived in the average human consciousness, the knowledge which is obtained through effort and mental development, whereas here, on the contrary, the knowledge he speaks of is the essential Knowledge, the supramental divine Knowledge, Knowledge by identity. And this is why he describes it here as "vast and eternal", which clearly indicates that it is not human knowledge as we normally understand it.

Many people have asked why Sri Aurobindo said that the river is "slender". This is an expressive image which creates a striking contrast between the immensity of the divine, supramental Knowledge — the origin of this inspiration, which is infinite — and what a human mind can perceive of it and receive from it. Even when you are in contact with these domains, the portion, so to say, which you perceive, is minimal, slender. It is like a tiny little stream or a few falling drops and these drops are so pure, so brilliant, so complete in themselves, that they give you the sense of a marvellous inspiration, the impression that you have reached infinite domains and risen very high above the ordinary human condition. And yet this is nothing in comparison with what is still to be perceived.

I have also been asked if the psychic being or psychic consciousness is the medium through which the inspiration is perceived.

Generally, yes. The first contact you have with higher regions is a psychic one. Certainly, before an inner psychic opening is achieved, it is difficult to have these inspirations. It can happen as an exception and under exceptional conditions as a grace, but the true contact comes through the psychic; because the psychic consciousness is certainly the medium with the greatest affinity with the divine Truth.

Later, when one has emerged from the mental consciousness into a higher consciousness beyond the mind, beyond even the higher mind, and when one opens oneself to the Overmind regions, and through the Overmind to the Supermind, one can receive inspirations directly. And naturally at that point they become more frequent, richer, if one may say so, more complete. There comes a time when inspiration can be obtained at will, but this obviously demands considerable inner development.

As we have just said, this inspiration from regions far above the mind surpasses in value and quality the highest achievements of the mind, such as reason. Reason is certainly at the apex of human mental activity. It can review and control the knowledge acquired with the help of the senses. It has often been said that the senses are altogether defective instruments of knowledge, that they are incapable of perceiving things as they are, that the information they supply is superficial and very often faulty. When it is fully developed, the human reason knows this and does not trust the knowledge of the senses. It is only if one is infrarational, if I may say so, that one believes that all one sees, hears, or touches is absolutely true. As soon as one is developed

On Thoughts and Aphorisms

in the region of higher reason, one knows that all these notions are almost essentially false, and that one can in no way rely on them. But the knowledge one receives from this supramental or divine region surpasses all that can be conceived or understood by reason, at least to the same extent that reason surpasses the knowledge of the senses.

Several questions concern a practical point: "How to develop the capacity for inspiration?"; "What are the conditions needed to receive inspiration and is it possible to have it constantly?"

I have already replied to this. When one opens oneself to the supramental regions, one puts oneself in the right state for receiving constant inspirations. Until then, the best method is to silence the mind as much as possible, to turn it upwards and to remain in a state of silent and attentive receptivity. The more one is able to establish a silent, perfect calm in the mind, the more one becomes capable of receiving inspirations.

It was also asked whether inspirations are of different qualities.

In their origin, no. They always come down from the regions of pure Knowledge and penetrate whatever part of the human being is most receptive, best adapted to receive them — but these inspirations may apply to different domains of action. They can be inspirations of pure knowledge, they can also be inspirations that contribute to one's effort to progress, and they can also be inspirations for action which help in the practical and outer realisation. But the question here is the use one makes of the inspiration, rather than of the quality of the inspiration — the inspiration is always like a drop of light and truth which succeeds in penetrating the human consciousness.

What the human consciousness does with this drop depends on the attitude, the need, the occasion, the circumstances; it does not alter the essential nature of the inspiration but it does alter the use one makes of it, its practical application.

Some of the other questions concern the difference between

inspiration and intuition. They are not the same thing; but I think that we will have the opportunity of returning to this subject in the course of our reading. When Sri Aurobindo tells us what he considers intuition to be, we shall come back to it.

In a general and almost absolute way, if you truly wish to profit from these readings, as from all of Sri Aurobindo's writings, the best method is this: having gathered your consciousness and focused your attention on what you are reading, you must establish a minimum of mental tranquillity — the best thing would be to obtain perfect silence — and achieve a state of immobility of the mind, immobility of the brain, I might say, so that the attention becomes as still and immobile as a mirror, like the surface of absolutely still water. Then what one has read passes through the surface and penetrates deep into the being where it is received with a minimum of distortion. Afterwards — sometimes long afterwards — it wells up again from the depths and manifests in the brain with its full power of comprehension, not as knowledge acquired from outside, but as a light one carried within.

In this way the faculty of understanding is at its highest, whereas if, while you read, the mind remains agitated and tries to understand at once what it is reading, you lose more than three-quarters of the force, the knowledge and the truth contained in the words. And if you are able to refrain from asking questions until this process of absorption and inner awakening is completed, well, then you will find that you have far fewer questions to ask because you will have a better understanding of what you have read.

19 September 1958

3 – When I speak, the reason says, "This will I say"; but God takes the word out of my mouth and the lips say something else at which reason trembles.

On Thoughts and Aphorisms

When Sri Aurobindo says "I", he speaks of himself and of his own experience. We would like to be able to say that what he says is symbolic and that it could apply to many people, but unfortunately this is not so at all.

This experience, of not saying what you had meant to say when you speak, but something else, is very common; but it is the opposite of what Sri Aurobindo speaks of here. That is to say, when you are sitting calmly at home using your reason to its full extent, you decide to say this or that, that this is the reasonable thing, but all too often, when you begin to speak, it is the lower impulses, the unreasonable emotions and the vital reactions which take hold of the tongue and make you say things which you should not say.

Here it is the same phenomenon, but, as I said, the other way round. Instead of infrarational impulses which make you speak with excitement and passion, it is, on the contrary, an inspiration coming from above, a light and a knowledge greater than those of the reason which take hold of the tongue and make you say things that you would have been incapable of saying even with the most enlightened reason.

Sri Aurobindo tells us that "the reason trembles" because these higher truths always appear in the human domain as paradoxes, revelations contrary to reason; not because reason is incapable of understanding what comes from the higher regions, but because these revelations are always ahead of, very much ahead of, that which reason has understood or accepted. What the human reason of today finds reasonable has been paradoxical and mad in the past; and probably — one may say, certainly — these unexpected, paradoxical, revolutionary revelations which are manifesting now and making the reason tremble, will in time to come be very reasonable knowledge, which in turn will tremble before new revelations.

It is this sense of something which is always moving, progressing, being transformed, that Sri Aurobindo is trying to give us with these compact phrases which for a time shake our understanding of things. It is to push us forward, to give us the sense of the complete relativity of all that manifests in the world, and of this universe which is always in motion, ever moving towards a higher and greater Truth.

For us, right now, the supramental transformation is the expression of the highest truth, it is the revolution we must bring about on earth; and certainly this revolution must be felt as an absolute by the majority of human beings, otherwise they will not be able to bring it about. But Sri Aurobindo insists that we should not forget that this absolute is still relative and that any manifestation must always be relative with regard to an Absolute which is even more absolute — the Unmanifest that will manifest later.

26 September 1958

4 – I am not a Jnani,[1] for I have no knowledge except what God gives me for His work. How am I to know whether what I see be reason or folly? Nay, it is neither; for the thing seen is simply true and neither folly nor reason.

"I am not a Jnani..." The Jnani is one who follows the path of Knowledge, one who wants to realise Yoga exclusively through Knowledge, and who follows a purely intellectual path with the will to go beyond it and attain Knowledge, which is no longer intellectual, but spiritual. And Sri Aurobindo says: I am not a Jnani.... I do not seek knowledge. I have given myself to the Divine to accomplish His work and, by the divine Grace, at every moment I know what must be known in order to accomplish this work.

It is an admirable state; it is perfect peace of mind. There is no longer any need to accumulate acquired knowledge, received ideas which have to be memorised; it is no longer necessary

---

[1] One who follows the path of Knowledge (*jñāna*) as opposed to the path of Love (*bhakti*), or the path of Works (*karma*).

to clutter one's brain with thousands and thousands of things in order to have at one's command, when the time comes, the knowledge that is needed to perform an action, to impart a teaching, to solve a problem. The mind is silent, the brain is still, everything is clear, quiet, calm; and at the right moment, by divine Grace a drop of light falls into the consciousness and what needs to be known is known. Why should one care to remember — why try to retain that knowledge? On the day or at the moment that it is needed one will have it again. At each second one is a blank page on which what must be known will be inscribed — in the peace, the repose, the silence of a perfect receptivity.

One knows what must be known, one sees what must be seen, and since what must be known and seen comes directly from the Supreme, it is Truth itself; and it completely eludes all notions of reason or folly. What is true is true — that is all. And one has to sink very low to wonder whether it is folly or reason.

Silence and a modest, humble, attentive receptivity; no concern for appearances or even any anxiety to be — one is quite modestly, quite humbly, quite simply the instrument which of itself is nothing and knows nothing, but is ready to receive everything and transmit everything.

The first condition is self-forgetfulness, a total self-giving, the absence of ego.

And the body says to the Supreme Lord: "What You want me to be, I shall be; what You want me to know, I shall know; what You want me to do, I shall do."

3 October 1958

5 – If mankind only caught a glimpse of what infinite enjoyments, what perfect forces, what luminous reaches of spontaneous knowledge, what wide calms of our being lie waiting for us in the tracts which our animal evolution has not yet conquered, they would leave all

and never rest till they had gained these treasures. But the way is narrow, the doors are hard to force, and fear, distrust and scepticism are there, sentinels of Nature, to forbid the turning away of our feet from her ordinary pastures.

What Sri Aurobindo has written, the words ["caught a glimpse"] which have been translated[2] as *entrevoyaient*, means to see something in its totality, but for a very brief moment. It is obvious that a constant vision of all these wonders would automatically compel you to set out on the path. It is also certain that a little fragmentary glimpse is not enough — it would not have enough weight to compel you to follow the path.

But if you had a total vision, however brief, you would not be able to resist the temptation of making the effort needed to realise it. But, in fact, the total vision is exceptional, and that is why Sri Aurobindo says to us: "If mankind only..."

To tell the truth, it very seldom happens that those who are ready, who are undoubtedly meant for realisation, do not have, at a certain moment in their lives, even if only for a few seconds, the experience of what this realisation is.

But even those whose destiny is certain have to struggle mightily, resolutely, against this "something" which one seems to take in with the very air one breathes: this fear, this dread of what may happen. And this is so stupid, because, in the final analysis, the destiny of each individual is the same: you are born, you live — more or less satisfactorily — and you die; then you wait for a certain length of time, and again you are born, you live — more or less satisfactorily — and again you die, and so on indefinitely, until you feel you have had enough of it.

Fear of what? Fear of coming out of the rut? Fear of being free? Fear of no longer being a prisoner?

And then, when you have enough courage to overcome this,

---

[2] In the French text of *Thoughts and Aphorisms* read by the Mother.

when you say, "Come what may! After all, there's not much to lose", then you become wary, you wonder if it is reasonable, if it is true, if all that is not an illusion, if you are not just imagining things, if there is really any substance to it.... And mind you, this mistrust seems stupid, but you encounter it even in the most intelligent, even in those who have repeatedly had conclusive experiences — it is something that you take in with the food you eat, the air you breathe, your contacts with others; and that is why you can speak of the "tentacles of Nature",[3] everywhere, in all things, like an octopus stealing in and catching you and binding you.

Even when you have overcome these two obstacles, when the experiences are so strong that you can no longer doubt, that doubt becomes impossible — like doubting one's own life — then there remains something awful, petty, dry, corrosive: scepticism. And this is founded on human pride, that is why it lasts so long. You want to think that you are above all these things, "Oh, I am not one to fall into those traps! I am a reasonable man, I see things from a practical point of view; I'm not so easily deceived." It is awful!... It is sordid. But it is dangerous.

Even in moments of greatest enthusiasm, even when one is filled with an exceptional, marvellous experience — it rises from the lowest depths. It is ugly, slimy, disgusting. And yet it rises, and spoils everything.

To conquer it, one must be a mighty warrior. One must struggle against all the obscurities of Nature, against all her tricks, all her temptations.

Why does she do this? It is as if she were moving away from her own goal. But I have already explained this to you many times. Nature knows very well where she is going and what the outcome is. She wants it, but... in her own way. She does not feel that any time is being wasted. She has all eternity before her. She

---

[3] The translation the Mother had before her was based on a text which read "tentacles of Nature" instead of "sentinels of Nature".

wants to follow her own way as she likes, meandering as much as she likes, going back on her tracks, straying from the straight path, starting the same thing all over again several times to see what will happen. And these enlightened cranks, who want to get there at once, as soon as possible, who thirst for truth, light, beauty, balance — they bother her, they urge her on, they tell her that she is wasting her time. Her time! She always replies, "But I have all eternity before me. Am I in a hurry? Why are you in such a hurry?" And again, with a smile: "Your haste is all too human; widen yourselves, become infinite, be eternal, and you will no longer be in a hurry."

There is so much fun on the way, for her... but not for everyone.

This is what happens when one sees things from a great height, from a great distance, when one's view is vast, almost infinite. Everything that upsets human beings and makes them suffer, disappears; so those who are very wise, who have abandoned life for the sake of higher wisdom tell you with a smile, "Why suffer? Come out of it and you will suffer no more." That is all very well individually but, in fact, if you think about others you may wish this rather tragic comedy would come to an end sooner. And it is very justifiable to feel tired of living like a beast at pasture, of roaming from one patch of grass to another, of ruminating in a corner, of having such narrow horizons and of missing all the splendours of life.

Perhaps it amuses Nature that we should be like that, but we are tired of it, we want to be different.

And that is it. When you have truly had enough of it and want things to be different, then you have the courage, the strength, the capacity to conquer these three terrible enemies: fear, doubt and scepticism. But I repeat, it is not enough to sit down one fine day, watch yourself be, and struggle with these things inside you once and for all. You have to do it and do it again and again and continue in a way which seems almost endless, to be sure that you have got rid of it all. In reality, you are perhaps never truly rid of it, but there comes a time when inside yourself, you are so different that you can no longer be touched by these things. You can see them, but you see them with a smile, and at a simple gesture they go away, back to where they came from, perhaps a little changed, perhaps a little less strong, less obstinate, less aggressive — until the time when the Light is so strong that all darkness vanishes.

As for the marvels Sri Aurobindo tells us about, it is better not to describe them, because each individual feels them, undergoes them, experiences them in his own way — and for each person that is the best way. One must not adopt another's way, one must go one's own way, then the experience has its full value, its full inestimable value.

And finally, I wish that you may all have these experiences yourselves. And for that, faith, confidence, much humaneness and great goodwill are needed.

Open, aspire, and... wait. It will surely come, the Grace is there. It asks only to be able to work for everyone.

10 October 1958

6 – Late, I learned that when reason died then Wisdom was born; before that liberation, I had only knowledge.

Once again I must repeat that the form of these aphorisms is purposely paradoxical in order to give the mind a little shock and awaken it enough for it to make an effort to understand. One must not take this aphorism literally. Some people seem worried by the idea that reason must disappear for one to become wise. It is not that, it is not that at all.

Reason must no longer be the summit and the master.

For a very long time in life, until one possesses anything resembling Knowledge, it is indispensable that reason be the master, otherwise one is the plaything of one's impulses, one's

Jnana

fancies, one's more or less disordered emotional imaginings, and one is in danger of being very far removed not merely from wisdom but even from the knowledge needed for conducting oneself acceptably. But when one has managed to control all the lower parts of the being with the help of reason, which is the apex of ordinary human intelligence, then if one wants to go beyond this point, if one wants to liberate oneself from ordinary life, from ordinary thought, from the ordinary vision of things, one must, if I may say so, stand upon the head of reason, not trampling it down disdainfully, but using it as a stepping stone to something higher, something beyond it, to attain to something which concerns itself very little with the decrees of reason; something which can allow itself to be irrational because it is a higher irrationality, with a higher light; something which is beyond ordinary knowledge and which receives its inspirations from above, from high above, from the divine Wisdom.

That is what this means.

As for the knowledge of which Sri Aurobindo speaks here, it is ordinary knowledge, it is not Knowledge by identity; it is knowledge that can be acquired by the intellect through thought, through ordinary means.

But once again — and in any case we shall have occasion to return to this when we study the next aphorism — do not be in a hurry to abandon reason in the conviction that you will immediately attain to Wisdom, because you must be ready for Wisdom; otherwise, by abandoning reason, you run a great risk of falling into unreason, which is rather dangerous.

Many times in his writings, particularly in *The Synthesis of Yoga*, Sri Aurobindo warns us against the imaginings of those who believe they can do sadhana without rigorous self-control and who heed all sorts of inspirations, which lead them to a dangerous imbalance where all their repressed, hidden, secret desires come out into the open under the pretence of liberation from ordinary conventions and ordinary reason.

On Thoughts and Aphorisms

One can be free only by soaring to the heights, high above human passions. Only when one has achieved a higher, selfless freedom and done away with all desires and impulses does one have the right to be free.

But neither should people who are very reasonable, very moral according to ordinary social laws, think themselves wise, for their wisdom is an illusion and holds no profound truth.

One who would break the law must be above the law. One who would ignore conventions must be above conventions. One who would despise all rules must be above all rules. And the motive of this liberation should never be a personal, egoistic one: the desire to satisfy an ambition, aggrandise one's personality, through a feeling of superiority, out of contempt for others, to set oneself above the herd and regard it with condescension. Be on your guard when you feel yourself superior and look down on others ironically, as if to say, "I'm no longer made of such stuff." That's when you go off the track and are in danger of falling into an abyss.

When one truly attains wisdom, the true wisdom, the wisdom Sri Aurobindo is speaking of here, there is no longer higher and lower; there is only a play of forces in which each thing has its place and its importance. And if there is a hierarchy it is a hierarchy of surrender to the Supreme. It is not a hierarchy of superiority with regard to what is below.

And with human understanding, human reason, human knowledge, one is unable to discern this hierarchy. Only the awakened soul can recognise another awakened soul, and then the sense of superiority disappears completely.

True wisdom comes only when the ego disappears, and the ego disappears only when you are ready to abandon yourself completely to the supreme Lord without any personal motive and without any expectation of profit — when you do it because you cannot do otherwise.

17 October 1958

7 – **What men call knowledge is the reasoned acceptance of false appearances. Wisdom looks behind the veil and sees. Reason divides, fixes details and contrasts them; Wisdom unifies, marries contrasts in a single harmony.**

All that Sri Aurobindo writes about knowledge, reason, Wisdom is said in order to bring us out of the rut of conventional thinking, and, if possible, make us perceive the reality behind the appearances.

As a general rule, with a few very rare exceptions, men are content to observe more or less accurately everything that happens around them, and sometimes within themselves, and to classify all these observations according to one superficial system of logic or another. And they call this organisation, these systems, "knowledge". It has never occurred to them, they have not even begun to perceive that all the things they see, touch, feel, experience, are false appearances and not reality itself.

The constant, general argument is, "But I see it, I touch it, I feel it — consequently it is true."

They should, on the contrary, tell themselves, "I see it, I touch it, I feel it — consequently it is false." We are at opposite poles and there is no way of coming to an understanding.

For Sri Aurobindo, true knowledge is precisely Knowledge by identity, and wisdom is the state one achieves when one is in this true knowledge. He says it here: Wisdom looks behind the veil of false appearances and sees the reality behind it. And Sri Aurobindo emphasises that when one defines something with the superficial, outer knowledge, it is always in opposition to something else; it is always by means of a contrast that one explains what one sees, feels, touches — and does not understand.

Reason always sets one thing against another and compels you to make a choice. People whose thought and reason are clear see all the differences between things. It is rather remarkable that reason can only work through differences; it is because one perceives the difference between this and that, one act and another, one object and another, that one makes decisions and that reason works.

But it is precisely true Knowledge, Knowledge by identity and the wisdom which results from it that always see the point where all apparently contradictory things harmonise, complement each other, form a perfectly coherent, coordinated whole. And naturally that changes entirely the point of view, the perception, and the consequences in action.

The first absolutely indispensable step is not to repeat, more or less mechanically and without quite knowing what you are saying, that "appearances are false". You say it because Sri Aurobindo has told us so — but without really understanding it. And yet, when you want to understand something, you continue to look, to observe, to touch, to taste and to feel, because you believe there are no other means of observation. It is only when you have had the experience of the "reversal of consciousness", when you have gone behind these things, when you can feel, experience, in the most concrete manner, their illusory appearance, that you are able to understand. But, unless you have had the experience, you can read all the aphorisms, repeat and learn them, have faith in them and still not perceive: they have no reality for you. All these appearances remain the only way of coming into contact with the outer world and of becoming aware of what it is. And sometimes you can spend a whole lifetime learning how things are in their appearances and be considered very cultured, very intelligent, highly knowledgeable, when you have observed all this in detail and remembered all that you have observed or learnt...

Strictly speaking, you can, when you have worked hard, have some slight effect on these appearances, change them a little — this is how, through science, you learn to manipulate matter — but there is no true change and there is no true power. And when you are in that state, you are wholly convinced that there is nothing you can do to change your character. You feel trapped in a kind of fatalism that weighs you down, you know neither whence nor how; you are born like this, in such and such a place, into such and such an environment, with such and such a character, and you get through life as best you can, adapting to things without having much influence on them, and trying to mitigate the drawbacks of your own character without having the power to transform it. You feel caught in a net, you are the slave of something of which you are unaware. You are the plaything of circumstances, of unknown forces, of a will you do not submit to, but which constrains you. Even the most rebellious are slaves, because the only thing that liberates you is precisely the act of passing behind the veil and discovering what lies beyond it. Once you have seen, you know who you are and once you have established your true identity, you have the key to the true transformation.

We read, we try to understand, we explain, we try to know. But a single minute of true experience teaches us more than millions of words and hundreds of explanations.

So the first question is: "How to have the experience?"

To go within yourself, that is the first step.

And then, once you have succeeded in going within yourself deeply enough to feel the reality of that which is within, to widen yourself progressively, systematically, to become as vast as the universe and lose the sense of limitation.

These are the first two preparatory movements.

And these two things must be done in the greatest possible calm, peace and tranquillity. This peace, this tranquillity brings about silence in the mind and stillness in the vital.

This effort, this attempt must be renewed very regularly, persistently. And after a certain lapse of time, which may be longer or shorter, you begin to perceive a reality that is different from the reality perceived in the ordinary, external consciousness.

Naturally, by the action of Grace, the veil may suddenly be rent from within, and at once you can enter the true truth; but even when that happens, in order to obtain the full value and full effect of the experience, you must maintain yourself in a state of inner receptivity, and to do that, it is indispensable for you to go within each day.

24 October 1958

> 8 – Either do not give the name of knowledge to your beliefs only and of error, ignorance or charlatanism to the beliefs of others; or do not rail at the dogmas of the sects and their intolerance.

The dogmas of sects and the intolerance of religions come from the fact that the sects and religions consider their beliefs alone to be knowledge, and the beliefs of others to be error, ignorance or charlatanism.

This simple movement causes them to set up what they believe to be true as dogma and to violently condemn what others believe to be true. To think that your knowledge is the only true one, that your belief is the only true one and that others' beliefs are not true, is to do precisely what is done by all sects and religions.

So, if you are doing exactly the same thing as the sects and religions, you have no right to mock them. You do the same thing without being aware of it because it seems quite natural to you. What Sri Aurobindo wants to make you understand is that when you say, "We are in possession of the truth and what is not this truth is an error" — though you may not dare say it in such a crude way — you are doing exactly the same thing as all the religions and all the sects.

If you objectify a little you will see that you have spontaneously, without realising it, established as knowledge everything you have learnt, everything you have thought, everything which has given you the impression of being particularly true and of major importance; and you are quite ready to contradict any different notion held by those who say, "No, no, it is like this, it is not like that."

If you watch yourself in action, you will understand the mechanism of this intolerance and you will immediately be able to put an end to all these useless discussions. This brings us back to what I have already told you once: the contact which you have had with the truth of things, your personal contact — a contact which is more or less clear, profound, vast, pure — may have given *you*, as an individual, an interesting, perhaps even a decisive experience; but although this contact may have given you an experience of decisive importance, you must not imagine that it is a universal experience and that the same contact would give others the same experience. And if you understand this, that it is something purely personal, individual, subjective, that it is not at all an absolute and general law, then you can no longer despise the knowledge of others, nor seek to impose your own point of view and experience upon them. This understanding obviates all mental quarrels, which are always totally useless.

Obviously, the first part of the aphorism can be taken as advice, but this is not what Sri Aurobindo meant when he wrote it; he wanted to make us conscious of the error we make ourselves but ridicule in others. This is a habit with us, not only in this particular case, but in all cases. It is rather remarkable that when we have a weakness — for example a ridiculous habit, a defect or an imperfection — since it is more or less part of our nature, we consider it to be very natural, it does not shock us. But as soon as we see this same weakness, this same imperfection, this same ridiculous habit in someone else, it seems quite shocking to us and we say, "What! He's like that?" — without noticing that we ourselves are "like that". And so to the weakness and imperfection we add the absurdity of not even noticing them.

There is a lesson to be drawn from this. When something in a person seems to you completely unacceptable or ridiculous — "What! He is like that, he behaves like that, he says things like that, he does things like that" — you should say to yourself, "Well, well, but perhaps I do the same thing without being aware of it. I would do better to look into myself first before criticising him, so as to make sure that I am not doing the very same thing in a slightly different way." If you have the good sense and intelligence to do this each time you are shocked by another person's behaviour, you will realise that in life your relations with others are like a mirror which is presented to you so that you can see more easily and clearly the weaknesses you carry within you.

In a general and almost absolute way anything that shocks you in other people is the very thing you carry in yourself in a more or less veiled, more or less hidden form, though perhaps in a slightly different guise which allows you to delude yourself. And what in yourself seems inoffensive enough, becomes monstrous as soon as you see it in others.

Try to experience this; it will greatly help you to change yourselves. At the same time it will bring a sunny tolerance to your relationships with others, the goodwill which comes from understanding, and it will very often put an end to these completely useless quarrels.

One can live without quarrelling. It seems strange to say this because as things are, it would seem, on the contrary, that life is made for quarrelling in the sense that the main occupation of people who are together is to quarrel, overtly or covertly. You do not always come to words, you do not always come to blows — fortunately — but you are in a state of perpetual irritation within because you do not find around you the perfection that you would yourself wish to realise, and which you find rather difficult to realise — but you find it entirely natural that others should realise it.

"How can they be like that?..." You forget how difficult you find it in yourself not to be "like that"!

Try, you will see.

Look upon everything with a benevolent smile. Take all the things which irritate you as a lesson for yourself and your life will be more peaceful and more effective as well, for a great percentage of your energy certainly goes to waste in the irritation you feel when you do not find in others the perfection that you would like to realise in yourself.

You stop short at the perfection that others should realise and you are seldom conscious of the goal you should be pursuing yourself. If you are conscious of it, well then, begin with the work which is given to *you*, that is to say, realise what you have to do and do not concern yourself with what others do, because, after all, it is not your business. And the best way to the true attitude is simply to say, "All those around me, all the circumstances of my life, all the people near me, are a mirror held up to me by the Divine Consciousness to show me the progress I must make. Everything that shocks me in others means a work I have to do in myself."

And perhaps if one carried true perfection in oneself, one would discover it more often in others.

7 November 1958

9 – What the soul sees and has experienced, that it knows; the rest is appearance, prejudice and opinion.

This amounts to saying that all knowledge which is not the result of the soul's vision or experience is without true value.

But the question immediately arises — it was, in fact, put to me — "How do we know what the soul sees?"

Obviously there is only one solution: to become conscious of one's soul. And this completes the aphorism: unless one is conscious of one's soul one does not have true knowledge. Therefore the first effort must be to find the soul within, to unite with it and allow it to govern one's life.

Some people ask, "How do we know whether this is the soul?" I have already answered this question several times. Those who ask this question, by the very fact of asking it, prove that they are not conscious of their souls, because as soon as you are conscious of your soul and identified with it, you have a positive knowledge of it and you no longer ask how you are to know. And that experience can neither be counterfeited nor imagined; you cannot pretend to be in contact with your soul — it is something which cannot be contrived or counterfeited. When the soul governs your life, you know it with absolute certainty and no longer ask any questions.

But the usefulness of the aphorism we have just read is to make you understand that everything you think you know, everything you have learnt, anything that has come to you in your life through personal observation, deduction, comparison — all that is a very relative knowledge on which you cannot found a durable and truly effective way of life.

How many times have we repeated this: all that comes from the mind is wholly relative. The more the mind is educated and has applied itself to various disciplines, the more it becomes capable of proving that what it puts forward or what it says is true. One can prove the truth of anything by reasoning, but that does not make it true. It remains an opinion, a prejudice, a knowledge based on appearances which are themselves more than dubious.

So there seems to be only one way out and that is to go in search of one's soul and to find it. It is there, it does not make a point of hiding itself, it does not play with you just to make things difficult; on the contrary, it makes great efforts to help you find it and to make itself heard. Only, between your soul and your active consciousness there are two characters who are in the habit of making a lot of noise, the mind and the vital. And because they make a lot of noise, while the soul does not, or, rather, makes as little as possible, their noise prevents you from hearing the voice of the soul.

When you want to know what your soul knows, you have to make an inner effort, to be very attentive; and indeed, if you are attentive, behind the outer noise of the mind and the vital, you can discern something very subtle, very quiet, very peaceful, which knows and says what it knows. But the insistence of the others is so imperious, while *that* is so quiet, that you are very easily misled into listening to the one that makes the most noise; most often you become aware only afterwards that the other one was right. It does not impose itself, it does not compel you to listen, for it is without violence.

When you hesitate, when you wonder what to do in this or that circumstance, there come the desire, the preference both mental and vital, that press, insist, affirm and impose themselves, and, with the best reasons in the world, build up a whole case for themselves. And if you are not on the alert, if you don't have a firm discipline, if you don't have the habit of control, they finally convince you that they are right. And as I was saying a little while ago, they make so much noise that you do not even hear the tiny voice or the tiny, very quiet indication of the soul which says, "Don't do it."

This "Don't do it" comes often, but you discard it as something which has no power and follow your impulsive destiny. But if you are truly sincere in your will to find and live the truth, then you learn to listen better and better, you learn to discriminate more and more, and even if it costs you an effort, even if it causes you pain, you learn to obey. And even if you have obeyed only once, it is a powerful help, a considerable progress on the path towards the discrimination between what is and what is not the soul. With this discrimination and the necessary sincerity you are sure to reach the goal.

But you must not be in a hurry, you must not be impatient, you must be very persevering. You do the wrong thing ten times for every time that you do the right thing. But when you do the wrong thing you must not give up everything in despair, but tell yourself that the Grace will never abandon you and that next time it will be better.

So, in conclusion, we shall say that in order to know things as they are you must first unite with your soul and to unite with your soul you must want it with persistence and perseverance.

Only the degree of concentration on the goal can shorten the way.

14 November 1958

10 – My soul knows that it is immortal. But you take a dead body to pieces and cry triumphantly, "Where is your soul and where is your immortality?"

It has often been repeated — but except in certain cases very rarely understood — that only like knows like. If this were understood, a great deal of ignorance would vanish.

Only the soul can know the soul, and on each level of being, only the equivalent level can recognise the other. Only the Divine can know the Divine, and because we carry the Divine in ourselves we are capable of seeing Him and recognising Him. But if we try to understand something of the inner life by using our senses and external methods, the result is sure to be total failure and we shall also deceive ourselves totally.

So when you imagine that you can know the secrets of Nature and still remain in a purely physical consciousness, you are entirely deceived. And this habit of demanding concrete, material proofs before accepting the reality of something, is one of the most glaring effects of ignorance. With that attitude any fool imagines that he can sit in judgment on the highest things and deny the most profound experiences.

It is certainly not by dissecting a body which is dead because the soul has departed from it that the soul can be found. Had the soul not departed, the body would not have been dead! It is to bring home to us the absurdity of this claim that Sri Aurobindo has written this aphorism.

It applies to all judgments of the critical mind and to all scientific methods when they would judge any but purely material phenomena.

The conclusion is always the same: the only true attitude

is one of humility, of silent respect before what one does not know, and of inner aspiration to come out of one's ignorance. One of the things which would make humanity progress most would be for it to respect what it does not know, to acknowledge willingly that it does not know and is therefore unable to judge. We constantly do just the opposite. We pass final judgments on things of which we have no knowledge whatsoever, and say in a peremptory manner, "This is possible. That is impossible", when we do not even know what it is we are speaking of. And we put on superior airs because we doubt things of which we have never had any knowledge.

Men believe that doubt is a sign of superiority, whereas it is really a sign of inferiority.

Scepticism and doubt are two of the greatest obstacles to progress; they add presumptuousness to ignorance.

21 November 1958

11 – **Immortality is not the survival of the mental personality after death, though that also is true, but the waking possession of the unborn and deathless Self of which body is only an instrument and a shadow.**

There are three statements here which have raised questions. First, "What is the mental personality?"

In each human being the body is animated by the vital being, and governed, or partially governed, by a mental being. This is a general rule, but the extent to which the mental being is formed and individualised varies greatly from one individual to the next. In the great mass of human beings the mind is something fluid which has no organisation of its own, and therefore it is not a personality. And as long as the mind is like that, fluid, unorganised, with no cohesive life of its own and without personality, it cannot survive. What made up the mental being dissolves in the mental region when the body, the substance which made up the body, dissolves in the physical substance.

But as soon as the mental being is formed, organised, individualised, and has become a personality, it does not depend, it no longer depends on the body for its existence, and it therefore survives the body. The earth's mental atmosphere is filled with beings, mental personalities which lead an entirely independent existence, even after the disappearance of the body; they can reincarnate in a new body when the soul, that is to say, the true Self, reincarnates, thus carrying with it the memory of its previous lives.

But this is not what Sri Aurobindo calls Immortality. Immortality is a life without beginning or end, without birth or death, which is altogether independent of the body. It is the life of the Self, the essential being of each individual, and it is not separate from the universal Self. And this essential being has a sense of oneness with the universal Self; it is in fact a personified, individualised expression of the universal Self and has neither beginning nor end, neither life nor death, it exists eternally and that is what is immortal. When we are fully conscious of this Self we participate in its eternal life, and we therefore become immortal.

But there is some misunderstanding about this word "Immortality" — and this is not something new; it is a misunderstanding which has recurred very frequently. When one speaks of immortality most people understand it as the indefinite survival of the body.

The body can survive indefinitely only if, in the first place, it becomes fully conscious of this immortal Self and unites with it, identifies with it to the extent of having the same capacity, the same faculty of constant transformation which would enable it to follow the universal movement. This is an absolutely indispensable condition if the body is to endure. Because the body is rigid, because it does not follow the movement, because it cannot transform itself rapidly enough to constantly identify itself with the universal evolution, it decomposes and dies. Its fixity, its rigidity, its incapacity to transform itself, make its destruction necessary, so that its substance may return to the general realm of physical substance and so that the body may be remoulded into new forms in order to become capable of further progress. But usually, when one speaks of immortality, people think of physical immortality — it goes without saying that this has not yet been realised.

Sri Aurobindo says that it is possible and even that it will happen, but he lays down one condition: the body must be supramentalised, it must have some of the qualities of the supramental being, which are qualities of plasticity and constant transformation. And when Sri Aurobindo writes that the body is "only an instrument and a shadow", he is speaking of the body as it is now and will probably continue to be for a long time to come. It is only the instrument of the Self, a very inadequate expression of this Self, and a shadow — a shadow, something vague and obscure in comparison with the light and precision of the eternal Self.

How this shadow, this instrument, can serve the development of the soul, and how by cultivating the instrument one can be of help to future lives, are questions which are not without interest.

Each time that the soul takes birth in a new body it comes with the intention of having a new experience which will help it to develop and to perfect its personality. This is how the psychic being is formed from life to life and becomes a completely conscious and independent personality which, once it has arrived at the summit of its development, is free to choose not only the time of its incarnation, but the place, the purpose and the work to be accomplished.

Its descent into the physical body is necessarily a descent into darkness, ignorance, unconsciousness; and for a very long time it must labour simply to bring a little consciousness into the material substance of the body, before it can make use of it for the experience it has come for. So, if we cultivate the body by a clear-sighted and rational method, at the same time we are helping the growth of the soul, its progress and enlightenment.

Physical culture is the process of infusing consciousness into the cells of the body. One may or may not know it, but it is a fact. When we concentrate to make our muscles move according to our will, when we endeavour to make our limbs more supple, to give them an agility, or a force, or a resistance, or a plasticity which they do not naturally possess, we infuse into the cells of the body a consciousness which was not there before, thus turning it into an increasingly homogeneous and receptive instrument, which progresses in and by its activities. This is the primary importance of physical culture. Of course, that is not the only thing that brings consciousness into the body, but it is something which acts in an overall way, and this is rare. I have already told you several times that the artist infuses a very great consciousness into his hands, as the intellectual does into his brain. But these are, as it were, local phenomena, whereas the action of physical culture is more general. And when one sees the absolutely marvellous results of this culture, when one observes the extent to which the body is capable of perfecting itself, one understands how useful this can be to the action of the psychic being which has entered into this material substance. For naturally, when it is in possession of an organised and harmonised instrument which is full of strength and suppleness and possibilities, its task is greatly facilitated.

I do not say that people who practise physical culture necessarily do it for this purpose, because very few are aware of this result. But whether they are aware of it or not, this is the result. Moreover, if you are at all sensitive, when you observe the moving body of a person who has practised physical culture in a methodical and rational way, you see a light, a consciousness, a life, which is not there in others.

There are always people with a wholly external view of things who say, "Workers, for example, who have to do hard physical labour and who are compelled by their work to learn to carry heavy weights — they too build up their muscles, and instead of spending their time like aristocrats doing exercises with no useful outward results, they at least produce something." This is ignorance. Because there is an essential difference between the muscles developed through specialised, local and limited use and muscles which have been cultivated deliberately and harmoniously according to an integral programme which leaves no part of the body without work or exercise.

People like workers and peasants, who have a specialised occupation and develop only certain muscles, always end up with occupational deformities. And this in no way helps their psychic progress because, although the whole of life necessarily contributes to the psychic development, it does so in such an unconscious way and so slowly that the poor psychic being must come back again and again and again, indefinitely, to achieve its purpose. Therefore we can say without fear of being mistaken that physical culture is the sadhana of the body and that all sadhana necessarily helps to hasten the achievement of the goal. The more consciously you do it, the quicker and more general the result, but even if you do it blindly, if you can see no further than the tips of your fingers or your feet or your nose, you help the overall development.

Finally, one can say that any discipline that is followed rigorously, sincerely, deliberately, is a considerable help, for it enables life on earth to attain its goal more rapidly and prepares it to receive the new life. To discipline oneself is to hasten the arrival of this new life and the contact with the supramental reality.

As it is, the physical body is truly nothing but a very disfigured shadow of the eternal life of the Self. But this physical body is capable of progressive development; through each individual formation, the physical substance progresses, and one day it will be capable of building a bridge between physical life as we know it and the supramental life which is to manifest.

28 November 1958

12 – They proved to me by convincing reasons that God did not exist, and I believed them. Afterwards I saw God, for He came and embraced me. And now which am I to believe, the reasonings of others or my own experience?

Sri Aurobindo is not asking a question, but rather making an ironic comment. It is to bring out clearly the stupidity of the reasonings of the mind, which imagines it can speak of what it does not know. It is nothing else.

You can prove anything with the mind. When you know how to use it and have mastered reasoning and deduction, you can prove anything. As a matter of fact, this is an exercise that is given in universities to make the mind supple: you are given a thesis to prove and immediately afterwards, with equal conviction, you have to prove its antithesis — in the hope that if you rise a little above both, you will discover the synthesis.

Therefore, once it is conceded that anything can be proved, it follows that reasoning leads nowhere; because if you can prove something and in the next moment prove its opposite, this is the proof that your proofs are worthless.

There is experience. For a simple heart, a sincere and honest nature, a nature which knows that its experience is sincere, that it is not a falsification of desire or of mental ambition, but a spontaneous movement which comes from the soul — the experience is absolutely convincing. It loses its power of conviction when the desire to have an experience, or the ambition to think oneself very superior, becomes mixed with it. If you have that in you, then beware, because desires and ambitions falsify experience. The mind is a formative power, and if you have a very strong desire for something very important and very interesting to happen to you, you can make it happen, at least in the eyes of those who see things superficially. But apart from these cases, if you are honest, sincere, spontaneous, and especially when experiences come to you without any effort on your part to have them, and as a spontaneous expression of your deeper aspiration, then these experiences carry with them the seal of an absolute authenticity; and even if the whole world tells you that they are nonsense and illusion, it does not change your personal convictions. But naturally, for this, you must not deceive yourself. You must be sincere and honest with a complete inner rectitude.

Someone has asked me, "How is it possible for God to reveal Himself to an unbeliever?" That's very funny; because if it pleases God to reveal Himself to an unbeliever, I don't see what would prevent Him from doing so!

On the contrary, He has a sense of humour — Sri Aurobindo has told us many times already that the Supreme has a sense of humour, that *we* are the ones who want to make Him into a grave and invariably serious character — and He may find it very amusing to come and embrace an unbeliever. Someone who has only the day before declared, "God does not exist. I do not believe in Him. All that is folly and ignorance....", He gathers him into His arms, He presses him to His heart — and He laughs in his face.

Everything is possible, even things which to our small and limited intelligence seem absurd.

Indeed, it is only when we have come to the end of these aphorisms that we will be able to understand them; because with each one, Sri Aurobindo places us in an entirely different position with regard to the truth to be discovered. There are innumerable facets. There are innumerable points of view. One can say the most contradictory things without being inconsistent or contradicting oneself. Everything depends on the way in which you look at it. And even once we have seen everything, from all the points of view accessible to us, around the central Truth, we will still have had only a very small glimpse — the

Truth will escape us on all sides at once. But what is remarkable is that once we have had the experience of a single contact with the Divine, a true, spontaneous and sincere experience, at that moment, in that experience, we will know everything, and even more. That is why it is so important to live the little you know in all sincerity in order to make yourself capable of having experiences, and of knowing by experience, not mentally, but because you live these things, because they become a part of your being and consciousness.

To put into practice the little you know is the best way to learn more; it is the most powerful means of advancing on the way — a little bit of really sincere practice. For example, not to do something that you know must not be done. When you have seen a weakness, a disability in your being, you must not allow it to happen again. When, if only for a moment, you have had the vision of what you must be, in an ardent aspiration, you must not — you must never forget to become that.

Some people are always complaining about their disabilities. But that doesn't lead you very far. If, once, you have truly seen your weaknesses and truly, sincerely understood, seen that you must not be like that — that's the end of complaining. Then there is the daily effort, the building up of the will, the vigilance of every moment — you must never allow a recognised mistake to renew itself. To err through ignorance, to err through unconsciousness, is obviously very unfortunate, but it can be put right. Whereas to go on making the same mistake, knowing that it must not be made, is an act of cowardice which we must not permit ourselves.

To say, "Oh, human nature is like this. Oh, we are in the inconscience. Oh, we are in the ignorance" — all this is laziness and weakness. And behind this laziness and weakness there is a huge bad will. There!

I say this because many people have made this remark to me, many. And it is always a way of justifying oneself: "Oh, we are doing what we can." It is not true. Because if you are sincere, once you have seen — as long as you have not seen, nothing can be said — but the moment you see is the moment when you receive the Grace, and once you have received the Grace, you no longer have the right to forget it.[4]

5 December 1958

---

[4] The "Friday Classes", which took place in the Ashram Playground, end here, and with them the first section of the Mother's commentaries.

Jnana

(Knowledge)

Second Period of Commentaries

(1960–1961)

Jnana (Knowledge)

Second Period of Commentaries (1960–1961)

13 – They told me, "These things are hallucinations." I inquired what was a hallucination and found that it meant a subjective or psychical experience which corresponds to no objective or no physical reality. Then I sat and wondered at the miracles of the human reason.

What does Sri Aurobindo mean by "the miracles of the human reason"?

In this aphorism, by "they" Sri Aurobindo means the materialists, the scientists and, in a general way, all those who only believe in physical reality and consider human reason to be the one infallible judge. Furthermore, the "things" he speaks of here are all the perceptions that belong to worlds other than the material, all that one can see with eyes other than the physical, all the experiences that one can have in subtle domains from the sense perceptions of the vital world to the bliss of the Divine Presence.

It was while discussing these and other similar "things" that Sri Aurobindo was told that they were "hallucinations". When you look up the word "hallucination" in the dictionary, you find this definition: "Morbid sensation not produced by any real object. Objectless perception." Sri Aurobindo interprets this or puts it more precisely: "A subjective or psychical experience which corresponds to no objective or no physical reality." There could be no better definition of these phenomena of the inner consciousness, which are most precious to man and make him something more than a mere thinking animal. Human reason is so limited, so down to earth, so arrogantly ignorant that it wants to discredit by a pejorative word the very faculties which open the gates of a higher and more marvellous life to man.... In the face of this obstinate incomprehension Sri Aurobindo wonders *ironically* at "the miracles of the human reason". For the power to change truth into falsehood to such a degree is certainly a miracle.

5 January 1960[1]

14 – Hallucination is the term of Science for those irregular glimpses we still have of truths shut out from us by our preoccupation with matter; coincidence for the curious touches of artist in the work of that supreme and universal Intelligence which in its conscious being, as on a canvas, has planned and executed the world.

What does the "artist" represent here?

Here Sri Aurobindo compares the work of the Supreme Lord, creator of the universe, to the work of an artist painting in his conscious being, with sweeping brush-strokes, as on a canvas, the picture of the world. And when by "curious touches" he paints one stroke over another, we have a "coincidence".

Usually the word "coincidence" suggests unconscious, meaningless chance. Sri Aurobindo wants to make us understand that chance and unconsciousness have nothing to do with this phenomenon; on the contrary, it is the result of a refinement of taste and consciousness of the kind that artists possess, and it can reveal a deep intention.

12 January 1960

---

[1] It should be noted that for the most part the dates in this section are those of the written questions. The Mother sometimes answered long after the question was submitted to her, without dating her reply. Some of the questions and answers towards the end of this section were oral.

15 – That which men term a hallucination is the reflection in the mind and senses of that which is beyond our ordinary mental and sensory perceptions. Superstition arises from the mind's wrong understanding of these reflections. There is no other hallucination.

Can hallucinations be compared to visions?

A vision is a perception, by the visual organs, of phenomena that really exist in a world corresponding to the organ which sees.

For example, to the individual vital plane there corresponds a cosmic vital world. When a human being is sufficiently developed he possesses an individualised vital being with organs of sight, hearing, smell, etc. So a person who has a well-developed vital being can see in the vital world with his vital sight, consciously and with the memory of what he has seen. This is what makes a vision.

It is the same for all the subtle worlds — vital, mental, overmental, supramental — and for all the intermediate worlds and planes of the being. In this way one can have visions that are vital, mental, overmental, supramental, etc.

On the other hand, Sri Aurobindo tells us that what is termed a hallucination is the reflection in the mind or the physical senses of that which is beyond our mind and our ordinary senses; it is therefore not a direct vision, but a reflected image which is usually not understood or explained. This character of uncertainty produces an impression of unreality and gives rise to all kinds of superstition. This is also why "serious" people, or people who think themselves serious, do not accord any value to these phenomena and call them hallucinations. And yet, in those who are interested in occult phenomena, this type of perception often precedes the emergence of the capacity of vision which may be in course of formation. But you must guard against mistaking this for true vision. For, I repeat, these phenomena occur most often in a state of almost complete ignorance and are too frequently accompanied by much error and wrong interpretation; not to mention the cases of unscrupulous people, who introduce into the account they give of their experiences many details and particulars not actually there, thus justifying the discredit with which these phenomena are received by rational and thoughtful people.

So we shall reserve the word "vision" for experiences that occur in awareness and sincerity. Nevertheless, in both cases, in "hallucination" as well as in vision, what is seen does correspond to something quite real, although it is sometimes much deformed in the transcription.

20 January 1960

16 – Do not like so many modern disputants smother thought under polysyllables or charm inquiry to sleep by the spell of formulas and cant words. Search always; find out the reason for things which seem to the hasty glance to be mere chance or illusion.

How can we find out the reason for things? If we try to do it with the mind, will it not be yet another illusion screening the Truth?

There are many planes or zones of the mind, from the plane of the physical mind, the lower zone of ordinary thoughts, full of error and ignorance and falsehood, to the plane of the higher mind which receives, in the form of intuitions, the rays of the supramental truth. Between these two extremes there is a gradation of countless intermediate planes that are superimposed one upon another and which influence each other. In one of the lower zones lies the practical reason, the common sense of which man is so proud and which, for ordinary minds, appears to be the expression of wisdom, although it still works wholly in the field of ignorance. To this region of practical reason belong

Jnana

the "polysyllables" of which Sri Aurobindo speaks, the commonplaces and clichés, all the ready-made phrases which run about in the mental atmosphere from one brain to another and which people repeat when they want to appear knowledgeable, or when they think themselves wise.

Sri Aurobindo puts us on our guard against this trite and inferior way of thinking when we are faced with a new or unexpected phenomenon and try to explain it. He tells us to search always, untiringly, using our highest intelligence, the intelligence which thirsts to know the true cause of things, and to go on searching without being satisfied by facile and popular explanations, until we have discovered a more subtle and truer truth. Then at the same time we shall find that behind everything, even what seems to be chance and illusion, there is a conscious will at work to express the Supreme Vision.

27 January 1960

17 – *Someone was laying down that God must be this or that or He would not be God. But it seemed to me that I can only know what God is and I do not see how I can tell Him what He ought to be. For what is the standard by which we can judge Him? These judgments are the follies of our egoism.*

Is it possible to know God, even with one's physical mind, once one has experienced identification?

After consciously identifying itself with the Divine, the entire being even in its external parts — mental, vital and physical — undergoes the consequences of this identification, and a change occurs which is sometimes even perceptible in the physical appearance. An influence is at work on the thoughts, the feelings, the sensations and even the actions. Sometimes, in all its movements, the being has a concrete and constant impression of the Divine Presence and its action through the outer instrument. But one cannot say that the physical mind *knows* God, for the very way of knowing that is characteristic of the mind is foreign to the Divine; one could even say that it is contrary to it. The physical mind itself can receive the divine influence and be transformed by it, but so long as it remains the physical mind, it can neither understand nor explain God, much less know Him; for to know God one must be identified with Him and for that the physical mind must cease to be what it is now, and consequently cease to be the physical mind.

The capacity to know God can be achieved in the lower triplicity — the mind, the vital and the physical — only with the supramental transformation, and this comes only just before the ultimate realisation which consists in becoming divine.

3 February 1960

> 18 – Chance is not in this universe; the idea of illusion is itself an illusion. There was never illusion yet in the human mind that was not the concealing and disfigurement of a truth.

What does this mean: "the idea of illusion is itself an illusion"?

We live in an illusion; no thoughtful person can deny this. But according to some people, behind the illusion that we see and live there exists nothing; there is nothingness, emptiness. Whereas others tell us that what we see and feel, the life we live, is a deceptive and illusory appearance behind which, beyond which, within which, there is a Reality, an eternal Truth which we do not see in our present state, but which we can experience, if we take the trouble and follow the appropriate methods.

In this aphorism, by "the idea of illusion", Sri Aurobindo means the philosophical theory which states that the material world has no real existence: it is merely an appearance created by an aberration of the ego and the senses, and when this aberration disappears the world will disappear at the same time.

Sri Aurobindo affirms, on the contrary, that behind all appearances, even the most illusory, there is a truth, a conscious will that presides over the unfolding of the universe. In this unfolding, each thing, each event, each circumstance is both the result of what has gone before and the cause of what is to follow. Chance and incoherence are only a deceptive appearance as seen by the human consciousness which is too partial and limited to see the truth of things. But this tangible and real truth exists behind all appearances and their illusory incoherence.

What Sri Aurobindo tells us is: The world is real, it is only our perception of it that is false.

10 February 1960

19 – **When I had the dividing reason, I shrank from many things; after I had lost it in sight, I hunted through the world for the ugly and the repellent, but I could no longer find them.**

Is there really nothing ugly and repellent in the world?
Is it our reason alone that sees things in that way?

To understand truly what Sri Aurobindo means here, you must yourself have had the experience of transcending reason and establishing your consciousness in a world higher than the mental intelligence. For from up there you can see, firstly, that everything that exists in the universe is an expression of Sachchidananda (Being-Consciousness-Bliss) and therefore behind any appearance whatever, if you go deeply enough, you can perceive Sachchidananda, which is the principle of Supreme Beauty.

Secondly, you see that everything in the manifested universe is relative, so much so that there is no beauty which may not appear ugly in comparison with a greater beauty, no ugliness which may not appear beautiful in comparison with a yet uglier ugliness.

When you can see and feel in this way, you immediately become aware of the extreme relativity of these impressions and their unreality from the absolute point of view. However, so long as we dwell in the rational consciousness, it is, in a way, natural that everything that offends our aspiration for perfection, our will for progress, everything we seek to transcend and surmount, should seem ugly and repellent to us, since we are in search of a greater ideal and we want to rise higher.

And yet it is still only a half-wisdom which is very far from the true wisdom, a wisdom that appears wise only in the midst of ignorance and unconsciousness.

In the Truth everything is different, and the Divine shines in all things.

17 February 1960

20 – **God had opened my eyes; for I saw the nobility of the vulgar, the attractiveness of the repellent, the perfection of the maimed and the beauty of the hideous.**

This aphorism is the complement and almost an explanation of the previous one.

Once again, Sri Aurobindo tells us clearly that behind the appearances there is a sublime Reality which is, one may say, the luminous opposite of all external deformations. Thus, when the inner eyes are open to this divine Reality, it is seen with such power that it is able to dissolve all that normally veils it to the ordinary vision.

24 February 1960

Jnana

21 – Forgiveness is praised by the Christian and the Vaishnava, but for me, I ask, "What have I to forgive and whom?"

When we ask forgiveness of the Divine, does He always forgive us?

Sri Aurobindo himself gives us the Divine's answer: "Forgive whom and what?" The Lord knows that all is Himself and therefore that all actions are His and all things are Himself. To forgive, one must be *other* than the one who is forgiven and the thing to be forgiven must have been done by someone other than oneself.

The truth is that when you ask forgiveness you hope that the dire consequences of what you have done will be wiped away. But that is possible only if the causes of the error you have committed have themselves disappeared. If you have made a mistake through ignorance, the ignorance must disappear. If you have made a mistake through bad will, the bad will must disappear and be replaced by goodwill. Mere regret will not do, it must be accompanied by a step forward.

For the universe is constantly evolving; nothing is at a standstill. Everything is perpetually changing, moving forward or backward. Things or acts that set us back seem bad to us, and cause confusion and disorder. The only remedy for them is a radical forward movement, a progress. This new orientation alone can annul the consequences of the backward movement.

Therefore it is not a vague and abstract forgiveness that one should ask of the Divine, but the power to make the necessary progress. For only an inner transformation can wipe out the consequences of the act.

2 March 1960

22 – God struck me with a human hand; shall I say then, "I pardon Thee thy insolence, O God"?

> 23 – God gave me good in a blow. Shall I say, "I forgive thee, O Almighty One, the harm and the cruelty, but do it not again"?

What does this mean: "God struck me with a human hand"?

These two aphorisms are illustrations of the affirmation of the Divine Presence in all things and all beings, and they also develop the idea which has already been touched on, that there is nothing and no one to forgive, since the Divine is the originator of all things.

This is how this sentence, "God struck me with a human hand", should be read and understood. If you see nothing but the appearances, it is only one man hitting another. But for one who sees and knows the Truth, it is the supreme Lord who gives the blow through that human hand, and the blow necessarily does good to the one who receives it, that is to say, brings about a progress in his consciousness, for the ultimate aim of creation is to awaken all beings to the consciousness of the Divine.

Once you have understood that, the rest of the two aphorisms is easily explained.

Are we to forgive the Lord for the good He does us, while, at the same time, asking Him not to do it again?

The self-contradiction and stupidity of such a formula are obvious.

9 March 1960

> 24 – When I pine at misfortune and call it evil, or am jealous and disappointed, then I know that there is awake in me again the eternal fool.

What is this "misfortune" and why does it come?

Jnana

If you act in order to obtain a result and if the result obtained is not the one you expected, you call this a misfortune. As a general rule, any event that is unexpected or feared is considered by ordinary minds to be a misfortune. Why does this misfortune come? In each case the reason is different; or rather, it is only after the event that the need to explain things makes us look for reasons. But most often our evaluation of circumstances is blind and mistaken. We judge in ignorance. It is only later on, sometimes very much later on, when we have the necessary perspective and view the train of events and the overall results, that we see things as they really were. Then we perceive that what seemed bad to us was in truth very useful and helped us to make the necessary progress.

Sri Aurobindo describes the state of one who is sunk in ignorance and desire and who judges everything from the point of view of his narrow and limited ego as that of "eternal fool". To be able to understand and feel things correctly one must have a universal vision and be conscious of the Divine Presence and Will in all things and in all circumstances.

Then we know that whatever happens to us is always for our good, if we take the point of view of the spirit in the unfolding of time.

16 March 1960

25 – *When I see others suffer, I feel that I am unfortunate, but the wisdom that is not mine, sees the good that is coming and approves.*

What is this "wisdom"?

It is the supreme wisdom, the wisdom of the Supreme. By this wisdom the present, the past and the future are all seen equally. It knows the causes of all effects and the effects of all causes. The sum total of all circumstances, perceived simultaneously in their entirety, is seen by it as Nature's sublime effort to express the Divine progressively, her ascending march towards divine perfection. That is "the good that is coming", everything tends towards that; and that is why the true wisdom approves.

For it is only our shortsightedness, our too limited perception and our misguided sensations that, for us, change into suffering what is a possibility and an opportunity for progress.

And this is proved by the fact that as soon as we understand and collaborate, suffering disappears.

23 March 1960

> **26** – Sir Philip Sidney said of the criminal led out to be hanged, "There, but for the grace of God, goes Sir Philip Sidney." Wiser, had he said, "There, by the grace of God, goes Sir Philip Sidney."

I have not understood the meaning of this aphorism.

Sir Philip Sidney was a statesman and a poet, but in spite of his success in life, he retained his humble nature. Seeing a criminal being taken to the gallows, he is supposed to have said the famous words which Sri Aurobindo quotes in his aphorism and which could be paraphrased like this, "That could have happened to me too, *but for* the Grace of God." Sri Aurobindo remarks that had Sir Philip Sidney been wiser he would have said, "That could have happened to me too, *by* the Grace of God." For the divine Grace is everywhere, always, behind everything and every event, whatever our reaction to that thing or event may be, whether it appears good or bad, catastrophic or beneficial.

And if Sir Philip had been a Yogi, he would have had the experience of human unity and he would have felt concretely that it was himself or a part of himself which was being led to the gallows and he would have known at the same time that everything that happens happens by the Grace of the Lord.

30 March 1960

27 – **God is a great and cruel Torturer because He loves. You do not understand this, because you have not seen and played with Krishna.**

What does "to play with Krishna" mean? What does "God is a great and cruel Torturer" mean?

Krishna is the immanent Divine, the Divine Presence in everyone and in all things. He is also, sovereignly, the aspect of Delight and Love of the Supreme; he is the smiling tenderness and the playful gaiety; he is at once the player, the play and all his playmates. And as both the game and its results are wholly known, conceived, willed, organised and played consciously in their entirety, there can be room for nothing but the delight of the play. Thus to see Krishna means to find the inner Godhead, to play with Krishna means to be identified with the inner Godhead and to share in his consciousness. When you achieve this state, you enter immediately into the bliss of the divine play; and the more complete the identification, the more perfect the state.

But if some corner of the consciousness keeps the ordinary perception, the ordinary understanding, the ordinary sensation, then you see the suffering of others, you find the play that causes so much suffering very cruel and you conclude that the God who takes pleasure in such a play must be a terrible Torturer; but on the other hand, when you have had the experience of identification with the Divine, you cannot forget the immense, the wonderful love which he puts into his play, and you understand that it is the limitation of our vision that makes us judge in this way, and that far from being a voluntary Torturer, he is the great beneficent love that guides the world and men, by the quickest routes, in their progressive march towards perfection, a perfection which, moreover, is always relative and is always being surpassed.

But a day will come when this apparent suffering will no longer be required to stimulate the advance and when progress can be made more and more in harmony and delight.

6 April 1960

28 – One called Napoleon a tyrant and imperial cutthroat; but I saw God armed striding through Europe.

Are all these wars necessary for the evolution of the earth?

At a certain stage of human development, wars are inevitable. In prehistoric times the whole of life was a war; and to the present day human history has been one long history of wars. Wars are the natural result of a state of consciousness dominated by the struggle for life and egoistic aggressiveness. And at the present time, in spite of some human efforts towards peace, there is, as yet, nothing to assure us that war is no longer an inevitable calamity. Indeed, does not a state of war, open or otherwise, exist at this moment in many parts of the world?

Besides, everything that happens on earth necessarily leads to its progress. Thus wars are schools of courage, endurance, fearlessness; they may serve to destroy a past which refuses to disappear although its time is over, and they make room for new things. Wars can, like Kurukshetra,[2] be a way to rid the earth of a domineering or destructive race so that justice and right may reign. They can, through the presence of danger,

---

[2] In the Bhagavad Gita, the legendary battle-field where the Pandavas, led by Sri Krishna, and the Kauravas confronted each other.

shake the apathy of a too tamasic[3] consciousness and awaken dormant energies. Finally they can, by contrast, and because of the horrors that accompany and follow them, drive men to seek an effective way to make such a barbarous and violent form of transformation unnecessary.

For everything that is unnecessary to the evolution of the earth automatically ceases to exist.

13 April 1960

You have written: "They [wars] may serve to destroy a past which refuses to disappear although its time is over, and they make room for new things." Now that the Supermind has descended upon earth will war be necessary to change the present state of the world?

All will depend on the receptivity of nations. If they open widely and quickly to the influence of the new forces and if they change rapidly enough in their conceptions and actions, war may be avoided. But it is always threatening and always in abeyance; every error, every darkening of the consciousness increases this threat.

And yet in the last analysis everything really depends on the Divine Grace and we should look towards the future with confidence and serenity, at the same time progressing as fast as we can.

15 April 1960

29 – I have forgotten what vice is and what virtue; I can only see God, His play in the world and His will in humanity.

---

[3] Governed by *tamas*, the principle of inertia and obscurity.

If everything is God's will, what is the use of personal will?

In the universe and more particularly upon earth everything is part of the divine plan executed by Nature and everything is necessary for its fulfilment. Personal will is one of Nature's means of action and indispensable for her working. So personal will is in a way part of God's will.

However, to understand properly, we must first agree on the meaning that is given to the word "will".

Will, as it is usually conceived, is the elaboration of a thought, to which is added a force, a power of fulfilment accompanied by an impulse to carry it out. That is the description of human will. Divine will is quite another thing. It is a vision united with a power of realisation. Divine will is omniscient and omnipotent, it is irresistible and immediate in its execution.

Human will is uncertain, often wavering, always in conflict with opposing wills. It is effective only when for some reason or other it is in accord with the will of Nature — itself a transcription of the divine will — or with the divine will itself, as a result of Grace or Yoga.

So one can say that personal will is one of the means that God uses to bring us back to Him.

20 April 1960

30 – I saw a child wallowing in the dirt and the same child cleaned by his mother and resplendent, but each time I trembled before his utter purity.

Can a child keep this purity even when he has grown up?

In theory, it is not impossible, and some people born away from cities, civilisations and cultures may maintain throughout the

Jnana

life of their earthly body this spontaneous purity, a purity of the soul that is not obscured by the mind's working.

For the purity of which Sri Aurobindo speaks here is the purity of instinct, that obeys Nature's impulses spontaneously, never calculating, never questioning, never asking whether it is good or bad, whether what one does is right or wrong, whether it is a virtue or a sin, whether the outcome will be favourable or unfavourable. All these notions come into play when the mental ego makes its appearance and begins to take a dominant position in the consciousness and to veil the spontaneity of the soul.

In modern "civilised" life, parents and teachers, by their practical and rational "good advice", lose no time in covering up this spontaneity which they call unconsciousness, and substituting for it a very small, very narrow, limited mental ego, withdrawn into itself, crammed with notions of misbehaviour and sin and punishment or of personal interest, calculation and profit; all of which has the inevitable result of increasing vital desires through repression, fear or self-justification.

And yet for the sake of completeness it should be added that because man is a mental being, he must necessarily in the course of his evolution leave behind this unconscious and spontaneous purity, which is very similar to the purity of the animal, and after passing through an unavoidable period of mental perversion and impurity, rise beyond the mind into the higher and luminous purity of the divine consciousness.

27 April 1960

31 – What I wished or thought to be the right thing does not come about; therefore it is clear that there is no All-Wise one who guides the world but only blind Chance or a brute Causality.

For some people events are always contrary to what they desire or aspire for or believe to be good for them. They

On Thoughts and Aphorisms

often despair. Is this a necessity for their progress?

Despair is never a necessity for progress, it is always a sign of weakness and *tamas*; it often indicates the presence of an adverse force, that is to say, a force that is purposely acting against sadhana.[4]

So, in all circumstances of life you must always be very careful to guard against despair. Besides, this habit of being sombre, morose, of despairing, does not truly depend on events, but on a lack of faith in the nature. One who has faith, even if only in himself, can face all difficulties, all circumstances, even the most adverse, without discouragement or despair. He fights like a man to the end. Natures that lack faith also lack endurance and courage.

Sri Aurobindo tells us that for human beings the degree of success in physical life depends on the degree of harmony between the individual and universal physical Nature. Some people have a will which is spontaneously in tune with the will of Nature, and they succeed in everything they undertake; others, on the contrary, have a will which is more or less totally out of tune with the will of cosmic Nature and they fail in everything they do or try to do.

As for the question of what is necessary for progress, in an evolving world everything is necessarily a help to progress; but individual progress extends over a considerable number of lives and through innumerable experiences. It cannot be judged on the basis of a single life between birth and death. On the whole, it is certain that the experience of a life of failure and defeat is just as useful to the soul's growth as the experience of a life of success and victory; even more so, no doubt, than the experience of an uneventful life, as human existence usually is, in which success and failure, satisfaction and disappointment, pleasure and pain mingle and follow one another — a life that

---
[4] The practice of Yoga.

seems "natural" and does not require any great effort.

4 May 1960

32 – The Atheist is God playing at hide and seek with Himself; but is the Theist any other? Well, perhaps; for he has seen the shadow of God and clutched at it.

What does "God playing at hide and seek with Himself" mean?

In the game of hide and seek, one person hides and the other seeks. So God hides from the atheist who says, "God? I do not see him, I do not know where he is; therefore he does not exist." But the atheist does not know that God is also in him; and therefore it is God who is denying his own existence. Isn't that a game? And yet a day will come when he will be brought face to face with himself and will be obliged to recognise that he exists.

The believer thinks himself very superior to the atheist, but all that he has been able to seize of God is His shadow and he clings to this shadow imagining that it is God himself. For if he truly knew God, he would know that God is all things and in everything; then he would cease to think himself superior to anybody.

11 May 1960

33 – O Thou that lovest, strike! If Thou strike me not now, I shall know that Thou lovest me not.

I have not understood this aphorism very well.

All who aspire for the divine perfection know that the blows which the Lord deals us in His infinite love and grace are the surest and quickest way to make us progress. And the harder the blows the more they feel the greatness of the divine Love.

Ordinary men, on the contrary, always ask God to give them an easy, pleasant and successful life. In every personal satisfaction they see a sign of divine mercy; but if on the contrary they meet with unhappiness and misfortune in life, they complain and say to God, "You do not love me."

In opposition to this crude and ignorant attitude, Sri Aurobindo says to the divine Beloved, "Strike, strike hard, let me feel the intensity of Thy love for me."

18 May 1960

34 – O Misfortune, blessed be thou; for through thee I have seen the face of my Lover.

If through misfortune one sees the face of God, then it is no longer misfortune, is it?

Obviously, far from being a misfortune, it is a blessing. And this is precisely what Sri Aurobindo means.

When things happen which are not what we expect, what we hope for, what we want, which are contrary to our desires, in our ignorance we call them misfortunes and lament. But if we were to become a little wiser and observe the deeper consequences of these very same events, we would find that they are leading us rapidly towards the Divine, the Beloved; whereas easy and pleasant circumstances encourage us to dally on the path, to stop along the way to pluck the flowers of pleasure which present themselves to us and which we are too weak or not sincere enough to reject resolutely, so that our march forward is not delayed.

One must already be very strong, very far along the way, to be able to face success and the little enjoyments it brings without giving way. Those who can do this, those who are strong, do not run after success; they do not seek it, and accept it with indifference. For they know and appreciate the value of the lashes given by unhappiness and misfortune.

But ultimately the true attitude, the sign and proof that we are near the goal, is a perfect equality which enables us to accept success and failure, fortune and misfortune, happiness and sorrow with the same tranquil joy; for all these things become marvellous gifts that the Lord in his infinite solicitude showers upon us.

25 May 1960

35 – Men are still in love with grief; when they see one who is too high for grief or joy, they curse him and cry, "O thou insensible!" Therefore Christ still hangs on the cross in Jerusalem.

36 – Men are in love with sin; when they see one who is too high for vice or virtue, they curse him and cry, "O thou breaker of bonds, thou wicked and immoral one!" Therefore Sri Krishna does not live as yet in Brindavan.[5]

I would like to have an explanation of these two aphorisms.

When Christ came upon earth, he brought a message of brotherhood, love and peace. But he had to die in pain, on the cross, so that his message might be heard. For men cherish suffering and hatred and want their God to suffer with them. They wanted this when Christ came and, in spite of his teaching and sacrifice, they still want it; and they are so attached to their pain that, symbolically, Christ is still bound to his cross, suffering perpetually for the salvation of men.

As for Krishna, he came upon earth to bring freedom and delight. He came to announce to men, enslaved to Nature, to

---

[5] The village where Sri Krishna spent his childhood, and where he danced with Radha and the other *Gopis*.

their passions and errors, that if they took refuge in the Supreme Lord they would be free from all bondage and sin. But men are very attached to their vices and virtues (for without vice there would be no virtue); they are in love with their sins and cannot tolerate anyone being free and above all error.

That is why Krishna, although immortal, is not present at Brindavan in a body at this moment.

3 June 1960

37 – **Some say Krishna never lived, he is a myth. They mean on earth; for if Brindavan existed nowhere, the Bhagavat[6] could not have been written.**

Does Brindavan exist anywhere else than on earth?

The whole earth and everything it contains is a kind of concentration, a condensation of something which exists in other worlds invisible to the material eye. Each thing manifested here has its principle, idea or essence somewhere in the subtler regions. This is an indispensable condition for the manifestation. And the importance of the manifestation will always depend on the origin of the thing manifested.

In the world of the gods there is an ideal and harmonious Brindavan of which the earthly Brindavan is but a deformation and a caricature.

Those who are developed inwardly, either in their senses or in their minds, perceive these realities which are invisible (to the ordinary man) and receive their inspiration from them.

So the writer or writers of the Bhagavat were certainly in contact with a whole inner world that is well and truly real and existent, where they saw and experienced everything they have described or revealed.

---

[6] The story of Krishna, as related in the Bhagavat Purana.

Whether Krishna existed or not in a human form, living on earth, is only of very secondary importance (except perhaps from an exclusively historical point of view), for Krishna is a real, living and active being; and his influence has been one of the great factors in the progress and transformation of the earth.

8 June 1960

38 – Strange! The Germans have disproved the existence of Christ; yet his crucifixion remains still a greater historic fact than the death of Caesar.

To what plane of consciousness did Christ belong?

In the *Essays on the Gita* Sri Aurobindo mentions the names of three Avatars, and Christ is one of them. An Avatar is an emanation of the Supreme Lord who assumes a human body on earth. I heard Sri Aurobindo himself say that Christ was an emanation of the Lord's aspect of love.

The death of Caesar marked a decisive change in the history of Rome and the countries dependent on her. It was therefore an important event in the history of Europe.

But the death of Christ was the starting-point of a new stage in the evolution of human civilisation. This is why Sri Aurobindo tells us that the death of Christ was of greater historical significance, that is to say, it has had greater historical consequences than the death of Caesar. The story of Christ, as it has been told, is the concrete and dramatic enactment of the divine sacrifice: the Supreme Lord, who is All-Light, All-Knowledge, All-Power, All-Beauty, All-Love, All-Bliss, accepting to assume human ignorance and suffering in matter, in order to help men to emerge from the falsehood in which they live and because of which they die.

16 June 1960

39 – Sometimes one is led to think that only those things really matter which have never happened; for beside them most historic achievements seem almost pale and ineffective.

I would like to have an explanation of this aphorism.

Sri Aurobindo, who had made a thorough study of history, knew how uncertain are the data which have been used to write it. Most often the accuracy of the documents is doubtful, and the information they supply is poor, incomplete, trivial and frequently distorted. As a whole, the official version of human history is nothing but a long, almost unbroken record of violent aggressions: wars, revolutions, murders or colonisations. True, some of these aggressions and massacres have been adorned with flattering terms and epithets; they have been called religious wars, holy wars, civilising campaigns; but they nonetheless remain acts of greed or vengeance.

Rarely in history do we find the description of a cultural, artistic or philosophical outflowering.

That is why, as Sri Aurobindo says, all this makes a rather dismal picture without any deep significance. On the other hand, in the legendary accounts of things which may never have existed on earth, of events which have not been declared authentic by "official" knowledge, of wonderful individuals whose existence is doubted by the scholars in their dried-up wisdom, we find the crystallisation of all the hopes and aspirations of man, his love of the marvellous, the heroic and the sublime, the description of everything he would like to be and strives to become.

That, more or less, is what Sri Aurobindo means in his aphorism.

22 June 1960

40 – There are four very great events in history, the siege

of Troy, the life and crucifixion of Christ, the exile of Krishna in Brindavan and the colloquy with Arjuna on the field of Kurukshetra. The siege of Troy created Hellas, the exile in Brindavan[7] created devotional religion (for before there was only meditation and worship), Christ from his cross humanised Europe, the colloquy at Kurukshetra will yet liberate humanity. Yet it is said that none of these four events ever happened.

(1) Were the meditation and worship of former times the same as those of today?
(2) What does this mean: "the colloquy at Kurukshetra will yet liberate humanity"?

(1) In ancient times, as in our own day, each religion had its own particular kind of meditation and worship. And yet everywhere, always, meditation is a special mode of mental activity and concentration, only the details of the practice vary. Worship is a series of ceremonies and rites that are scrupulously and exactly performed in honour of a deity.

Here Sri Aurobindo refers to the worship and meditation of ancient India, in Vedic and Vedantic times.

(2) The colloquy at Kurukshetra is the Bhagavad Gita.

Sri Aurobindo considers the message of the Gita to be the basis of the great spiritual movement which has led and will lead humanity more and more to its liberation, that is to say, to its escape from falsehood and ignorance, towards the truth.

From the time of its first appearance, the Gita has had an immense spiritual action; but with the new interpretation that Sri Aurobindo has given to it, its influence has increased considerably and has become decisive.

29 June 1960

---

[7] The child Krishna had to take refuge at Brindavan in order to escape his uncle Kansa, the tyrant king of Mathura.

41 – They say that the gospels are forgeries and Krishna a creation of the poets. Thank God then for the forgeries and bow down before the inventors.

What is the role of the Gospels in the life of man?

The Gospels were the starting-point of the Christian religion. To say what they have brought to the world it would be necessary to give a historical and psychological account of the development of the life of Christianity and the action of the Christian religion upon earth. That would take a long time and be somewhat out of place here.

I can only say that the writers of the Gospels have tried to reproduce exactly what Christ taught and that they have in a certain measure succeeded in transmitting his message. It is a message of peace, brotherhood and love.

But it is better to keep silent about what men have done with this message.

6 July 1960

42 – If God assigns to me my place in Hell, I do not know why I should aspire to Heaven. He knows best what is for my welfare.

Do Heaven and Hell exist?

Heaven and Hell are at once real and unreal. They both exist and do not exist.

Human thought is creative; it gives more or less lasting forms to mental, vital and even subtle physical substance. These forms are appearances rather than realities; but for those whose thoughts they are, and still more for those who believe in them, they have a concrete enough existence to give them an illusion of reality. Thus, for the believers of religions which assert the existence of a hell, a paradise, or various heavens, these places do exist objectively, and when they die they can go there for a longer or shorter period. But still these things are only impermanent mental formations; they carry no eternal truth in themselves.

I have seen the heavens and hells where some people have gone after death, and it is very difficult to make them understand that there is no truth in them. Once it took me more than a year to convince someone that his so-called hell was not hell and to get him out of it.

The hell which Sri Aurobindo speaks of here is more a state of consciousness than a place, it is a psychological condition that one creates for oneself.

Just as you can carry within you a heaven of blissful communion with the Divine, you can, if you do not take care to master the asuric[8] tendencies in your nature, also carry in your consciousness a hell of misery and desolation.

There are moments in life when everything around you, people and circumstances, is so obscure, so adverse, so ugly that all hope of a higher realisation seems to vanish. The world seems irremediably doomed to a night of cruel hatred, unconscious and obstinate ignorance and intractable bad will. Then one may say with Sri Aurobindo, "God has assigned to me a place in hell"; and, with him too, in all circumstances, however terrible they may seem, one should dwell in the peaceful joy of total surrender to the Divine and say to the Lord in all sincerity, "Let Thy will be done."

13 July 1960

43 – If God draw me towards Heaven, then, even if His other hand strive to keep me in Hell, yet must I struggle upwards.

---

[8] Of the Asuras, hostile beings of the mentalised vital plane.

On Thoughts and Aphorisms

> *Does not God know what He wants for us? Why should He want to pull us in two opposite directions?*

God knows perfectly well what He wants for us. He wants to bring us all back to Him in a perfect union. The goal is one, the same for all; but the means, the methods and the procedures for reaching it are innumerable. There are just as many as there are beings on earth; and each one of these means is an exact expression of the will of the Supreme Lord, who, in his integral vision and perfect wisdom, does what is needful for each person.

So if someone needs a contradiction, an inner opposition to intensify his aspiration and effort, the Lord, in His infinite Grace, even while drawing this being upward and giving him the power to rise, will at the same time hold him down to create in him the resistance needed to intensify his aspiration and effort.

And if, like Sri Aurobindo, you can see that both movements have the same divine origin, then, instead of lamenting and being alarmed, you rejoice and keep a firm and luminous faith.

19 July 1960

44 – Only those thoughts are true the opposite of which is also true in its own time and application; indisputable dogmas are the most dangerous kind of falsehoods.

> *Why are indisputable dogmas the most dangerous ones?*

The absolute, infinite, eternal Truth is unthinkable for the mind, which can conceive only what is spatial, temporal, fragmentary and limited.

Thus, on the mental plane the absolute Truth is divided into innumerable fragmentary and contradictory truths which, in their entirety, strive to reproduce, insofar as possible, the original Truth.

If one element of this totality is taken separately and affirmed as the only true one, however central or comprehensive it may be, it necessarily becomes a falsehood, since it denies all the rest of the Total Truth.

This is precisely how indisputable dogmas are created and this is why they are the most dangerous kind of falsehood — because each one asserts that it is the sole truth to the exclusion of all other truths which, in their innumerable and complementary totality, express progressively, in the becoming, the infinite, eternal, absolute Truth.

27 August 1960

45 – Logic is the worst enemy of Truth, as self-righteousness is the worst enemy of virtue; for the one cannot see its own errors nor the other its own imperfections.

What is the role of logic and reason in our lives?

The best answer I can give to your question is this quotation from *The Synthesis of Yoga*: "The characteristic power of the reason in its fullness is a logical movement assuring itself first of all available materials and data by observation and arrangement, then acting upon them for a resultant knowledge gained, assured and enlarged by a first use of the reflective powers, and lastly assuring itself of the correctness of its results by a more careful and formal action, more vigilant, deliberate, severely logical which tests, rejects or confirms them according to certain secure standards and processes developed by reflection and experience. The first business of the logical reason is therefore a right, careful and complete observation of its available material and data."[9]

But in this aphorism Sri Aurobindo does not speak of reason. He speaks of logic, which is the partner and instrument of reason.

[9] *The Synthesis of Yoga*, Cent. Vol. 21, p. 820.

Logic is the art of correctly deducing one idea from another and inferring from a fact all its consequences. But logic does not itself possess the capacity to discern the truth. So your logic may be indisputable, but if your starting-point is wrong, your conclusions will also be wrong, in spite of the correctness of your logic, or rather, because of it. The same holds true for self-righteousness, which is a feeling of virtuous superiority. Your virtue makes you disdainful of others, and this pride — which fills you with disdain for those who, according to you, are less virtuous than you are — makes your virtue completely worthless.

That is why Sri Aurobindo tells us in his aphorism that logic is the worst enemy of Truth, just as the feeling of virtuous superiority is the worst enemy of virtue.

24 August 1960

46 – When I was asleep in the Ignorance, I came to a place of meditation full of holy men and I found their company wearisome and the place a prison; when I awoke, God took me to a prison and turned it into a place of meditation and His trysting-ground.

Is Sri Aurobindo speaking here of his own experience in prison during his political life?

Yes. Sri Aurobindo is referring here to his experience in Alipore jail.

But what is interesting in this aphorism is the contrast he points out between the material prison where only his body was confined, while his spirit, unfettered by social conventions and prejudice, free from all preconceived ideas and all doctrinaire limitations, had a direct and conscious contact with the Divine and a first revelation of the integral Yoga; and, on the other hand, the mental prison of narrow rules which excludes life

Jnana

and within which people often confine themselves when they renounce ordinary existence in order to devote themselves to a spiritual life based on traditional dogmatic ideas.

So Sri Aurobindo is here, as always, the champion of the real freedom beyond all rules and limitations, the total freedom of perfect union with the supreme and eternal Truth.

24 October 1960

> 47 – When I read a wearisome book through and with pleasure, yet perceived all the perfection of its wearisomeness, then I knew that my mind was conquered.

How is it possible to read a wearisome book with pleasure?

It is possible when your pleasure no longer depends on what you do or what happens to you, when your pleasure is the spontaneous outward expression of the unchanging joy which you carry within yourself with the Divine Presence. Then it is a constant state of consciousness in all activities and in all circumstances. And, as of all wearisome things one of the most wearisome is a wearisome book, Sri Aurobindo gives us this example as an irrefutable proof of the conquest and transformation of the mind.

10 November 1960

> 48 – I knew my mind to be conquered when it admired the beauty of the hideous, yet felt perfectly why other men shrank back or hated.

What does "the beauty of the hideous" mean?

It is always the same realisation presented from different angles, expressed through various experiences: the realisation that everything is a manifestation of the Supreme, the Eternal, the Infinite, immutable in his total perfection and in his absolute reality. That is why, by conquering our mind and its ignorant and false perceptions we can, through all things, enter into contact with this Supreme Truth which is also the Supreme Beauty and the Supreme Love, beyond all our mental and vital notions of beauty and ugliness, the good and the bad.

Even when we say "Supreme Truth, Supreme Beauty, Supreme Love", we should give to these words a meaning other than the one which is attributed to them by our intellect. It is to emphasise this fact that Sri Aurobindo writes, paradoxically, "the beauty of the hideous".

14 November 1960

What is this other meaning?

I meant that we cannot conceive the Divine intellectually. It is only when we leave the mental world and enter into the spiritual world, and, instead of thinking things, we live them and become them, that we can truly understand them. But even then, when we want to express our experience we have only those words that express our mental experiences, and in spite of all our efforts these words are inapt to convey what we want to express.

That is why Sri Aurobindo so often uses paradoxes to lift the mind out of the rut of ordinary thinking and, behind the apparent absurdity of what is said, to make us see the light of what is felt and perceived.

26 November 1960

49 – To feel and love the God of beauty and good in the ugly and the evil, and still yearn in utter love to heal it of its ugliness and its evil, this is real virtue and morality.

Jnana

How can one help to cure the evil and the ugliness that one sees everywhere? Through love? What is the power of love? How can an individual phenomenon of consciousness act on the rest of mankind?[10]

How can one help to cure evil and ugliness?... One may say that there is a kind of hierarchy of collaboration or action: there is a negative help and a positive help.

To begin with, there is a way that might be called negative, the way provided by Buddhism and kindred religions: not to see. First of all, to be in such a state of purity and beauty that you do not perceive ugliness and evil — it is like something that does not touch you because it does not exist in you.

That is the perfection of the negative method. It is quite elementary: never to notice evil, never to speak of the evil in others, not to perpetuate these vibrations by observation, by criticism, by insistence on what is bad. That is what the Buddha taught: each time you speak of an evil, you help to spread it.

This barely touches the problem.

Yet it should be a very general rule. But people who criticise have an answer for that; they say, "If you do not see the evil, you will never be able to cure it. If you leave someone in his ugliness, he will never get out of it." This is not true, but that is how they justify their behaviour. So in this aphorism Sri Aurobindo forestalls these objections: it is not because of ignorance or unconsciousness or indifference that you do not see the evil — you are quite capable of seeing it, even of feeling it, but you refuse to help to spread it by giving it the force of your attention and the support of your consciousness. And for that you must yourself be above this perception and feeling; you must be able to see the evil or the ugliness without suffering from it, without being shocked or disturbed by it. You see it from a height where these things do not exist, but you have the conscious perception

---

[10] Oral question and answer.

of it, you are not affected by it, you are free. This is the first step.

The second step is to be *positively* conscious of the supreme Good and supreme Beauty behind all things, which sustains all things and enables them to exist. When you see Him, you are able to perceive Him behind this mask and this distortion; even this ugliness, this wickedness, this evil is a disguise of Something which is essentially beautiful or good, luminous, pure.

Then comes the *true* collaboration, for when you have this vision, this perception, when you live in this consciousness, it also gives you the power to *draw* That down into the manifestation, to the earth, and to bring It into contact with what now distorts and disguises, so that little by little this distortion and this disguise are transformed by the influence of the Truth that is behind.

Here we are at the very summit of the scale of collaboration.

In this way it is not necessary to introduce the principle of love into the explanation. But if you want to know or understand the nature of the Force or the Power that enables or brings about this transformation — particularly where evil is concerned, but also with ugliness to a certain extent — you see that love is obviously the most potent and integral of all powers — integral in the sense that it applies in all cases. It is even more powerful than the power of purification which dissolves all bad will and which is, as it were, the master of the adverse forces, but which has not the direct power of transformation. The power of purification first dissolves in order to allow the transformation afterwards. It destroys one form in order to be able to create a better one, whereas love need not dissolve in order to transform; it possesses the direct power of transformation. Love is like a flame that changes what is hard into something malleable and even sublimates this malleable thing into a kind of purified vapour — it does not destroy, it transforms.

In its essence, in its origin, love is like a flame, a white flame which overcomes *all* resistances. You can experience this yourself: whatever the difficulty in your being, whatever the burden of accumulated error, ignorance, incapacity and bad will, a single *second* of this pure, essential, supreme love dissolves it as in an all-powerful flame; a single moment and a whole past can disappear; a single instant in which you *touch* it in its essence and a whole burden is consumed.

And it is very easy to explain how a person who has this experience can spread it, can act on others; because to have the experience you must touch the one, supreme Essence of the whole manifestation, the Origin and the Essence, the Source and the Reality of all that is; and at once you enter the realm of Unity — there is no longer any separation of individuals, there is only one single vibration that can be repeated indefinitely in external form.[11]

If you rise high enough, you find yourself at the heart of all things. And what is manifest in this heart can manifest in all things. That is the great secret, the secret of the divine incarnation in an individual form, because in the normal course of things what manifests at the centre is realised in the external form only with the awakening and the response of the will in the individual form. Whereas if the central Will is represented constantly and permanently in an individual being, this individual being can serve as an intermediary between this Will and all beings, and will for them. Everything this individual being perceives and offers in his consciousness to the supreme Will is answered as if it came from each individual being. And if for any reason the individual elements have a more or less conscious and voluntary relation with that representative being, their relation increases the efficacy, the effectiveness of the representative individual; and thus the supreme Action can act in

---

[11] Later the disciple asked Mother: "Is it one single vibration which *can be repeated* indefinitely or which *is repeated* indefinitely?" Mother answered: "I meant several things at the same time. This single vibration is static everywhere, but when one realises it consciously, one has the power of making it active wherever one directs it; that is to say, one doesn't move anything, but the stress of the consciousness makes it active wherever one directs one's consciousness."

Matter in a much more concrete and permanent manner. That is the reason for these descents of consciousness — which we may describe as "polarised", for they always come to earth with a definite purpose and for a special realisation, with a mission — a mission which is decided upon, determined before the incarnation. These are the great stages of the supreme incarnations on earth.

And when the day comes for the manifestation of supreme love, for the crystallised, concentrated descent of supreme love, that will truly be the hour of transformation. For nothing will be able to resist That.

But since it is all-powerful, some receptivity must be prepared on earth so that the effects are not shattering. Sri Aurobindo has explained this in one of his letters. Someone asked him, "Why does it not come immediately?" He answered something like this: if divine love were to manifest in its essence upon earth, it would be like a bombshell; because the earth is neither supple nor receptive enough to be able to widen itself to the dimensions of this love. It not only needs to open, but to widen itself and to become more supple — Matter is still too rigid. And even the substance of the physical consciousness — not only the most material Matter, but the substance of the physical consciousness — is too rigid.

January 1961

50 – **To hate the sinner is the worst sin, for it is hating God; yet he who commits it glories in his superior virtue.**

When we enter into a certain state of consciousness, we see clearly that we are capable of anything and that in fact there is not a single "sin" that is not potentially our sin. Is this impression correct? And yet we revolt against and feel an aversion for certain things: there is always something somewhere which we cannot accept. Why?

Jnana

What is the true attitude, the effective attitude in face of evil?[12]

There is not a single sin that is not our sin.... You have this experience when for some reason or other — depending on the case — you come into contact with the universal state of consciousness — not in its limitless essence, but on any level of Matter. There is an atomic consciousness; there is a purely material consciousness; and there is, even more, a general psychological consciousness. When by going within, by a kind of withdrawal from the ego, you come into contact with this zone of consciousness, let us say, a terrestrial or collective human psychological zone — there is a difference, "collective human" is restrictive, whereas "terrestrial" includes many animal movements, even plant movements; but as in the present case the moral notion of guilt, sin, evil belongs exclusively to the human consciousness, we will say simply the collective human psychological consciousness — when you come into contact with that through this identification, naturally you feel or see or know that you are capable of any human movement anywhere. It is to some extent a truth-consciousness — this egoistic sense of what belongs and does not belong to you, of what you can do and cannot do, disappears at that time; you become aware that the fundamental structure of the human consciousness is such that any human being is capable of doing anything at all. And since you are in a truth-consciousness, at the same time you have the feeling that judgments or aversions, or rejection, are absurd. *Everything* is potentially there. And if certain currents of force — which you usually cannot trace; you see them come and go, but as a rule their origin and direction are unknown — if any one of these currents enters into you, it can make you do anything.

If you could always remain in this state of consciousness, after some time — provided you maintained within you the flame

---

[12] Oral question and answer.

of Agni, the flame of purification and progress — you would be able not only to prevent these movements from taking an active form in you and expressing themselves materially, but also to act on the very nature of the movement and transform it. But, of course, unless you have attained a very high degree of realisation, it will be practically impossible to maintain this state of consciousness for long. Almost immediately you fall back into the egoistic consciousness of the separate self. And then all the difficulties come back: the disgust, the revolt against certain things, the horror they arouse in you, etc.

It is probable — it is even certain — that until you are yourself completely transformed, these movements of disgust and revolt are needed so that you can do *in yourself* what has to be done to shut the door. For after all, the problem is not to allow them to manifest themselves.

In another aphorism Sri Aurobindo says — I no longer remember his exact words — that sin is merely something which is not in its right place. In this perpetual Becoming nothing ever repeats itself, and there are things that disappear, so to speak, into the past; and when their disappearance becomes necessary these things become, for our very limited consciousness, bad and repulsive. And we revolt against them because their time is over. But if we had the overall view, if we could contain within ourselves the past, the present and the future all at once — as it is somewhere above — we would see the relativity of these things and that it is above all the progressive Force of evolution that gives us the will to reject; and that wherever they are in their right place, they are quite acceptable. Only, it is practically impossible to have this experience unless you have the total vision, that is to say, the vision that belongs to the Supreme alone! Therefore you must first of all identify yourself with the Supreme; then, afterwards, with this identification, you can return to a sufficiently exteriorised consciousness and see things as they are. But that is the principle, and to the extent that you are capable of realising it, you reach a state of consciousness where you can look at everything with a smile of total certitude that everything is as it should be.

Naturally, people who do not think deeply enough will say, "Ah, but if we saw that everything is as it should be, nothing would move!" No, you cannot prevent things from moving! Even for a fraction of a second they do not stop moving. It is a continuous, total transformation, a movement that never ceases. And because it is difficult for us to feel like this, it is possible for us to imagine that if we were to enter into certain states of consciousness, things would not change. But even if we were to enter into an apparently total inertia, things would continue to change and so would we!

Basically, disgust, revolt, anger, all these movements of violence are necessarily movements of ignorance and limitation, with all the weakness that limitation represents. Revolt is a weakness — it is the feeling of an impotent will. You will — or you think you will — you feel, you see that things are not as they should be and you revolt against whatever does not agree with what you see. But if you were all-powerful, if your will and your vision were all-powerful, there would be no occasion for you to revolt, you would always see that all things are as they should be. If we go to the highest level and unite with the consciousness of the supreme Will, we see, at every second, at every moment of the universe, that all is exactly as it should be, exactly as the Supreme wills it. That is omnipotence. And all movements of violence become not only unnecessary but utterly ridiculous.

Therefore there is only one solution: to unite ourselves by aspiration, concentration, interiorisation and identification with the supreme Will. And that is both omnipotence and perfect freedom at the same time. And that is the only omnipotence and the only freedom; everything else is an approximation. You may be on the way, but it is not the entire thing. So if you experience this, you realise that with this supreme freedom and supreme power there is also a total peace and a serenity that never fails. Therefore, if you feel something which is not that, a revolt, a disgust, something which you cannot accept, it means that *in you* there is a part which has not been touched by the transformation, something which has kept the old consciousness, something which is still on the path — that is all.

In this aphorism Sri Aurobindo speaks of those who hate the sinner. One must not hate the sinner.

It is the same problem seen from another angle. But the solution is the same.

Not to hate the sinner is not so difficult, but not to hate the virtuous is much more difficult. It is easy to understand a sinner, it is easy to understand a poor wretch, but the virtuous...

But in reality, what you hate in them is their complacency, it is only that. Because after all they are right not to do evil — you cannot blame them for that! But because of that they think themselves superior. And that is what is so difficult to tolerate: their feeling of superiority, the way in which they look down from their heights on all these poor devils — who are no worse than they are!

Oh, I have seen such marvellous examples of this!

Take, for example, a person who has friends, whose friends are very fond of her because they see special capacities in her, because it is pleasant to be in her company, one can always learn from her. Then all of a sudden, by a concurrence of circumstances, this person is shunned by society because she has been with another man or because she is living with someone else without being officially married, in short, because of all these social things which have no value in themselves. And all her friends — I am not speaking of those who truly loved her — all her acquaintances, all those who received her kindly, who welcomed her and greeted her with a warm smile when they met her in the street, now turn their heads the other way and walk right past her without a glance — this has happened even here in the Ashram! I do not want to give any details, but anyway, several times something happened which contravened accepted social laws, and people who had shown so much affection and sympathy — oh, they would sometimes say, "This person is lost!"

When such things happen in the world at large, I find it quite natural, but when it happens here, I always get a little shock, in the sense that I say to myself: "Well, well, they haven't gone beyond that!"

Even people who profess to be broad-minded, to be above all these "conventions", fall straight into the trap, immediately. Then to protect their conscience, they say: "Mother does not allow it. Mother does not permit it. Mother does not tolerate it!" — adding one more stupidity to all the others.

It is very difficult to get out of this state. This is truly self-righteousness, this sense of social dignity. But it is narrow-mindedness, because a person with a little intelligence is not going to be caught out by something like that. For example, people who have travelled the world and seen that all these social rules depend entirely on climate, race, custom, and even more on time and period, can smile at all that. But right-minded people — phew!

It is an elementary stage. Until you come out of this state you are unfit for yoga. Because, truly, you are not ready for yoga when you are in that state. It is a rudimentary state.

January 1961

51 – When I hear of a righteous wrath, I wonder at man's capacity for self-deception.

When one deceives oneself, one always does it in good faith. One is always acting for the good of others or for

On Thoughts and Aphorisms

> *the welfare of humanity and to serve you — that goes without saying! How does one deceive oneself?*[13]

I feel like asking you a question myself! Because your question can be understood in two ways. One can take it in the same spirit of irony and humour that Sri Aurobindo has put in his aphorism, when he marvels at man's capacity for self-deception. That is to say, you are putting yourself in the place of someone who is deceiving himself and you say, "But I am acting in good faith! I always want the good of others, etc. — the welfare of humanity, to serve the Divine, that goes without saying! And how can I be deceiving myself?"

But actually there are two ways of deceiving oneself, which are very different. For example, you may very well be shocked by certain things, not for personal reasons, but precisely in your goodwill and eagerness to serve the Divine, when you see people behaving badly, being selfish, unfaithful and treacherous. There is a stage where you have overcome these things and no longer allow them to manifest in yourself, but to the extent that you are linked to the ordinary consciousness, the ordinary point of view, the ordinary life, the ordinary way of thinking, they are still possible, they exist latently because they are the reverse of the qualities that you are striving to attain. And this opposition still exists — until you rise above it and no longer have either the quality or the defect. So long as you have the virtue, its opposite is always latent in you; it is only when you are above both the virtue and the defect that it disappears.

So this kind of indignation that you feel comes from the fact that you are not altogether above it; you are at the stage where you thoroughly disapprove and could not do it yourself. Up to that point there is nothing to say, unless you give a violent outer expression to your indignation. If anger intervenes, it is because there is a complete contradiction between the feeling you want

---

[13] Oral question and answer.

to have and how you react to others. Because anger is a deformation of the vital power, an obscure and wholly unregenerated vital, a vital that is still subject to all the ordinary actions and reactions. When this vital power is used by an ignorant and egoistic individual will and this will meets with opposition from other individual wills around it, this power, under the pressure of opposition, changes into anger and tries to obtain by violence what cannot be achieved solely by the pressure of the force itself.

Besides, anger, like every other kind of violence, is always a sign of weakness, impotence and incapacity.

And here self-deception comes solely from the approval given to it or the flattering epithet attached to it — because anger can only be something blind, ignorant and asuric, that is to say, contrary to the light.

But this is still the best case.

There is another one. There are people who without knowing it — or because *they want* to ignore it — always follow their personal interest, their preferences, their attachments, their conceptions; people who are not wholly consecrated to the Divine and who make use of moral and yogic ideas to conceal their personal impulses. But these people are deceiving themselves doubly; not only do they deceive themselves in their external activities, in their relation with others, but they also deceive themselves in their own personal movement; instead of serving the Divine, they serve their own egoism. And this happens constantly, constantly! They serve their own personality, their own egoism, while pretending to serve God. Then it is no longer even self-deception, it is hypocrisy.

This mental habit of always endowing everything with a very favourable appearance, of giving a favourable explanation to all movements — sometimes it is rather subtle, but sometimes it is so crude that nobody is deceived except oneself. It is a habit of excusing oneself, the habit of giving a favourable mental excuse, a favourable mental explanation to everything one does, to everything one says, to everything one feels. For example, those who have no self-control and slap someone's face in great indignation would call that an almost divine wrath!

It is amazing, amazing — this power of self-deception, the mind's skill in finding an admirable justification for any ignorance, any stupidity whatsoever.

This is not an experience that comes only now and then. It is something which you can observe from minute to minute. And you usually see it much more easily in others! But if you look at yourself closely, you catch yourself a thousand times a day, looking at yourself just a little indulgently: "Oh! But it is *not the same thing.*" Besides, it is never the same for you as it is for your neighbour!

January 1961

52 – This is a miracle that men can love God, yet fail to love humanity. With whom are they in love then?

Is it possible to reach the Divine through philanthropy?[14]

It depends on what you mean by philanthropy. Normally, we call philanthropists those who do charitable works.

Here Sri Aurobindo does not use the word philanthropy, for, as it is usually understood, philanthropy is a social and conventional attitude, a kind of magnified egoism which is not love but a condescending pity which assumes a patronising air.

In this aphorism Sri Aurobindo refers to those who follow the ascetic path in solitary search of a solitary God, by trying to cut themselves off completely from the world and men.

But for Sri Aurobindo men form part of the Divine; and if you truly love the Divine, how can you not love men, since they are an aspect of Himself?

18 January 1961

---

[14] Written question and answer.

53 – The quarrels of religious sects are like the disputing of pots, which shall be alone allowed to hold the immortalising nectar. Let them dispute, but the thing for us is to get at the nectar in whatever pot and attain immortality.

54 – You say that the flavour of the pot alters the liquor. That is taste; but what can deprive it of its immortalising faculty?

(1) What is this immortalising nectar of which Sri Aurobindo speaks? What, in this nectar, gives us the power of immortality? Is it physical immortality?
(2) When we find this nectar, what happens to the religious sects? Do they reach their goal?[15]

The immortalising nectar is the supreme Truth, the supreme Knowledge, the Union with the Supreme which gives the consciousness of immortality.

Each religious sect has its own way of approaching the Divine and this is why Sri Aurobindo compares them to different pots. But he says: No matter which path you follow, the goal alone is important, and the goal is the same whatever the path you follow. The nectar is the same in whichever pot it is contained.

Some say that the flavour of the pot, the path you follow changes the taste of the nectar, that is to say, affects your union with the Divine. Sri Aurobindo answers: The approach may be different, each one chooses the one he prefers or which most suits his taste, but the nectar itself, the union with the Divine, always keeps its power of immortality.

Now when we say that by union with the Divine we gain the consciousness of immortality, it means that the consciousness in us unites with what is immortal and therefore feels itself to be

---

[15] Written question and answer.

immortal. We become conscious of the domains where immortality exists. But this does not imply that our physical substance is transformed and becomes immortal. For that quite another procedure has to be followed. You must not only first obtain this consciousness, but bring it down into the material world and let it work not only on the transformation of the physical consciousness, but also on the transformation of the physical substance, which is quite a considerable task.

Finally, you must not confuse personal realisation with the realisation of humanity as a whole. When *we* have found the nectar we are above all religious sects; they no longer have any meaning or use for us. But in a general way, for men in general, these things continue to have their value and usefulness as a path, until they achieve realisation.

28 January 1961

55 – Be wide in me, O Varuna; be mighty in me, O Indra; O Sun, be very bright and luminous; O Moon, be full of charm and sweetness. Be fierce and terrible, O Rudra; be impetuous and swift, O Maruts; be strong and bold, O Aryama; be voluptuous and pleasurable, O Bhaga; be tender and kind and loving and passionate, O Mitra. Be bright and revealing, O Dawn; O Night, be solemn and pregnant. O Life, be full, ready and buoyant; O Death, lead my steps from mansion to mansion. Harmonise all these, O Brahmanaspati. Let me not be subject to these gods, O Kali.

Why does Sri Aurobindo give more importance to Kali?

It is good and necessary to possess all the divine qualities that these gods represent and symbolise; that is why Sri Aurobindo invokes them and asks them to take possession of his nature. But for one who wants union with the Supreme, for one who

Jnana

aspires for the supreme Realisation, this cannot be sufficient. This is why at the end he calls upon Kali to give him the power to go beyond them all.

For Kali is the most powerful aspect of the universal Mother and her power is greater than that of all the gods in her creation. To unite with her means therefore to become more vast, more complete, more powerful than all the gods together and that is why Sri Aurobindo places union with her above and beyond all the others.

2 February 1961

56 – When, O eager disputant, thou hast prevailed in a debate, then art thou greatly to be pitied; for thou hast lost a chance of widening knowledge.

What is the use of discussions? What is the best way to make other people understand what one feels to be true?[16]

In general, those who like to discuss things are those who need the stimulant of contradiction to clarify their ideas.

It is obviously the sign of an elementary intellectual stage.

But if you can "attend" a discussion as an impartial spectator — even while you are taking part in it and while the other person is talking with you — you can always benefit from this opportunity to consider a question or a problem from several points of view; and by attempting to reconcile opposite views, you can widen your ideas and rise to a more comprehensive synthesis.

As for the best way of proving to others what one feels to be true, one must *live it* — there is no other way.

---

[16] Oral question and answer.

How is it that we lose a chance to widen our knowledge by prevailing in a debate?[17]

A debate is never anything but a conflict of opinions; and opinions are nothing but very fragmentary aspects of the truth. Even if you were able to put together and synthesise all opinions on a given subject, you still would not achieve anything but a very imperfect expression of the truth.

If you prevail in a debate, it means that your opinion has prevailed over the opinion of another, not necessarily because yours was truer than his, but because you were better at wielding the arguments or because you were a more stubborn debater. And you come out of the discussion convinced that you are right in what you assert; and so you lose a chance to see a view of the question other than your own and to add an aspect of the truth to the one or the ones you already possess. You remain imprisoned in your own thought and refuse to widen it.

17 March 1961

57 – Because the tiger acts according to his nature and knows not anything else, therefore he is divine and there is no evil in him. If he questioned himself, then he would be a criminal.

What would be the truly natural state for man? Why does he question himself?[18]

On earth[19] man is a transitional being. Therefore, in the course of his evolution, he has had several natures in succession, which

---

[17] Written question and answer.
[18] Oral question and answer.
[19] Mother added: "This precise detail is not superfluous; I said 'on earth' meaning that man does not belong merely to earth: in essence man is a universal being, but he has a special manifestation on earth."

have followed an ascending curve and will continue to follow it until he reaches the threshold of the supramental nature and is transformed into the superman. This curve is the spiral of mental development.

We tend to call "natural" any spontaneous manifestation which is not the result of a choice or a preconceived decision, that is to say, without the intrusion of any mental activity. This is why when a man has a vital spontaneity which is very little mentalised, he seems more "natural" in his simplicity. But this naturalness is very much like that of the animal and is at the very bottom of the human evolutionary scale. He will only regain this spontaneity free from mental intrusion when he attains to the supramental stage, that is to say, when he transcends mind and emerges into the higher Truth.

Until then all his behaviour is, naturally, natural! But with the mind evolution has become, one cannot say twisted, but distorted, because by its very nature the mind was open to perversion and almost from the beginning it became perverted, or, to be more precise, it was perverted by the Asuric forces. And this state of perversion gives us the impression that it is unnatural.

Why does he question himself? Simply because this is the nature of the mind!

With the mind individualisation began and a very acute feeling of separation, and also a kind of impression, more or less precise, of freedom of choice — all that, all these psychological states are the natural consequences of mental life and they open the door to everything we see now, from aberrations to the most rigorous principles. Mind has the impression that it can choose between one thing and another, but this impression is the distortion of a true principle which would be completely realisable only when the soul or psychic being appears in the consciousness and if the soul were to take up the governance of the being. Then man's life would truly become the manifestation of the supreme Will expressing itself individually, consciously. But in the normal human state this is something extremely exceptional which to the ordinary human consciousness does not seem at all natural — it seems almost supernatural!

Man questions himself because the mental instrument is intended to see all possibilities. And the immediate consequence of this is the concept of good and evil, or of what is right and what is wrong, and all the miseries that follow from that. One cannot say that it is a bad thing; it is an intermediate stage — not a very pleasant one, but still... one which was certainly inevitable for the complete development of the mind.

17 March 1961

58 – **The animal, before he is corrupted, has not yet eaten of the tree of the knowledge of good and evil; the god has abandoned it for the tree of eternal life; man stands between the upper heaven and the lower nature.**

Is it true that there was an earthly paradise? Why was man driven out of it?[20]

From the historical point of view (I am not speaking from the psychological but from the historical point of view), if I base myself on my memories — only I cannot prove it; nothing can be proved, and I do not think there is any truly historical proof, that is to say, one which has been preserved, or at any rate none has yet been found — but according to what I remember, there was certainly a moment in earth's history when there existed a kind of earthly paradise, in the sense that it was a perfectly harmonious and natural life; that is to say, the manifestation of the mind was in accord, was *still* in complete accord with the ascending march of Nature and totally harmonious, without perversion or distortion. This was the first stage of mind's manifestation in material forms.

---

[20] Oral question and answer.

Jnana

How long did it last? It is difficult to say. But for man it was a life that was like a kind of outflowering of animal life. I have a memory of a life in which the body was perfectly adapted to its natural environment and the climate adapted to the needs of the body, the body to the needs of the climate. Life was wholly spontaneous and natural, just as a more luminous and more conscious animal life would be; but there were none of the complications and distortions that the mind brought in later in the course of its development. I have the memory of that life — I had it, I relived it when I became conscious of the life of the earth as a whole. But I cannot say how long it lasted nor what area it covered. I do not know. I can only remember the condition, the state, what material Nature was like, what the human form and the human consciousness were like at that time and this kind of harmony with all the other elements on earth — harmony with animal life, and such a great harmony with plant life. There was a kind of spontaneous knowledge of how to use the things of Nature, of the properties of plants, of fruits and everything vegetable Nature could provide. No aggressiveness, no fear, no contradictions nor frictions and no perversions at all — the mind was pure, simple, luminous, uncomplicated.

It is only with the progress of evolution, the march of evolution, when the mind began to develop in itself, *for itself*, that all the complications and distortions began. So that the story of Genesis which seems so childish contains some truth. In the old traditions like that of Genesis, each letter[21] stood for a specific knowledge, it was a graphic summary of the traditional knowledge of that time. But apart from that, even the symbolic story had a reality in the sense that there truly was a period of life on earth — the first manifestation of mentalised matter in human forms — which was still in complete harmony with all that preceded it. It was only later...

And the symbol of the tree of knowledge represents the kind

---

[21] Of the Hebrew alphabet.

of knowledge which is no longer divine, the material knowledge that comes from the sense of division and which started spoiling everything. How long did this period last? Because in my memory too it was like an almost immortal life, and it seems that it was an accident of evolution that made it necessary for forms to disintegrate... for progress. So I cannot say how long it lasted. And where? According to certain impressions — but they are only impressions — it would seem that it was in the vicinity of... I do not know exactly whether it was on this side of Ceylon and India or on the other (*Mother points to the Indian Ocean, first to the west of Ceylon and India and then to the east, between Ceylon and Java*), but it was certainly a place which no longer exists, which has probably been swallowed up by the sea. I have a very clear vision of this place and a very clear awareness of this life and its forms, but I cannot give any material details. To tell the truth, when I relived these moments I was not curious about details. One is in a different state of mind and one has no curiosity about these material details; everything changes into psychological factors. And it was... it was something so simple, so luminous, so harmonious, beyond all our preoccupations — precisely beyond all these preoccupations with time and place. It was a spontaneous, extremely beautiful life, and so close to Nature, like a natural flowering of the animal life. And there were no oppositions, no contradictions, or anything like that — everything happened in the best way possible.

(Silence)

Repeatedly, in different circumstances, several times, I have had the same memory. It was not exactly the same scene or the same images, because it was not something that I saw, it was *a life* that I was living. For some time, by night or by day, in a certain state of trance I went back to a life that I had lived and had the full consciousness that it was the outflowering of the human form on earth — the first human forms capable of embodying the divine Being. It was that. It was the first time I could manifest in an earthly form, in a particular form, in an individual form — not a "general" life but an individual form — that is to say, the first time that the Being above and the being below were joined by the mentalisation of this material substance. I lived this several times, but always in similar surroundings and with a very similar feeling of *such* joyful simplicity, without complexity, without problems, without all these questions; there was nothing, absolutely nothing of the kind! It was an outflowering of the joy of living, simply that, in universal love and harmony — flowers, minerals, animals: all were in harmony.

It was only long afterwards — but this is a personal impression — long afterwards that things went wrong. Probably because some mental crystallisations were necessary, inevitable for the general evolution, so that the mind might be prepared to move on to something else. This is where... Faugh! It is like falling into a hole, into ugliness, into obscurity; everything becomes so dark afterwards, so ugly, so difficult, so painful, it is really — it really feels like a fall.

(*Silence*)

I knew an occultist who used to say that it was not — how to put it? — inevitable. In the total freedom of the manifestation it is the deliberate separation from the Origin that is the cause of all disorder. But how to explain it? Our words are so poor that we cannot speak of these things. We can say that it was "inevitable" because it happened; but if we go outside the creation, we can conceive — or we could have conceived — of a creation in which this disorder would not have happened. Sri Aurobindo also said practically the same thing, that it was a kind of "accident", if you like, but an "accident" which has given the manifestation a much greater and much more complete perfection than if it had never occurred. But this still belongs to the realm of speculation and these speculations are useless, to say the least. In any case, the experience, the feeling is this: a... (*Mother indicates an abrupt fall*) oh! all of a sudden.

For the earth it probably happened like that, all of a sudden: a kind of ascent, then a fall. But the earth is only a very small point of concentration. For the universe it is something else.

(*Silence*)

So the memory of that time is preserved somewhere, in the earth's memory, in the region where all the memories of the earth are recorded, and those who are able to communicate with this memory can say that the earthly paradise still exists somewhere; but I know nothing about it, I do not see.

What about the story of the serpent? Why does the serpent have such an evil reputation?

The Christians say that it is the spirit of Evil.

(*Silence*)

But all this is a misunderstanding.

The occultist I spoke of used to say that the true interpretation of the Bible story about Paradise and the serpent is that man wanted to rise from a state of animal divinity — like the animals — to a state of conscious divinity through the development of the mind — and that is what the symbol means when it is said that they ate of the fruit of the tree of knowledge. And the serpent — he always used to say that it was iridescent, that is to say, it was all the colours of the rainbow — it was not at all the spirit of Evil, it was the evolutionary force, the force, the power of evolution, and of course it was the power of evolution that had made them taste of the fruit of knowledge.

And so, according to him, Jehovah was the chief of the Asuras, the supreme Asura, the egoistic god who wanted to dominate everything and have everything under his control. And once he had taken the position of supreme lord in relation to earthly realisation, of course he was not pleased that man should make this mental progress, for it would bring him a knowledge that enabled him not to obey any longer! This made him furious! For it would enable man to become a god by the evolutionary power of consciousness. And that is why they were driven out of Paradise.

There is a good deal of truth in that, a good deal.

And Sri Aurobindo fully agreed. He said the same thing. It is the evolutionary power — the power of the mind — that led man towards knowledge, a separative knowledge. And it is a fact that man became conscious of himself with the sense of good and evil. But, of course, that spoiled everything and he could not stay there. He was driven out by his own consciousness. He could no longer stay there.

But were they driven out by Jehovah or by their own consciousness?

It is just two different ways of saying the same thing.

According to me, all these old Scriptures and these old traditions have different levels of meaning (*Mother makes a gesture to show the different levels*); and according to the period, the people, the needs, one symbol or another has been selected and used. But there comes a time — when you transcend all these things and see them from what Sri Aurobindo calls "the other hemisphere" — when you become aware that these are merely ways of speaking to establish a contact — a kind of bridge or link between the lower way of seeing and the higher way of knowing.

And people who argue and say, "Oh, no! it is like this; it is like that" — there comes a time when it seems so funny, so funny! And just that, the spontaneous retort of so many people, "Oh, that is impossible" — the word itself is so funny! For the slightest, I might even say, the most elementary intellectual development enables you to realise that you could not even think of it if it were not possible.

(Silence)

Oh! If we could only find that again, but how?

Really, they have spoilt the earth, they have spoilt it — they have spoilt the atmosphere, they have spoilt everything! And now, for the atmosphere to come back to what it should be — oh! we have a long way to go, and above all psychologically. But even the very structure of matter (*Mother feels the air around her*), with their bombs and experiments, oh, they have made a mess of it all!... They have really made a mess of matter.

Probably — no, not probably — it is quite certain that it was necessary to knead it, to churn it, to prepare it so that it can receive *this*, the new thing which is not yet manifested.

It was very simple, very harmonious, very luminous, but not complex enough. And this complexity has spoilt everything, but it will bring a realisation that is *infinitely* more conscious — infinitely. And so when the earth again becomes so harmonious, simple, luminous, pure — simple, pure, purely divine — and with this complexity, then we shall be able to do something.

As the Mother was leaving she noticed a brilliant crimson Canna flower.

There were so many flowers just like this in the landscape of the earthly paradise, red, so beautiful.

11 March 1961

> 59 – One of the greatest comforts of religion is that you can get hold of God sometimes and give him a satisfactory beating. People mock at the folly of savages who beat

their gods when their prayers are not answered; but it is the mockers who are the fools and the savages.

How can one give a satisfactory beating to God?

Religion always tends to make God in the image of man, a magnified and aggrandised image, but in the end it is always a god with human qualities. This is what makes it possible for people to treat him as they would treat a human enemy. In some countries, when their god does not do what they want, they take him and throw him into the river!

But are these idols not merely human creations? Do they have any existence in themselves?[22]

Whatever the image — what we disdainfully call an idol — whatever the external form of the deity, even if to our physical eye it appears ugly or commonplace or horrible, a caricature, there is always within it the presence of the thing it represents. And there is always someone, a priest or an initiate, or a sadhu, a sannyasin, who has the power and who draws — this is usually the work of the priests — who draws the force, the presence within. And it is real: it is quite true that the force, the presence is there; and it is that, not the form of wood or stone or metal, which people worship — it is the presence.

But people in Europe do not have this inner sense, not at all. For them everything is like a surface — not even that, just a thin outer film with nothing behind — so they cannot feel it. And yet it is a fact that the presence is there; it is an absolutely real fact, I guarantee it.

Many people say that the teaching of Sri Aurobindo is a

---

[22] Mother replied orally to this second question and in writing to the first and third questions.

new religion. Would *you say that it is a religion?*

People who say that are fools who don't even know what they are talking about. You only have to read all that Sri Aurobindo has written to know that it is impossible to base a religion on his works, because he presents each problem, each question in all its aspects, showing the truth contained in each way of seeing things, and he explains that in order to attain the Truth you must realise a synthesis which goes beyond all mental notions and emerge into a transcendence beyond thought.

So the second part of your question is meaningless. Besides, if you had read what was published in the last *Bulletin*,[23] you could not have asked this question.

I repeat that when we speak of Sri Aurobindo there can be no question of a teaching nor even of a revelation, but of an action from the Supreme; no religion can be founded on that.

But men are so foolish that they can change anything into a religion, so great is their need of a fixed framework for their narrow thought and limited action. They do not feel secure unless they can assert this is true and that is not; but such an assertion becomes impossible for anyone who has read and understood what Sri Aurobindo has written. Religion and Yoga do not belong to the same plane of being and spiritual life can exist in all its purity only when it is free from all mental dogma.

26 April 1961

60 – There is no mortality. It is only the Immortal who can die; the mortal could neither be born nor perish.

---

[23] "What Sri Aurobindo represents in the world's history is not a teaching, not even a revelation; it is a decisive action direct from the Supreme."
Bulletin of Sri Aurobindo International Centre of Education, April 1961, p. 169

Does a being carry his mental, vital and physical experiences from one life to another?

Each case is different. It all depends on the degree of the individual's development in his different parts and on how well these parts are organised around the psychic centre. The more organised the being, the more consciously lasting it becomes. We can say in a general way that each person brings into his present life the consequences of his previous lives, without, however, preserving the memory of these lives. Apart from a few very rare exceptions, only when you are united with your psychic being and become fully conscious of it do you obtain, at the same time, the memory of past lives, which the psychic preserves in its consciousness.

Otherwise, even in those who are most sensitive, these memories are fragmentary, uncertain and intermittent. Most often they are hardly recognisable and seem to be nothing more than indefinable impressions. And yet a person who knows how to see through appearances will be able to perceive a kind of similarity in the sequence of events in his life.

4 May 1961

61 – There is nothing finite. It is only the Infinite who can create for Himself limits. The finite can have no beginning nor end, for the very act of conceiving its beginning and end declares its infinity.

How can we have the experience of the Infinite?

The only way is to come out of the consciousness of the finite.

It is in the hope of achieving this that all yogic disciplines have been developed and undertaken from time immemorial until now. Much has been written on the subject, but little has been done. Only a very small number of individuals have so far succeeded in escaping from the finite to plunge into the Infinite.

And yet, as Sri Aurobindo has written, the Infinite alone exists; only the falsehood of our superficial perception makes us believe in the existence of the finite.

20 May 1961

62 – I heard a fool discoursing utter folly and wondered what God meant by it; then I considered and saw a distorted mask of truth and wisdom.

How can folly be a distorted mask of truth?

It is the very definition of folly that Sri Aurobindo gives here. A mask is something that conceals, that makes invisible what it covers. And if the mask is distorted, it not only renders invisible what it conceals but also totally changes its nature. So, according to this definition, folly is something that veils and distorts beyond all recognition the Truth which is at the origin of all things.

23 June 1961

Does Sri Aurobindo mean that there is no absolute falsehood, no absolute untruth?[24]

There can be no absolute untruth. In actual fact it is not possible, because the Divine is behind all things.

It is like people who ask whether certain elements will disappear from the universe. What could "the destruction of a universe" mean? If we come out of our folly, what can we call "destruction"? Only the form, the appearance is destroyed — and indeed, all appearances are destroyed, one after another. It is also said — it is written everywhere, so many things are

---

[24] The Mother replied orally to this question.

said — that the adverse forces will either be converted, that is to say, they will become conscious of the Divinity within them and become divine, or they will be destroyed. But what does "destroyed" mean? Their form? Their form of consciousness can be dissolved, but that "something" which makes them exist, which makes all things exist — how could that be destroyed? The universe is an objectivisation, an objective self-discovery of That which *is* from all eternity. So? How can the All cease to be? The infinite and eternal All, that is to say, That which has no limits of any kind — what can go outside That? There is no place to go! Go where? There is nothing but *That*.

Furthermore, when we say, "There is only That", we are locating it somewhere, which is absolutely stupid. So, what can be taken away from there?

One can conceive of a universe being projected outside the present manifestation. One can conceive of universes having succeeded each other and that which was in the earlier ones would no longer be in the later ones — that is even obvious. One can conceive that a whole mass of falsehood and untruth — things which are falsehood and untruth for us *now* — will no longer belong to the world as it will be in its unfolding; all this one can understand — but "destroy"? Where can it go to be destroyed? When we speak of destroying, we think only of the destruction of a form — it may be a form of consciousness or a material form, but it is always a form. But how could what is without form be destroyed?

So to speak of an absolute falsehood that will disappear would simply mean that a whole set of things will live eternally in the past but will not belong to future manifestations, that is all.

One cannot go outside *That*!

But they will remain in the past?

We are told that there is a state of consciousness, when we rise above, when we are able to go beyond both the aspect of Nothingness or Nirvana and the aspect of Existence — there is the Nirvana aspect and the Existence aspect, the two simultaneous and complementary aspects of the Supreme — where all things exist eternally and simultaneously; so one can conceive — God knows! This may well be another stupidity — one can conceive of a certain number of things passing into Non-Being, and that to our consciousness would be a disappearance or a destruction.

Is that possible? I do not know. You would have to ask the Lord, but usually He does not answer such questions. He smiles!

There comes a time when really one can no longer say anything: one has the feeling that whatever one says, even if it isn't absolutely inane, is not far short of it, and that it would actually be better to keep quiet. That is the difficulty. In some of these aphorisms you feel that he has suddenly caught hold of something above and beyond everything that can be thought — so what can one say?

(*Silence*)

Naturally, when one comes down here again, one can — oh, one can say many things!

As a joke — one can always joke, but one hesitates to do so because people take your jokes so seriously — one could very well say, without being completely wrong, that one sometimes learns much more by listening to a madman or a fool than by listening to a reasonable man. I am quite sure of it. There is nothing that withers you more than reasonable people.

27 June 1961

63 – God is great, says the Mahomedan. Yes, He is so great that He can afford to be weak, whenever that too is necessary.

64 – God often fails in His workings; it is the sign of His illimitable godhead.

65 – Because God is invincibly great, He can afford to be weak; because He is immutably pure, He can indulge with impunity in sin; He knows eternally all delight, therefore He tastes also the delight of pain; He is inalienably wise, therefore He has not debarred Himself from folly.

Why does God need to be weak?

Sri Aurobindo does not say that God has any need of weakness. He says that in any particular whole, for the perfection of the play of forces, a moment of weakness may be just as necessary as a display of strength. And he adds, somewhat ironically, that since God is almighty force, He can at the same time afford to be weak, if necessary.

This is to widen the outlook of certain moralists who attribute definite qualities to God and will not permit Him to be otherwise.

Strength as we see it and weakness as we see it are both an equally distorted expression of the Divine Truth which is secretly present behind all physical manifestations.

30 June 1961

Does God ever really fail? Is God ever really weak? Or is it simply a game?[25]

It is not like that! That is precisely the distortion in the Western attitude as opposed to the attitude of the Gita. It is extremely difficult for the Western mind to understand in a living and concrete manner that *everything* is the Divine.

---

[25] The Mother replied orally to this question.

People are so deeply imbued with the Christian idea of "God the Creator" — the creation on one side and God on the other. When you think about it you reject it, but it has penetrated into the sensations and feelings; so, spontaneously, instinctively, almost subconsciously, you attribute to God everything you consider to be best and most beautiful and, above all, everything you want to attain, to realise. Naturally, each one changes the content of his God according to his own consciousness, but it is always what he considers to be best. And that is also why instinctively and spontaneously, subconsciously, you are shocked by the idea that God can be things that you do not like, that you do not approve of or do not think best.

I put that rather childishly, on purpose, so that you can understand it properly. But it is like that — I am sure, because I observed it in myself for a very long time, because of the subconscious formation of childhood, environment, education, etc. You must be able to press into this body the consciousness of Oneness, the absolute exclusive Oneness of the Divine — exclusive in the sense that nothing exists except in this Oneness, even the things we find most repulsive.

And this is what Sri Aurobindo is fighting, for he too had this Christian education, he too had to struggle; and these aphorisms are the result — the flowering, as it were — of this necessity of fighting a subconscious formation. For that is what makes you ask such questions: "How can God be weak? How can God be foolish? How...?" But there is nothing other than God, only He exists, there is nothing outside Him. And if something seems ugly to us, it is simply because He no longer wants it to exist. He is preparing the world so that this thing may no longer be manifested, so that the manifestation can move from that state to something else. So naturally, within us, we violently repulse everything that is about to go out of the active manifestation — there is a movement of rejection.

But it is Him. There is nothing but Him. This is what we should repeat to ourselves from morning to evening and from evening to morning, because we forget it at each moment.

There is only Him. There is nothing but Him — He alone exists, there is no existence without Him, there is only Him!

So, to ask a question like this is still to react like those who make a distinction between what is and what is not Divine or rather between what is and what is not God. "How can He be weak?" It is a question I cannot ask.

I understand, but they speak of the Lila, the divine play; so He is standing back, as it were. He is not really entirely "involved", not really absolutely in the play.

Yes, yes, He is! He is totally in it. He himself is the Play.

We speak of God, but we should remember that there are all these gradations of consciousness; and when we speak of God and His Play, we mean God in His transcendent state, beyond all the levels of matter, and when we speak of the Play we speak of God in his material state. So we say: Transcendent God is watching and playing — in Himself, by Himself, with Himself — His material game.

But all language is a language of ignorance. Our entire way of expressing ourselves, everything we say and the way in which we say it, is necessarily ignorance. And that is why it is so difficult to express something which is concretely true; this would require explanations which would themselves be full of falsehood, of course, or else extremely long. This is why Sri Aurobindo's sentences are sometimes very long, precisely because he strives to escape from this ignorant language.

Our very way of thinking is wrong. The believers, the faithful, all of them — particularly in the West — when they speak of God, think of Him as "something else", they think that He cannot be weak, ugly or imperfect — they think wrongly, they divide, they separate. It is subconscious, unreflecting thought; they are in the habit of thinking like this instinctively; they do not watch themselves thinking. For example, when they speak of "perfection" in a general way, they see or feel or postulate precisely the sum-total of everything they consider to be virtuous, divine, beautiful, admirable — but it is not that at all! Perfection is something which lacks nothing. The divine perfection is the Divine in His entirety, which lacks nothing. The divine perfection is the Divine as a whole, from whom nothing has been taken away — so it is just the opposite! For the moralists divine perfection means all the virtues that they represent.

From the true point of view, perfection is the whole (*Mother makes a global gesture*), and it is precisely the fact that there can be nothing outside the whole. It is impossible that anything should be missing, because it is impossible for anything not to form part of the whole. There can be nothing which is not in the whole. Let me explain. A given universe may not contain everything, for a universe is a mode of manifestation; but there is every possible kind of universe. So I always come back to the same thing: there can be nothing which does not form part of the whole.

Therefore one can say that each thing is in its place, exactly as it should be, and that relations between things are exactly as they should be.

But perfection is only one special way of approaching the Divine; it is one side, and in the same way there are innumerable sides, angles or aspects, innumerable ways of approaching the Divine, for example: will, truth, purity, perfection, unity, immortality, eternity, infinity, silence, peace, existence, consciousness, etc. The number of approaches is almost unlimited. With each one you approach or draw near or enter into contact with the Divine through one aspect and if you really do it, you find that the difference is merely in the most external form, but the contact is identical. It is as if you were turning around a centre, a globe, and seeing it from many different angles as in a kaleidoscope; but once the contact is made, it is the same thing.

Perfection is therefore a global way of approaching the Divine: everything is there and everything is as it should be

— "should be", that is to say, a perfect expression of the Divine; one cannot even say of His Will, for if you say "His Will" it is still something outside Him.

One can also say — but this is far, far below it — that He is what He is and exactly as He wants to be — with this "exactly as He wants to be", one has come down by a considerable number of steps! But this is to give you the point of view of perfection.

Besides, divine perfection implies infinity and eternity; that is to say, everything coexists outside time and space.

It is like the word "purity"; one could hold forth interminably on the difference between divine purity and what people call purity. The divine purity, at the lowest, allows no influence other than the divine influence — at the lowest. But that is already very much distorted; the divine purity means that there is only the Divine, nothing else — it is perfectly pure, there is only the Divine, there is nothing other than Him.

And so on.

7 July 1961

66 – Sin is that which was once in its place, persisting now it is out of place; there is no other sinfulness.

Has cruelty, for example, ever been in its place?[26]

This very question of yours came to my vision, since I receive in my consciousness all the questions people ask.

To kill out of cruelty? To make others suffer out of cruelty? And yet it is an expression of the Divine — we always come back to the same thing — but an expression which is distorted in its appearance. Can you tell me what lies behind it?

Cruelty was one of the things that was most repugnant to Sri Aurobindo, but he always said that it was the distortion of

---

[26] Oral question and answer.

an intensity, one could almost say the distortion of an intensity of love, something which is not satisfied with a middle course, which wants extremes — and that is justifiable.

I had always known that cruelty, like sadism, is a need for violent, extremely strong sensation, to penetrate a thick layer of tamas that feels nothing — tamas needs something extreme in order to be able to feel. The explanation may lie in this direction.

But at the origin there is still the problem that has never been solved: "Why has it become like this? Why this distortion? Why has it all been perverted?" Behind, there are beautiful things, very intense, infinitely more powerful than what we can even bear, wonderful things, but why has all that become so frightful here? This is what came to me immediately when I read this aphorism.

The concept of sin is something that I do not understand and have never understood; original sin seems to me one of the most monstrous ideas that man could ever have — sin and I don't go together! So naturally, I fully agree with Sri Aurobindo that there is no sin, this is understood, but...

Certain things, like cruelty, could be called "sin", but I can only see this explanation, that it is a distortion of the taste or need for an extremely strong sensation. I have observed in cruel people that they feel Ananda at that moment; they find an intense joy in it. So that is its justification, only it is in such a state of distortion that it is repugnant.

As for the idea that things are not in their place, I understood it even when I was a child. It was only later that I was given the explanation by the person who taught me occultism, for, in his cosmogonic system, he explained the successive *pralayas*[27] of the various universes by saying that with each universe an aspect of the Supreme would manifest itself, that each universe was built on one aspect of the Supreme and that one after another they had all returned into the Supreme. He enumerated all the

---

[27] Pralaya: the end or destruction of a universe.

aspects that were manifested successively and with what logic! It was extraordinary — I have kept it somewhere, I forget where. And he said that this time, it was — I do not remember exactly what number in the series — but it would be the universe which would not be withdrawn again, which would follow a progressive course of becoming that would be, so to say, indefinite. And this universe represented equilibrium, not static but progressive equilibrium, that is to say, each thing in its place, exactly, each vibration, each movement in its place. The further down one goes, the more each form, each activity, each thing is exactly in its place in relation to the whole.

I was extremely interested, because later Sri Aurobindo said the same thing, that nothing is bad, it is just that things are not in their place — their place not only in space but also in time; their place in the universe, beginning with the worlds, the stars, etc., each thing exactly in its place. And so, when each thing is exactly in its place, from the most stupendous to the most microscopic, the whole will express the Supreme progressively, without any need of being withdrawn to be emanated again. On this Sri Aurobindo based the fact that in this creation, in this universe, the perfection of a divine world — what Sri Aurobindo calls the Supermind — will be able to manifest. Equilibrium is the essential law of this creation and this is why perfection can be realised in the manifestation.

In this connection what are the very first things that the Supramental Force intends to drive out, or is trying to drive out, so that everything may be in its place, individually and cosmically?

Drive out? But will it "drive out" anything? If we accept Sri Aurobindo's idea, it will put each thing in its place, that's all.

One thing must necessarily cease, and that is the distortion, that is to say, the veil of falsehood upon Truth, because that is what is responsible for everything we see here. If this is removed, things will be completely different, completely. They will be what we feel them to be when we come out of this consciousness. When one comes out of this consciousness and enters into the Truth-consciousness; the difference is such that one wonders how there can be anything like suffering and misery and death and all that. There is a kind of astonishment in the sense that one does not understand how it can happen — when one has really tipped over to the other side. But this experience is usually associated with the experience of the unreality of the world as we know it, whereas Sri Aurobindo says that this perception of the unreality of the world is not necessary to live in the supramental consciousness — it is only the unreality of Falsehood, not the unreality of the world. That is to say, the world has a reality of its own, independent of Falsehood.

I suppose that is the first effect of the Supermind — the first effect in the individual, because it will begin with the individual.

18 July 1961

67 – There is no sin in man, but a great deal of disease, ignorance and misapplication.

68 – The sense of sin was necessary in order that man might become disgusted with his own imperfections. It was God's corrective for egoism. But man's egoism meets God's device by being very dully alive to its own sins and very keenly alive to the sins of others.

At what phase of his development will man be able to rid himself of egoism?

When egoism will no longer be necessary to make man a conscious individuality.

27 July 1961

Jnana

(Knowledge)

Third Period of Commentaries

(1962–1966)

Jnana (Knowledge)

Third Period of Commentaries (1962–1966)

69 – Sin and virtue are a game of resistance we play with God in His efforts to draw us towards perfection. The sense of virtue helps us to cherish our sins in secret.

These aphorisms clearly express the futility of our ideas of sin and virtue. You had also said, following your experience of 3 February 1958,[1] "I saw that what helps people to become supramental or prevents them from doing so, is very different from what our usual moral notions imagine." You said besides, "What is very clear is that our appraisal of what is divine or undivine is not correct.... At that time I had the impression... that the relation between this world and the other completely changed the standpoint from which things should be evaluated or appraised. This standpoint had nothing mental about it and it gave a strange inner feeling that many things we consider to be good or bad are not really so. It was very clear that everything depended on the capacity of things, on their ability to express the supramental world or to be in relation with it."

What is this supramental standpoint like? What is this capacity or this aptitude to express the supramental world or to be in relation with it?

I have already spoken a little about that in connection with

---

[1] See the Mother's comments on her experience in *Questions and Answers 1957-58* (19 February 1958).

the story of the stag going through the forest.[2] There was an indication there.

Then I put myself in contact again with this experience of the supramental boat. My vision of things has not changed since. And I realised that the experience had had a decisive effect on the situation; it established the required conditions very clearly, very precisely, very definitively.

Once and for all it swept away not only all the ordinary notions of morality, but everything that is considered here in India as necessary for the spiritual life. From this point of view it was very instructive. First of all this kind of so-called ascetic purity. Ascetic purity is simply the rejection of all vital movements; instead of taking up these movements and turning them towards the Divine, that is to say, instead of seeing the supreme Presence in them and letting the Supreme act freely on them, you tell Him, "No, that is not your concern." He is not allowed to interfere with them.

As for the physical, it is an old story, everyone knows: the ascetics have always rejected it, but then they added the vital. Only the things that were classically recognised as sacred or permitted by religious tradition, as for example, the sanctity of marriage and things like that, were accepted, but to live freely — oh! that was incompatible with any religious life.

So all that was completely swept away once and for all.

Which is not to say, however, that what is required is any easier. It is probably much more difficult.

First of all, from the psychological point of view, there must be the condition I spoke about in the story of the stag: perfect equality. It is an absolute condition. I have observed since 1956, for years, that no supramental vibration can be transmitted except in this perfect equality. If there is the least opposition to this equality — in fact the least movement of ego, any preference of

---

[2] See *Bulletin of Sri Aurobindo International Centre of Education*, Vol. XIII: 2 (April 1961), p. 23.

the ego, it does not come through, it is not transmitted. This is already difficult enough.

Added to this, there are two conditions for the realisation to become total and they are not easily fulfilled. It is not very difficult on the intellectual plane — I am not speaking here of just anyone at all but of people who have already practised yoga and followed a discipline — it is relatively easy; on the psychological plane too, if you bring in this equality, it is not very difficult. But as soon as you come to the material plane, that is, the physical and then the body, it is not easy. The two conditions are: first, a power of expansion, of widening, that is unlimited, so to say, so that you can widen yourself to the dimension of the supramental consciousness, which is total. The supramental consciousness is the consciousness of the Supreme in His totality — when I say "His totality", I mean the Supreme in His aspect of Manifestation. Naturally, from the higher point of view, the point of view of the essence — the essence of what becomes the Supermind in the Manifestation — there must be a capacity for total identification with the Supreme, not only in His aspect of Manifestation, but also in his static or nirvanic aspect, beyond the Manifestation — Non-Being. But in addition to this, one must be able to identify oneself with the Supreme in the Becoming. This implies two things: first a widening that is at least unlimited, as I have said, and at the same time a total plasticity in order to be able to follow the Supreme in His Becoming. It is not at one particular moment that one must be as wide as the universe, but indefinitely, in the Becoming. These are the two conditions; they must be there potentially.

So long as there is no question of physical transformation, the psychological and, in a large measure, subjective point of view is sufficient. And that is relatively easy. But when it comes to including Matter in the work, Matter as it is in this world, where the very starting-point itself is wrong — we start from Inconscience and Ignorance — then it is very difficult. Because, in fact, so that this Matter could reach the individualisation needed to recover the lost Consciousness, it was made with a certain fixity indispensable to make forms last and precisely to maintain this possibility of individuality. And that is the chief obstacle to the widening, the plasticity, the suppleness needed to be able to receive the supermind. I am constantly faced with this problem, which is a very concrete, absolutely material one, when one is dealing with these cells which must remain cells and not evaporate into a reality which is no longer physical. And at the same time, they must have this suppleness, this lack of fixity which enables them to widen indefinitely.

(*Silence*)

The experience of the boat took place in the subtle physical. And the people who had dark patches and who had to be taken back were always the ones who lacked the suppleness needed for these two movements, but especially the movement of widening, more than the movement of progression to follow the Becoming; this seemed to be a preoccupation later, for those who had landed, after the landing. But the preparation on the boat was for this capacity for widening.

There was also something else which I did not mention when I described my experience: the boat had no machines. Everything, everything was set in motion by the will — individuals and things — even people's dress was a result of their will. And this gave a great suppleness to all these things and to the forms of individuals; because one was conscious of this will, which is not a mental will but a will of the Self, or a spiritual will, one might say, a will of the soul, if one gives that meaning to the word soul. But this is something which can be experienced here when one acts with an absolute spontaneity, that is to say, when an action, such as speech or movement, is not determined by the mind — I am not speaking of thought and intellect — not even by the mind which usually makes us act. Usually, when we do something, we perceive within us the will to do this thing —

Jnana

when we are conscious and observe ourselves doing it, we can see that; there is always — it may be very fleeting — the will to do it. It is the intervention of the mind, the habitual intervention, the order in which things happen. Whereas the supramental action is decided by overleaping the mind. It is not necessary to pass through the mind, it is direct. Something enters into direct contact with the vital centres and makes them act — without passing through the thought, but with full consciousness. The consciousness does not work in the usual order, it goes directly from the centre of spiritual will to Matter.

As long as one can keep this absolute immobility of the mind, the inspiration is absolutely pure, it comes pure. If one can catch it and keep it while speaking, what comes through is also unmixed, it remains pure.

It is an extremely delicate working, probably because it is unfamiliar — the least movement, the smallest mental vibration disturbs everything. But as long as it lasts it is perfectly pure. And that must be the *constant* state of a supramentalised life. The mentalised spiritual will should no longer intervene; because one may very well have a spiritual will, one can live constantly expressing the spiritual will — that is what happens to all those who feel that they are guided by the Divine within — but that comes through a mental transcription. And so long as it is like that, it is not the supramental life. The supramental life *no longer* passes through the mind. The mind is an immobile zone of transmission. The slightest twitch is enough to disturb it.

(*Silence*)

One could say that the constant state that is needed for the Supermind to be able to express itself through a terrestrial consciousness is the perfect equality that comes from spiritual identification with the Supreme. Everything becomes the Supreme in a perfect equality. And it is automatic — not the equality achieved by the conscious will, by intellectual effort or an understanding prior to the state; it is not that. It must be spontaneous and automatic; one should no longer respond to everything that comes from outside as if one were responding to something coming from outside. This kind of reflection and response should be replaced by a state of constant perception — which I cannot call identical because each thing necessarily calls for a special response — but free from any rebound, if one may say so. It is the difference that exists between something coming from outside, that strikes you and that you respond to, and something which is circulating and which quite naturally brings with it the vibrations needed for the general action. I do not know whether I am making myself clearly understood.... It is the difference between a vibratory movement circulating in a *unitary* field of action and a movement coming from something outside, striking from outside and obtaining a response — that is the usual state of human consciousness. On the other hand, when the consciousness is identified with the Supreme, the movements are internal, so to say, in the sense that nothing comes from outside; there are only things that circulate and naturally bring about certain vibrations in the course of their circulation, by similarity and necessity — or that change the vibrations in the medium of circulation.

It is something very familiar to me, because it is my constant state at present — I never have the impression of things coming from outside and striking, but of inner, multiple and sometimes contradictory movements, and of a constant circulation bringing about the inner changes needed for the movement.

That is the indispensable basis.

The widening follows almost automatically, demanding adjustments in the body itself which are difficult to resolve. This is a problem in which I am still completely immersed.

And then the suppleness needed to follow the movement of Becoming; suppleness, that is, the capacity for decrystallisation — the whole period of life spent in individualisation is a period of conscious and deliberate crystallisation, which later has to be undone. Becoming a conscious and individual being is a constant crystallisation — constant and deliberate — of all things; and afterwards one must make the opposite movement, constantly, and also, even more so, deliberately. At the same time, one must not lose the benefit, in the consciousness, of what one has acquired by individualisation.

I must say that it is difficult.

From the point of view of thought it is elementary, very easy. And even from the point of view of feelings, it is not difficult; for the heart, that is, the emotional being, to widen itself to the dimension of the Supreme is relatively easy. But the body! It is very difficult, very difficult without the body losing — how to put it? — its centre of coagulation; without it dissolving into the surrounding mass. And even then, if one were in the midst of Nature with mountains, forests and rivers, and great natural beauty, plenty of space, it would be rather pleasant! But one cannot take a single step materially, out of one's body, without coming across things that are painful. It occasionally happens that one comes in contact with a substance that is pleasing, harmonious, warm, that vibrates with a higher light. But this is rare. Yes, flowers, sometimes flowers — sometimes, not always. But this material world, oh!... You get knocked everywhere — scratched, scratched, scraped, knocked by all kinds of things that *won't unfold*. Oh, how difficult it is! How little human life has blossomed! It is shrivelled up, hardened, without light, without warmth — to say nothing of joy.

But sometimes, when one sees flowing water or a ray of sunlight in the trees — oh, everything sings, the cells sing, they are happy.

But if the physical transformation is so difficult, would it not be preferable to act in an occult way, to materialise something, to create a new body by occult processes?

The idea is that first of all some beings must reach a certain realisation here in the physical world that would give them the power to materialise a supramental being.

I told you that once I endowed a vital being with a body, but I would never have been able to... it would have been impossible to make this body material: something is missing, something is missing. Even if it could be made visible, it probably could not be made permanent — at the very first opportunity it would dematerialise. It is this permanence that we cannot obtain.

I had discussed this with Sri Aurobindo — "discussed" is a manner of speaking — we had talked about it and he saw it the same way as I did, that is, there is a power we do not have, the power to fix the form here on earth. Even for those who have the capacity to materialise things, they do not remain, they cannot remain, they do not have the quality of physical things.

So the continuity of creation could not be assured without something which possessed that quality.

I knew the whole occult process in detail, but I could never have made the thing more material, even if I had tried — visible, yes, but impermanent, incapable of progressing.

12 January 1962

70 – Examine thyself without pity, then thou wilt be more charitable and pitiful to others.

Very good!

It is very good, very good for everybody, particularly for people who think themselves very superior.

But this really corresponds to something very profound.

In fact, this is an experience which I have been having for some time. It is almost like a reversal of attitude.

Indeed, men have always considered themselves victims harassed by adverse forces; those who are courageous fight, the others complain. But I have an increasingly concrete vision of the role that the adverse forces play in the creation, of the almost absolute necessity for them, so that there can be progress and for the creation to become its Origin once again — and such a clear vision that instead of asking for the conversion or abolition of the adverse forces one must realise one's own transformation, pray for it and carry it out. This is from the terrestrial point of view, I am not taking the individual standpoint. We know the individual standpoint; this is from the terrestrial point of view. It was the sudden vision of all the error, all the misunderstanding, all the ignorance and obscurity, and even worse, all the bad will in the terrestrial consciousness which felt responsible for the perpetuation of these adverse beings and forces and which offered them in a great aspiration — more than an aspiration, a kind of holocaust — so that the adverse forces might disappear and have no further reason to exist, so that they might no longer be there to point out everything that has to be changed.

Their presence was made unavoidable by all these things that were negations of the divine life. And this movement of offering of the earth consciousness to the Supreme, in an extraordinary intensity, was like a redemption so that the adverse forces might disappear.

It was a very intense experience which expressed itself like this: "Take all the faults I have committed, take them all, accept them, efface them so that these forces may disappear."

This aphorism is the same thing from the other end, it is the same thing in essence. As long as it is possible for a human consciousness to feel, act, think or be contrary to the great divine Becoming, it is impossible to blame anyone else for it; it is impossible to blame the adverse forces which are maintained in creation as the means of making you see and feel all the progress that has yet to be made.

(Silence)

The state I found myself in was like a memory — a memory that is eternally present — of that Consciousness of supreme

Love which the Lord emanated upon earth, in the earth — *in the earth* — to bring it back to Him. For that was truly a descent into the most total negation of the Divine, the negation of the very essence of the divine Nature, and therefore a renunciation of the divine state in order to accept earth's obscurity and bring earth back to the divine state. And unless this supreme Love becomes all-powerfully conscious here on earth, the return can never be final.

This experience came after the vision of the great divine Becoming,[3] and I asked myself, "Since this world is progressive, since it is becoming more and more the Divine, will there not always be this intensely painful feeling of the thing which is undivine, of the state which is undivine compared to the one which is to come? Will there not always be what we call 'adverse forces', that is, something which is not following the movement harmoniously?" Then the answer came, the vision came: no, indeed the time for this possibility is near, the time for the manifestation of that essence of perfect Love which can transform this unconsciousness, this ignorance and the bad will which results from it into a progression that is luminous, joyful, eager for perfection and all-inclusive.

It was very concrete.

And this corresponds to a state in which one is so *perfectly* identified with all that is, that one becomes all that is anti-divine in a concrete way, and that one can offer it — one can offer it and truly transform it by offering it.

Basically, this kind of will for purity, for good, in men — which expresses itself in the ordinary mentality as the need to be virtuous — is the *great obstacle* to true self-giving. This is the origin of Falsehood and even more the very source of hypocrisy — the refusal to accept to take upon oneself one's own share of the burden of difficulties. And in this aphorism Sri Aurobindo has gone straight to this point in a very simple way.

---

[3] See the commentary on the preceding aphorism.

Do not try to appear virtuous. See how much you are united, one with everything that is anti-divine. Take your share of the burden, accept yourselves to be impure and false and in that way you will be able to take up the Shadow and offer it. And in so far as you are capable of taking it and offering it, then things will change.

Do not try to be among the pure. Accept to be with those who are in darkness and give it all with total love.

21 January 1962

71 – A thought is an arrow shot at the truth; it can hit a point, but not cover the whole target. But the archer is too well satisfied with his success to ask anything farther.

But it is obvious! It is so obvious for us.

Yes, but what must we do to cover the whole target?

Stop being an archer!

It is a fine image. This is good for people who are in a state where they imagine they have discovered the Truth.

It is a good thing to say to those who think they have found the Truth because they have touched one point.

But so often, we have said something else.

One wonders how far it is possible to act once one is able to include the whole target, that is, to know all points of view and the usefulness of each thing, since one can see that everything is useful, that everything is in its place. In order to act, doesn't one need to be in some way exclusive or combative?

You know the story of the philosopher who lived in the south of France — I do not remember his name, a very well-known man who was a professor at the University of Montpellier and who lived on the outskirts of the city? There were several roads leading to his house. Every day this man would leave his university and arrive at the crossroads where all the roads leading to his house branched out — this way, that way, another way. And every day he would stop and ask himself, "Which one shall I take?" Each one had its advantages and disadvantages. And all this went on in his head, the advantages and disadvantages, and this and that, and he would waste half an hour choosing his way home.

He used to give that as an example of the thought's incapacity for action: if one begins to think, one can no longer act.

It is all right down here, on this plane, as long as one is the archer and hits only one point. But above it is not true — quite the contrary! All intelligence below is like that; it sees all kinds of things, and as it sees all kinds of things, it cannot choose in order to act. But in order to see the whole target, to see the Truth in its entirety, you must cross over to the other side. And when you cross over to the other side, you do not see a sum of multiple truths nor a countless number of truths added one to another, which you see one after another so that you cannot grasp the whole all at once. When you rise above, it is the whole that you see first; the whole presents itself all at once, in its entirety, in its wholeness, without division. And then you no longer have to make a choice, you have a vision: *this* is what has to be done. It is not a choice between this and that, or this or that, because it is no longer like that. You no longer see things successively, one after another; you have the simultaneous vision of a whole that exists as a unity. Then the choice is simply a vision.

But as long as you are in the state of the archer, you cannot see the whole — you cannot see the whole successively, you cannot see the whole by adding one truth to another. That is precisely the incapacity of the mind. The mind cannot do it. It will always see successively, it will always see a sum of things

Jnana

and it is not that — something will escape, the very meaning of the truth will elude it.

It is only when one has a global, simultaneous perception of the whole in its oneness that one can possess the truth in its entirety.

And then action is no longer a choice subject to error, rectification and discussion, but the clear vision of what is to be done — which is infallible.

3 February 1962

72 – **The sign of dawning Knowledge is to feel that as yet I know little or nothing; and yet, if I could only know my knowledge, I already possess everything.**

In sleep one occasionally has a very accurate knowledge of what is going to happen, with an extraordinary precision in the material details, as if everything were already there complete down to the smallest details, on an occult plane. Is that correct? What is this plane of knowledge? Is there one or several? What should one do to gain access to it consciously in the waking state? And how is it that people who are serious, who have a divine realisation, sometimes make such gross mistakes in their predictions?

But it is a whole world in itself! It is not one question, but twenty!

There are all kinds of premonitory dreams. There are premonitory dreams that are fulfilled immediately, that is to say, you dream in the night what will happen on the next day, and there are premonitory dreams that are fulfilled over varying lengths of time. And according to their position in time, these dreams are seen on various planes.

The higher we rise towards absolute certainty, the greater

the distance is, because these visions belong to a region which is very close to the Origin and the length of time between the revelation of what is going to be and its realisation may be very great. But the revelation is certain, because it is very close to the Origin. There is a place — when one is identified with the Supreme — where one knows everything absolutely, in the past, the present, the future and everywhere. But usually people who go there forget what they have seen when they return. An extremely strict discipline is needed to remember. And that is the only place where one cannot make a mistake.

But the links of the chain of communication are not always all there and one very rarely remembers.

To come back to what I was saying, according to the plane on which one has seen, one can more or less judge the time that the vision will take to be fulfilled. And the immediate things are already realised, they already exist in the subtle physical and they can be seen there — they simply are, they exist there. They are only the reflection — not even a transcription — the reflection or projection of the image in the material world which will appear on the next day or in a few hours. There you see the exact thing in all its details, because it already exists; so everything depends on the accuracy of the vision and the power of vision. If you have a power of vision that is objective and sincere, you see the thing accurately; if you add your own feelings and impressions to it, it is coloured by them. So accuracy in the subtle physical depends exclusively on the instrument, that is to say, on the one who sees.

But as soon as you enter a more subtle region, such as the vital — and even more so in the mental, but already in the vital there is a small margin of possibility — then there you can see roughly what is going to happen, but in detail it may be like this or like that; there are wills and influences that may possibly intervene and create a difference.

And this is because the original Will is reflected, so to say, in the various regions, and each region alters the organisation and the relation of the images. The world we live in is a world of images. It is not the thing itself in its essence, it is the reflection of the thing. One could say that we are, in our material existence, only a reflection, an image of what we are in our essential reality. And the modalities of these reflections bring in every error and falsification — what you see in the essence is perfectly true and pure and exists from all eternity; the images are essentially variable. And according to the degree of falsehood that enters into the vibrations, the degree of distortion and alteration increases. One could say that every circumstance, every event, every thing has a pure existence, which is the true existence, and a considerable number of impure or distorted existences, which are the existence of the same thing in the various domains of being. For example, in the intellectual domain, there is already a good deal of distortion; in the mental domain there is a considerable amount of distortion, and as all the emotional and sensorial domains come in, the distortions increase. And once you reach the material plane, it is most often unrecognisable. It is completely distorted — so much so that it is sometimes very difficult to know that this is the material expression of that — they are no longer very much alike.

It is a rather novel way of approaching the problem and it may be the key to many things.

Thus when you know someone well and you often see him physically, if you see him in the subtle physical, already there are things which become more marked, more visible, more outstanding, which you had not seen physically, because in the greyness of the material world they had merged with many other things on the same plane. There are characteristics or expressions of character which become outstanding enough to be quite visible, although they had not been physically apparent. When you look at a person physically, there is the complexion, the features, the expression; at the same moment, if you see this face in the subtle physical, you suddenly notice that one part of the face is one colour, another part another colour; that in the eyes there is an expression and a kind of light which were not at all visible; and that the whole has quite a different appearance and, above all, gives a very different feeling, which to our physical eyes would seem rather extravagant, but which to the subtle vision is very expressive and revealing of the character, or even of the influences acting on this person. What I say here is the record of an experience that I had again a few days ago.

So according to the degree to which you are conscious and the extent to which you see, you perceive images, see events that are more or less near, and you see them more or less accurately. The only vision that is true and sure is the vision of the divine Consciousness. So the problem is to become aware of the divine Consciousness and to keep this consciousness in all details all the time.

Until then, there are all sorts of ways of receiving indications. The precise, accurate, familiar vision that certain people have may come from several sources. It may be a vision by identity with circumstances and things, when you are used to extending your consciousness all around you. It may be an indication given by a talkative being from the invisible world who amuses himself by informing you of what is going to happen; this happens very often. Then everything depends on the moral character of your "informant"; if he is amusing himself at your expense, he tells you all kinds of tales — and this is what happens most of the time to people who get information from entities. To lure people on, they may very often tell them things as they really will be, since they have a universal vision in some domain of the vital or of the mind; and then when they are quite sure that you will trust them, they may start telling you tales and you make a fool of yourself. This happens very often. You yourself should be in a higher state of consciousness than these individuals or entities or these little gods, as some people call them, and be able to verify from above what their statements are worth.

If you have a universal mental vision, you can see all mental formations. Then you see—and it is very interesting—how the mental world is organised to realise itself on the physical plane. You see the various formations, the way in which they approach and fight each other, combine together and organise themselves, the ones that prevail and gain influence and achieve a more complete realisation. Now if you really want to have a higher vision, you must rise above the mental world and see the original wills as they descend to express themselves. In this case, you may not possess all the details, but the central *fact*, the fact in its central truth, is indisputable, undeniable, absolutely correct.

Some people also have the power to predict things which already exist on earth, but at a distance, at a great distance, very far from the physical eyes. These are usually people who are capable of widening and extending their consciousness. They have a physical, but slightly more subtle vision, which depends on an organ that is more subtle than the purely material one—what might be called the life of this organ—and so, by projecting their consciousness with a will to see, they can see very well, they can see things: these things already exist, only they are not within the field of our ordinary vision. People who have this capacity and who tell what they see, who are sincere and who are not bluffers, see in a way that is absolutely precise and exact.

In fact, an important factor for those who predict or see, is their absolute sincerity. Unfortunately, because of people's curiosity, their insistence, the pressure they apply—which very few can resist—what happens, when there is something they do not see exactly and precisely, is that there is an almost involuntary faculty of inner imagination, which adds the little missing element. This is what causes the flaws in their predictions. Very few have the courage to say, "Oh no, I do not know about that, it eludes me." They do not even have the courage to say it to themselves. And then, just a touch of imagination, acting almost subconsciously, and they fill in the vision, the information—anything can happen. Very few people can resist that. I have known many, many clairvoyants, I have known many people who had a marvellous gift; very few of them would stop when they come to the end of their knowledge. Or else they would add some little detail. This is what always gives these faculties a rather doubtful quality. One must truly be a saint — a great saint, a great sage — and completely free, not at all influenced by other people. Naturally, I am not speaking of those who seek fame, because there they fall into the crudest traps; but even goodwill, the wish to make people happy, to please them, to help them, is enough to create a distortion.

When events are already prepared in the subtle physical and you have a vision of them, is it too late to change things? Can one still act?

I know of a very interesting example. There was a time when in the newspaper *Le Matin* — it was a long time ago, you must have been very young — every day there was a little cartoon of a boy pointing to something — a kind of page-boy dressed like that — and always showing the date or something — a little cartoon. Now the gentleman in this story was travelling and he was staying in a big hotel, I do not remember in which town, and one night or early in the morning, very early, he had a dream. He saw this page-boy pointing to his funeral carriage — you know, when they take people to the cemetery, in Europe — and inviting him to step into it! He saw that and then in the morning when he was ready, he left his room which was on the top floor, and there, on the landing, the same boy, dressed in the same way, was pointing out the lift for him to go down. That gave him a shock. He refused and said, "No thank you." The lift fell and crashed, killing the people inside.

He told me that after that he believed in dreams.

It was a vision. He saw the boy, but instead of the lift, the boy was showing him his hearse. So when he saw the same gesture, the same boy — like the cartoon, you see — he said, "No thank you, I'll walk down", and the machine — it was one of those hydraulic lifts — broke and fell. It was right at the top. It was crushed to a pulp.

My explanation is that an entity had forewarned him. The image of the page-boy seems to indicate that an intelligence, a consciousness had intervened; it does not seem to have been his own subconscient. Or it might be that his subconscient was aware and had seen in the subtle physical that this was going to happen. But why did his subconscient give him an image like that? I do not know. Perhaps something in the subconscient knew, because it was already there, it was already in the subtle physical. The accident already existed before it happened — the law of the accident.

Obviously, there is always, in every case, some difference, sometimes a few hours — but that is the maximum — sometimes a few seconds. And very often, things tell you that they are there, and it takes them sometimes a few minutes, sometimes a few seconds to come into contact with your consciousness. Constantly, constantly I know what is going to happen, and for things that are of absolutely no interest — there is no advantage in knowing it beforehand, it changes nothing; but it exists, it is all around you. If your consciousness is wide enough, you know all that, for example, that a certain person is going to bring you a parcel, things like that. And it is like that every day. Or that a certain person is about to arrive. It is because the consciousness is extended, so it contacts things.

But in that case we cannot say that it is a premonition, for it already exists, only the contact with our senses takes a few seconds to be realised, because there is a door or a wall or something that prevents us from seeing.

But several times I have had experiences like this. For example, once when I was walking in the mountains, I was on a path where there was only room for one — on one side the precipice, on the other sheer rock. There were three children behind me and a fourth person bringing up the rear. I was leading. The path ran along the edge of the rock; we could not see where we were going — and besides, it was very dangerous; if anyone had slipped, he would have been over the edge. I was walking in front when suddenly I saw, with other eyes than these — although I was watching my steps carefully — I saw a snake, there, on the rock, waiting on the other side. Then I took one step, gently, and indeed on the other side there was a snake. That spared me the shock of surprise, because I had seen and I was advancing cautiously; and as there was no shock of surprise, I was able to tell the children without giving them a shock, "Stop, keep quiet, don't stir." If there had been a shock, something might have happened. The snake had heard a noise, it was already coiled and on the defensive in front of its hole, with its head swaying — it was a viper. This was in France. Nothing happened, whereas if there had been any confusion or commotion, anything could have happened.

    This kind of thing has happened to me very, very often — with snakes it happened to me four times. Once, it was completely dark, here, near the fishing village of Ariankuppam. There was a river and it happened just at the place where it flows into the sea. It was dark — the night had fallen very quickly. We were walking along the road and just as I was about to put my foot down — I had already lifted my foot and I was going to put it down — I distinctly heard a voice in my ear: "Be careful!" And yet nobody had spoken. So I looked and saw, just as my foot was about to touch the ground, an enormous black cobra, which I would have comfortably stepped on — those people don't like that. He streaked away and across the water — what a beauty, my child! His hood open, head erect above the water, he went across like a king. Obviously, I would have been punished for my impertinence.

    I have had hundreds and hundreds of experiences like that; at the very last moment, not a second too soon, I was informed. And in the most varied circumstances. Once, in Paris, I was crossing the Boulevard Saint Michel. It was during the last weeks; I had decided that within a certain number of months I would achieve union with the psychic Presence, the inner Divine, and I no longer had any other thought, any other concern. I lived near the Luxembourg Gardens and every evening I used to walk there — but always deeply absorbed within. There is a kind of intersection there, and it is not a place to cross when one is deeply absorbed within; it was not very sensible. And so I was like that, I was walking, when I suddenly received a shock, as if I had received a blow, as if something had hit me, and I jumped back instinctively. And as soon as I had jumped back, a tram went past — it was the tram that I had felt at a little more than arm's length. It had touched the aura, the aura of protection — it was very strong at that time, I was deeply immersed in occultism and I knew how to keep it — the aura of protection had been hit and that had literally thrown me backwards, as if I had received a physical shock. And what insults from the driver! I jumped back just in time and the tram went by.

I could tell scores of such stories, if I could remember them.

The protection may come from many different sources. Very often it was someone who informed me: a little entity, or some kind of being; sometimes it was the aura that protected me. And it was for all kinds of things. That is to say, life was seldom limited to the physical body — this is convenient, this is good. It is necessary, it increases your capacities. This is what the person who taught me occultism told me straightaway: "You are depriving yourself of senses which are most useful *even for the most ordinary life.*" And this is true, quite true. We can know infinitely more things than we usually do, simply by using our own senses. And not only from the mental point of view, but also from the vital and even the physical point of view.

But what is the method?

Oh, the method is very easy. There are disciplines. It depends on what you want to do.

It depends. For each thing there is a method. And the first method is to want it, to begin with, that is, to take a decision. Then you are given a description of all these senses and how they work — that takes some time. You take one sense or several, or the one which is easiest for you to start with, and you decide. Then you follow the discipline. It is the equivalent of exercises for developing the muscles. You can even succeed in creating a will in yourself.

But for more subtle things, the method is to make for yourself an exact image of what you want, to come into contact with the corresponding vibration, and then to concentrate and do exercises — such as to practise seeing through an object or hearing through a sound,[4] or seeing at a distance. For example, once, for a long time, for several months, I was confined to bed and I found it rather boring — I wanted to see. I was in a room and at one end there was another little room and at the end of the little room there was a kind of bridge; in the middle of the garden the bridge became a staircase leading down into a very big and very beautiful studio, standing in the middle of the garden. I wanted to go and see what was happening in the studio, for I was feeling bored in my room. So I would remain very quiet, close my eyes and send out my consciousness, little by little, little by little, little by little. And day after day — I chose a fixed time and did the exercise regularly. At first you make use of your imagination and then it becomes a fact. After some time I really had the physical sensation that my vision was moving; I followed it and then I could see things downstairs which I knew nothing about. I would check afterwards. In the evening I would ask, "Was this like that? And was that like this?"

---

[4] Mother explained later: "To hear behind the sound is to come into contact with the subtle reality which is behind the material fact, behind the word or the physical sound or behind music, for example. One concentrates and then one hears what is behind. It means coming into contact with the vital reality which is behind the appearances. There can also be a mental reality, but generally, what lies immediately behind the physical sound is a vital reality."

But for each one of these things you must practise for months with patience, with a kind of obstinacy. You take the senses one by one, hearing, sight, and you can even arrive at subtle realities of taste, smell and touch.

From the mental point of view it is easier, for there you are accustomed to concentration. When you want to think and find a solution, instead of following the deductions of thought, you stop everything and try to concentrate and concentrate, intensify the point of the problem. You stop everything and wait until, by the intensity of the concentration, you obtain an answer. This also requires some time. But if you used to be a good student, you must be quite used to doing that and it is not very difficult.

There is a kind of extension of the physical senses. Red Indians, for example, possess a sense of hearing and smell with a far greater range than our own — and dogs! I knew an Indian — he was my friend when I was eight or ten years old. He had come with Buffalo Bill, at the time of the Hippodrome — it was a long time ago, I was eight years old — and he would put his ear to the ground and was so clever that he knew how far away... according to the intensity of the vibration, he knew how far away someone's footsteps were. After that, the children would immediately say, "I wish I knew how to do that!"

And then you try. That is how you prepare yourself. You think you are playing but you are preparing yourself for later on.

27 February 1962

73 – When Wisdom comes, her first lesson is, "There is no such thing as knowledge; there are only *aperçus* of the Infinite Deity."

This is very good.
There is no need for any questions.

74 – Practical knowledge is a different thing; that is real and serviceable, but it is never complete. Therefore to systematise and codify it is necessary but fatal.

75 – Systematise we must, but even in making and holding the system, we should always keep firm hold on this truth that all systems are in their nature transitory and incomplete.

I have looked at this very, very often. There was even a time when I thought that if one could have a total, complete and perfect knowledge of the entire working of physical Nature as we perceive it in the world of Ignorance, that might be a way to rediscover or to re-attain the truth of things. After my latest experience[5] I cannot think this any more.

I do not know if I am making myself clear. There was a time — for a very long period — when I thought that if science were to realise its full potential, but in an absolute way, if that were possible, it would reach true Knowledge. For example, in its study of the composition of Matter, by pushing and pushing its investigations further and further, a time would come when the two would meet. Well, when I had the experience of passing from the eternal Truth-consciousness to the consciousness of the individualised world, it became clear to me that this was impossible. And if you ask me now, I think that both these things, the possibility of a meeting by carrying science to its extreme and the impossibility of any true conscious connection with the material world, are equally incorrect. There is something else.

And these last few days, more and more, I find myself faced with the total problem, as if I had never seen it before.

Perhaps they are two paths leading to a third point, and at the moment perhaps it is this third point that I am not exactly

---

[5] A particular yogic experience which took place on 13 April 1962.

studying, but searching for, where the two would meet in a third one which would be the True Thing.

But certainly, objective, scientific knowledge carried to its extreme, if it is possible for it to become absolutely total, leads at least to the threshold. That is what Sri Aurobindo says. Only he says that it is fatal, because all those who have devoted themselves to that knowledge, have believed in it as an absolute truth, and for them this has closed the door to the other approach. In that way it is fatal.

But according to my personal experience, I could say that for all those who believe in the *exclusive* spiritual approach, the approach through inner experience, at least if it is exclusive, is also fatal — because it shows them *one* aspect, *one* truth of the Whole, not the Whole. The other aspect seems equally indispensable to me, in the sense that while I was so totally immersed in the supreme Realisation, it was absolutely indisputable that the other realisation, the outer, the illusory one, was only a distortion, probably accidental, of something that was *just as* true as that one.

It is this "something" that we are searching for — perhaps not only searching for it, but *making* it.

We are being used so that we can participate in the manifestation of "that", of "that" which is still inconceivable to everyone, because it is not yet there. It is an expression that is yet to come.

This is all I can say.

(Silence)

That is really the state of consciousness I am living in at present. It is as if I were confronted with this eternal problem, but *from another standpoint.*

These standpoints, the spiritual and the "materialist", if one may say so, that think they are exclusive — exclusive and unique, so that one denies the value of the other, from the point of view of Truth — are insufficient, not only because they do not accept one another, but also because to accept both and to unite both is not enough to solve the problem. It is something else — a third thing which is not the result of these two, but something that is yet to be discovered, which will probably open the door to the total Knowledge.

This is the point I have reached.

I cannot say more because that is where I am.

In practice, how can we participate in this...?

This discovery?

Well!... Basically, it is always the same thing. It is always the same thing: to realise one's own being, to enter into conscious relation with the supreme Truth of one's own being, in *any* form, by *any* path — it does not matter at all — but this is the only way. We carry, each individual carries within him a truth, and this is the truth he must unite with, this is the truth he must live; and so the path he must follow to reach and realise this truth is the path that will lead him *as near as possible* to Knowledge. That is to say, the two are absolutely one: the personal realisation and the Knowledge.

Who knows, perhaps this very multiplicity of approach will yield the secret — the secret that will open the door.

I do not think that a single individual on the earth as it is now, a single individual, however great, however eternal his consciousness and origin, can on his own change and realise — change the world, change the creation as it is and realise this higher Truth which will be a new world, a world more true, if not absolutely true. It would seem that a certain number of individuals — until now it seems to have been more in time, as a succession, but it could also be in space, a collectivity — are indispensable so that this Truth can become concrete and realise itself.

Practically, I am sure of it.

That is to say, however great, however conscious, however

Jnana

powerful he may be, *one* Avatar cannot by himself realise the supramental life on earth. It is either a group in time, extending over a period of time, or a group spread out in space — perhaps both — that are indispensable for this Realisation. I am convinced of it.

The individual can give the impulsion, indicate the path, *walk* on the path himself — that is to say, show the path by realising it himself — but he cannot fulfil. The fulfilment obeys certain group laws which are the expression of some aspect of Eternity and Infinity — naturally, it is all the same Being! They are not different individuals or different personalities, it is all the same Being. And it is all the same Being expressing Himself in a way which for us becomes a body, a group, a collectivity.

There. Do you have another question on the same subject?

In what way has your vision become different since this experience?

I repeat. For a very long time it seemed to me that if a perfect union could be achieved between the scientific approach carried to its extreme and the spiritual approach carried to its extreme — its extreme realisation — if both could be joined, we would find, we would naturally obtain the Truth we are seeking, the total Truth. But with the two experiences I have had — the experience of external life, with universalisation, impersonalisation, in short, all the yogic experiences one can have in the physical body, and on the other hand the experience of total and perfect union with the Origin — now that I have had these two experiences and that something has happened, which I cannot describe yet, I know that the knowledge of the two and the union of the two is not enough; that they lead to a third thing and it is this third thing which is in the making, in course of elaboration. It is this third thing that can lead to the Realisation, to the Truth we seek.

Is it clear this time?

On Thoughts and Aphorisms

I had something else in mind.... In what way has your vision of the physical world changed since then?

One can only give an approximation of that consciousness.

Through yoga, I had achieved a kind of relationship with the material world, based on the notion of the fourth dimension — inner dimensions, which become innumerable in yoga — and the use of this attitude and this state of consciousness. I studied the relationship between the material world and the spiritual world with a sense of the inner dimensions, and by perfecting the consciousness of these inner dimensions — that was my experience until the latest one.

Naturally, for a long time, there has no longer been any question of three dimensions — this belongs *absolutely* to the world of illusion and falsehood. But now the whole use of the sense of the fourth dimension with all that it entails seems superficial to me! This is so strong that I have lost it. The other one, the three-dimensional world is absolutely unreal; and this one seems to be — how to put it? — conventional. As if it were a conventional interpretation that allows you to make a certain kind of approach.

And as for saying what the other one is, the true poise... it is so far beyond any intellectual state that I am unable to formulate it.

Yet the formula will come, I know. But it will come through a series of experiences that must be lived and which I have not yet had.

(*Silence*)

This approach, which was very convenient, very helpful to me, which I used in my yoga, which gave me a hold on Matter, appeared to me as a method, a means, a process, but it is not *that*.

This is my present state.

More I cannot say.

24 May 1962

76 – Europe prides herself on her practical and scientific organisation and efficiency. I am waiting till her organisation is perfect; then a child shall destroy her.[6]

When these aphorisms were published in the Bulletin *you said that this one should be omitted. It is a rather mysterious aphorism, which I would very much like to understand. But I would like to know whether now we should publish it or not?*

Where did Sri Aurobindo write that?

In the Aphorisms.

Yes, but he did not write a special book; these texts were collected from here and there.

No, no, not at all. Sri Aurobindo had a special notebook in which he wrote the aphorisms as they came.[7] And this one was among the others.

(*Silence*)

"A child"... What did he put in English at the beginning?

"Prides herself."

Prides herself...
I would put it in.

---

[6] The following conversation took place in December 1971, nearly ten years after the Mother's commentaries on this group of aphorisms.
[7] There is, in fact, one notebook which contains all the aphorisms, but it is in all likelihood a fair copy and not the first draft of the aphorisms.

But what did he mean?

I don't know.
   Of course, only the power can be destroyed, because one cannot destroy the earth.

Yes, the earth cannot be destroyed, but a civilisation can be destroyed.

Yes.

He says: Europe will be destroyed.

Yes... but which child?
   I have the impression that it came as something absolutely true, an absolutely true prediction — but I don't know.

You had said that it would be better to leave it out.

But now, on the contrary, I feel that it *must* be said.
   But I do not think that the time has come yet, I mean "come" for the realisation; the time has come to say it, but not for the realisation.

"The child"... perhaps it is the child of the new world — with a smile, he will bring the whole thing tumbling down.

Yes, it is possible — it is possible.

(Silence)

There is a terrifying power in it... something tremendous. You cannot imagine the power that is in it; it is really as if the Divine himself were speaking: "I am waiting... I am waiting..."

11 December 1971

77 – Genius discovers a system; average talent stereotypes it till it is shattered by fresh genius. It is dangerous for an army to be led by veterans; for on the other side God may place Napoleon.

78 – When knowledge is fresh in us, then it is invincible; when it is old, it loses its virtue. This is because God moves always forward.

Sri Aurobindo is speaking here of knowledge by inspiration or revelation, when something suddenly descends and illumines the understanding. You suddenly have the impression that you know something for the first time, because it comes directly from the domain of Light, of true Knowledge, and it comes with all its innate power of truth — it illumines you. And when you have just received it, it seems indeed that nothing can resist that Light. And if you take care to allow it to act within you, it accomplishes all the transformation it can achieve in its own domain.

This is an experience one may often have. When it comes, for some time — not very long — everything seems to organise itself quite naturally around that Light. And then, little by little, it mingles with the rest; the intellectual knowledge remains — it is formulated in one way or another — it remains, but it is just as if it were empty. It no longer has that driving power which transforms all the movements of the being into the image of this Light. That is what Sri Aurobindo means: the world moves quickly, the Lord is always moving onward and all this is the trail He leaves behind Him, but it no longer has the same immediate and almighty power as when He projected it into the world.

It feels like a rain of truth falling; everyone who can catch even a drop of it receives a revelation. But unless they themselves are moving forward at a fantastic speed, the Lord with His rain of truth is already very far ahead and they must run very fast to catch up with it! This is what he means.

On Thoughts and Aphorisms

> *Yes, but for this knowledge to have a real power of transformation...*

Yes, it is the higher Knowledge, the Truth expressing itself, what Sri Aurobindo calls the true Knowledge, and it is this Knowledge that transforms all creation. But it is as if He were pouring it down all the time and you have to make great haste so as not to be too late!

But haven't you ever had the feeling of a dazzling light in your head? And then it is translated by, "Oh, but of course!" Sometimes it is something you knew intellectually, but it was dull, lifeless, and it suddenly comes like a tremendous power that arranges everything within the consciousness around that Light. It does not last very long. Sometimes it lasts only a few hours, sometimes a few days, but never more than that, unless you are very slow in your movement. And in the meanwhile the source of the truth is moving, moving, moving....

> *These are all psychological transformations, but where Matter and the body are concerned, what kind of knowledge is needed?*

For the moment, I can't say anything about that, my child, because I do not know.

> *Is it another kind of knowledge?*

No, I do not think so.

(Silence)

It may be another kind of action, but it is not another kind of knowledge.

(Silence)

In truth, we shall only be able to speak of what transforms Matter when Matter is at least a little transformed, when there is a beginning of transformation. Then we shall be able to speak of the process. But for the moment...

(Silence)

But any transformation in the being, on any plane, always has some repercussion on the lower planes. There is always an effect; even things which seem to be purely intellectual certainly have some repercussion on the structure of the brain.

This kind of revelation can only occur in a silent mind — at least in a mind that is at rest, completely quiet and still, otherwise they do not come. Or if they come, you do not notice them, because of all the noise you are making. And of course, they help this quiet, this silence, this receptivity to become better and better established. This feeling of something so still — but not closed, still but open, still but receptive — is something which becomes established through repeated experiences. There is a great difference between a silence that is dead, dull, unresponsive and the receptive silence of a quietened mind. That makes a great difference. But that is the result of these experiences. All the progress we make always results, quite naturally, from truths coming from above.

They have an effect, all these things have an effect on the functioning of the body — the functioning of the organs, of the brain, of the nerves, etc. That will surely happen before — long before — there is any effect on the external form.

In reality, when people speak of transformation they are thinking mainly of a glamorous transformation, no? A beautiful appearance! luminous, supple, plastic, changing at will. But this rather unaesthetic business of transforming the organs — they don't give it much thought! And yet that will certainly be

On Thoughts and Aphorisms

the first thing to happen, long before the transformation of the appearance.

Sri Aurobindo spoke of replacing the organs by the functioning of the chakras.[8]

Yes, yes. He said three hundred years! (*Mother laughs.*)

(*Silence*)

Because if you think it over, you will understand quite easily. If it were only a matter of stopping one thing and starting something else, it could be done quite rapidly. But to keep a body alive, so that it goes on functioning, and *at the same time* to bring in a new functioning, sufficient for it to stay alive, and a transformation — that makes a kind of combination which is very difficult to realise. I am very much aware of this, very much so... the immense amount of time required to do this without catastrophe.

Especially when we come to the heart: the heart replaced by the centre of power, a tremendous dynamic power! (*Mother laughs.*) Precisely when are we going to cut off the circulation and release the Force?

It is difficult.

(*Silence*)

In ordinary life, you think things over and then you do them — it is just the opposite! In this life, first you must do the thing and then, afterwards, you understand, long afterwards. First you must do it — without thinking. If you think, you do nothing worthwhile; that is, you fall back into the old way.

6 October 1962

---

[8] Centres of consciousness in the subtle body.

79 – God is infinite Possibility. Therefore Truth is never at rest; therefore, also, Error is justified of her children.

80 – To listen to some devout people, one would imagine that God never laughs; Heine was nearer the mark when he found in Him the divine Aristophanes.

Yes, he means that what is true at one time is no longer true at another. And this is why "Error is justified of her children."

Perhaps he means that there is no error.

Yes, it is the same thing, another way of saying the same thing. That is to say, what we call Error was Truth at a certain time.
Error is a concept in time.

Some things may really appear to be errors.

For a moment.
The impression is this: all our judgments are momentary. They are... one moment, it is like this; the next moment, it is no longer like this. And for us they are errors, because we see things one after another. But to the Divine they cannot appear like this, because everything is within Him.
Now just try to imagine that you are the Divine, for a moment! Everything is within you; you simply amuse yourself by bringing it out in a certain order. But for you, in your consciousness, everything is there at the same time; there is no time — neither past nor future nor present — everything is together. And every possible combination. He amuses Himself by bringing out first one thing and then another, like that. So the poor fellows down below who can see only a tiny part — they can see only so much of it — say, "Oh, that is an error!" In what way is it an error? Simply because they can only see a tiny part.

This is clear, isn't it? It is easy to understand. This concept of error is a concept that belongs to time and space.
It is like the feeling that something cannot *be* and *not be* at the same time. And yet this is true, it is and it is not. It is the concept of time which introduces the concept of error — of time and space.

What do you mean, that a thing is and is not at the same time? How is that?

It is, and at the same time there is its opposite. So, for us, it cannot be yes and no at the same time. But for the Lord it is *all the time* yes and no at the same time.
It is like our concept of space; we say, "I am here, therefore you are not here." But I am here, you are here and everything is here! (*Mother laughs.*) Only you must be able to leave the concept of space and time behind in order to understand.
This is something that can be felt very concretely, but not with our way of seeing.
Certainly, many of these aphorisms were written at the point where the higher mind suddenly emerges into the Supermind. It has not yet forgotten how it is in the ordinary way, but it also sees how it is in the supramental way. And so the result is this kind of thing, this paradoxical form. Because the one is not forgotten and the other is already perceived.

(*Long silence*)

And yet if one looks attentively, one has to think that the Lord is staging a fantastic play for Himself! That the Manifestation is a play which He is acting for Himself and with Himself.
He has taken the stand of the spectator and He looks at Himself. And so in order to look at Himself, He must accept the

concept of time and space, otherwise He cannot! And immediately the whole comedy begins. But it is a comedy, nothing more.

But we take it seriously, because we are puppets! But as soon as we stop being puppets, we can see quite clearly that it is a comedy.

For some people it is also a real tragedy.

Yes, we are the ones who make it tragic. *We are the ones* who make it tragic.

Recently, I have been looking at this carefully. I looked at the difference between similar incidents when they happen to men and when they happen to animals. If you identify yourself with the animals you see quite clearly that they do not take it tragically at all — except the ones which have come into contact with man; but then it is not their natural state, it is a transitional state. They become transitional beings between animal and man.... And the first things they naturally learn from man are his defects — they are always the easiest things to learn! And so they make themselves unhappy — for nothing.

So many things... So many things... Man has made a terrible tragedy out of death. These last few days, I have seen this, because last night or the night before I spent at least two hours in a world which is subtle physical, where the living and the dead intermingle without feeling any difference — it doesn't make any difference. There, there is no difference. The living were there — those whom we call the "living" and those whom we call the "dead". They were there together, they ate together, they moved together, they played together; and all this was in a pretty light, quiet and very pleasant, it was very pleasant. I said to myself, "There, men have made a break, like this, and then they say, 'Now, dead.'" And "dead" — the best part of it is that they treat them as they would treat something unconscious — yet the body is still conscious.

On Thoughts and Aphorisms

(*Silence*)

Where, where is Error? Where is Error?
    That is to say, there is no error. Things only seem to be impossible, because we do not know that the Lord is all possibility and that He can do whatever He likes, as He likes. We cannot get that into our heads, we always say, "This is possible and that is not possible." But it is not true! For our imbecility, it is not possible; but everything is possible.

(*Silence*)

You see, only the one who is watching the play is not worried, because he knows everything that is going to happen and he has an absolute knowledge of everything — everything that happens, everything that has happened and everything that is going to happen — and it is all there, as *one* presence for him. And so it is the others, the poor actors who do not even know, they do not even know their parts! And they worry a great deal, because they are being made to act something and they do not know what it is. This is something I have just been feeling very strongly: we are all acting a play, but we do not know what the play is, nor where it is going, nor where it comes from, nor what it is as a whole; we barely know — imperfectly — what we are supposed to do from moment to moment. Our knowledge is imperfect. And so we worry! But when one knows everything, one can no longer worry, one smiles — He must be having great fun, but we... And yet we are given the *full power* to amuse ourselves like Him.
    We simply do not take the trouble.

It is not easy!

Oh, if it were easy... if it were easy, we would get tired of it!
    One also sometimes wonders why, why is this life so tragic? But if it were like a perpetual enchantment, first of all we would

not even appreciate it, because it would be quite natural — mainly that, we would not appreciate it because it would be absolutely natural — and then, who is to say that we would not enjoy a little confusion just for a change? One cannot be sure.

Perhaps this is the story of the earthly paradise.... In paradise they had a spontaneous knowledge, that is to say, they lived, they had the same consciousness as the animals, just enough to be able to enjoy life a little, like that, to have the joy of living. But they started wanting to know why, how, where they were going, what they should do, etc., and then all the worries began — they got tired of being quietly happy.

(Silence)

I think that Sri Aurobindo meant that error is an illusion like all the rest — that there is no error, that all possibilities are there, that they are often — and *necessarily* — contradictory if they are all there. They appear contradictory. But one only has to look at oneself and say, "What do I call error?" If you look it in the face you see immediately that it is a stupidity — there is no error, it slips through your fingers.

(Silence)

I have a feeling that Sri Aurobindo was in his ascension; the intuitive mind was piercing a hole and coming into contact with the Supermind, and so it would come like that, pop! like an explosion in the thought, and he would write these things. And if you follow the movement you see the Origin.

Obviously what he meant is that Error is one of the innumerable, infinite possibilities. "Infinite" means that absolutely nothing is beyond possibility. So where does error fit into it? We call it error, but it is completely arbitrary. We say, "This is an error" — in relation to what? In relation to our judgment that "this is true", but certainly not in relation to the judgment of the Lord, since it is a part of Himself!

Very few people can bear this widening of the understanding.

Now, when I start looking like this (*Mother closes her eyes*), two things are there at the same time: this smile, this joy, this laughter are there, and such peace! Such *full*, luminous, total peace, in which there are no more conflicts, no more contradictions. There are no more conflicts. It is *one single* luminous harmony — and yet everything we call error, suffering, misery, everything is there. *It eliminates nothing.* It is another way of seeing.

(*Long silence*)

There can be no doubt that if you sincerely want to get out of it, it is not so difficult after all: you have nothing to do, you only have to allow the Lord to do everything. And He does everything. He does everything. It is so wonderful, so wonderful!

He takes anything, even what we call a very ordinary intelligence and he simply teaches you to put this intelligence aside, to rest: "There, be quiet, don't stir, don't bother me, I don't need you." Then a door opens — you don't even feel that you have to open it; it is wide open, you are taken over to the other side. All that is done by Someone else, not you. And then the other way becomes impossible.

All this... oh, this tremendous labour of the mind striving to understand, toiling and giving itself headaches!... It is absolutely useless, absolutely useless, no use at all, it merely increases the confusion.

You are faced with a so-called problem: what should you say, what should you do, how should you act? There is nothing to do, nothing, you only have to say to the Lord, "There, You see, it is like that" — that's all. And then you stay very quiet. And then quite spontaneously, without thinking about it, without reflection, without calculation, nothing, nothing, without the slightest effort — you do what has to be done. That is to say, the Lord does it, it is no longer you. He does it, He arranges the circumstances, He arranges the people, He puts the words into your mouth or your pen — He does everything, everything, everything, everything; you have nothing more to do but to allow yourself to live blissfully.

I am more and more convinced that people do not really want it.

But clearing the ground is difficult, the work of clearing the ground beforehand.

But you don't even need to do it! He does it for you.

But they are constantly breaking in: the old consciousness, the old thoughts....

Yes, they try to come in again, by habit. You only have to say, "Lord, You see, You see, You see, it is like that" — that's all. "Lord, You see, You see this, You see that, You see this fool" — and it is all over immediately. And it changes automatically, my child, without the slightest effort. Simply to be sincere, that is to say, to *truly* want everything to be right. You are perfectly conscious that you can do nothing about it, that you have no capacity. I feel more and more that this amalgam of matter, like this, of cells, all that, is pitiful. It is pitiful! I do not know whether there are certain states in which people feel powerful, wonderful, luminous, capable; but for me it is because they do not really know what they are like! When you really see how you are made — it is really nothing, nothing. But it is capable of everything, provided... provided that you allow the Lord to act. But there is always something that wants to do it by itself; that's the trouble, otherwise...

No, you may be full of an excellent goodwill and then *you*

want to do it. That's what complicates everything. Or else you don't have faith, you believe that the Lord will not be able to do it and that you must do it yourself, because He does not know! (*Mother laughs.*) This, this kind of stupidity is very common. "How can He see things? We live in a world of Falsehood, how can He see Falsehood and see..." But He sees the thing as it is! Exactly!

I am not speaking of people of no intelligence, I am speaking of people who are intelligent and who try — there is a kind of conviction, like that, somewhere, even in people who know that we live in a world of Ignorance and Falsehood and that there is a Lord who is All-Truth. They say, "Precisely because He is All-Truth, He does not understand. (*Mother laughs.*) He does not understand our falsehood, I must deal with it myself." That is very strong, very common.

Ah! we make complications for nothing.

There is something I have often wondered about: when one prays to the Lord, when one wants to make Him understand that something is wrong, I always have the impression that one must concentrate very hard and that after all one is calling to something far away. Is that right? Or is it really...

That depends on us!

Now I can feel Him everywhere, all the time, all the time... even a physical contact — it is subtle physical, but physical — in things, in the air, in people, in... like this. (*Mother presses her hands to her face.*) And then, it is not far to go, all I have to do is this (*Mother turns her hands slightly inwards*), one second of concentration — He is there! He is there, He is everywhere. He is far away only when we think He is far away.

Naturally, when we begin to think of all the zones, all the planes of universal consciousness and that it is at the very end, at the very end, right at the very end, then it becomes very far away, very, very far! (*Mother laughs*.) But when we think that He is everywhere, that He is everything and that it is only our perception that prevents us from seeing Him and feeling Him and that we only have to do this (*Mother turns her hands inwards*); it is a movement like this and like that (*Mother turns her hands alternately inwards and outwards*), it becomes very concrete: you do this (*outward movement*), everything becomes artificial, hard, dry, false, untrue, artificial; you do this (*inward movement*), everything becomes wide, tranquil, luminous, peaceful, vast, joyful. And it is simply this, that (*Mother turns her hands alternately inwards and outwards*). How? Where? It cannot be described, it is only, *only* a movement of consciousness, nothing else. A movement of consciousness. And the difference between the true consciousness and the false consciousness becomes more and more precise, and at the same time, *thin* — you don't have to do "great things" to come out of it. Before that, one has the impression that one is living inside something and that a great interiorisation, concentration, absorption, is needed to get out of it; but now the impression is of something one accepts (*Mother screens her face with her hand*), something like a thin little peel that is very hard — very hard but malleable, very, very dry, very thin, very thin, something like putting on a mask; and then one does this (*gesture*), and it disappears.

One can foresee the time when it will not be necessary to be aware of the mask; it will be so thin that one will be able to see, to feel, to act through it with no need to put the mask on again. That is what has just begun.

But this Presence in all things.... It is a vibration, but it is a vibration that contains everything — a vibration which contains a kind of infinite power, infinite delight and infinite peace, of vastness, vastness, vastness; there are no limits.... But it is only a vibration, it does not... Oh, Lord! it cannot be thought, so it cannot be said. If you think, as soon as you think, the whole muddle begins again. That is why one cannot speak.

No, He is very far away because you think He is very far

On Thoughts and Aphorisms

away. Even, you know, if you think He is there, like this (*gesture close to her face*) touching you... if you could feel — it is not like the touch of a person, it is not like that. It is not something alien, external, which comes in from outside. It is not that.... It is everywhere.

Then you feel — everywhere, everywhere, everywhere: inside, outside, everywhere, everywhere — Him, nothing but Him — Him, His vibration.

No, you must stop that (*the head*), until you stop that, you cannot see the True Thing — you look for comparisons, you say, "It is like this, it is like that." Oh!

(*Silence*)

And how often, how often the impression... there is no form — there is a form and there is no form, it cannot be put into words. And the impression of a look and there are no eyes — there are no eyes, but there is a look — a look and a smile, and there is no mouth, there is no face! And yet there is a smile, there is a look and (*Mother laughs*) one cannot help saying, "Yes, O Lord, I am stupid!" But He laughs, one laughs, one is happy.

One cannot! It cannot be explained. It cannot be put into words. One cannot say anything. Whatever one says is nothing, nothing.

12 October 1962

81 – God's laughter is sometimes very coarse and unfit for polite ears; He is not satisfied with being Molière, He must needs also be Aristophanes and Rabelais.

82 – If men took life less seriously, they could very soon make it more perfect. God never takes His works seriously; therefore one looks out on this wonderful Universe.

83 – Shame has admirable results and both in aesthetics and in morality we could ill spare it; but for all that it is a badge of weakness and the proof of ignorance.

One might ask how taking things seriously has prevented life from being more perfect.

Virtue has always spent its time eliminating whatever it found bad in life, and if all the virtues of the various countries of the world had been put together, very few things would remain in existence.

Virtue claims to seek perfection, but perfection is a totality. So the two movements contradict each other. A virtue that eliminates, reduces, fixes limits, and a perfection that accepts everything, rejects nothing but puts each thing in its place, obviously cannot agree.

Taking life seriously generally consists of two movements: the first one is to give importance to things that probably have none, and the second is to want life to be reduced to a certain number of qualities that are considered pure and worthy of existence. In some people — for example, those Sri Aurobindo speaks about here, the "polite" or the puritans — this virtue becomes dry, arid, grey, aggressive and it finds fault everywhere, in everything that is joyful and free and happy.

The only way to make life perfect — I mean here, life on earth, of course — is to look at it from high enough to see it as a whole, not only in its present totality, but in the whole of the past, present and future: what it has been, what it is and what it will be — one must be able to see everything at once. Because that is the only way to put everything in its place. Nothing can be eliminated, nothing *should* be eliminated, but each thing must be in its place in total harmony with all the rest. And then all these things that seem so "bad", so "reprehensible", so "unacceptable" to the puritan mind, would become movements of delight and freedom in a totally divine life. And then nothing would prevent us from knowing, understanding, feeling and living this wonderful laughter of the Supreme who takes infinite delight in watching Himself live infinitely.

This delight, this wonderful laughter that dissolves every shadow, every pain, every suffering! You only have to go deep enough within yourself to find the inner Sun, to let yourself be flooded by it; and then there is nothing but a cascade of harmonious, luminous, sunlit laughter, which leaves no room for any shadow or pain.

In fact, even the greatest difficulties, even the greatest sorrows, even the greatest physical pain — if you can look at them from that standpoint, from there, you see the unreality of the difficulty, the unreality of the sorrow, the unreality of the pain — and there is nothing but a joyful and luminous vibration.

In fact, this is the most powerful way of dissolving difficulties, overcoming sorrows and removing pain. The first two are relatively easy — I say relatively — the last one is more difficult because we are in the habit of considering the body and its feelings to be extremely concrete, positive; but it is the same thing, it is simply because we have not learnt, we are not in the habit of regarding our body as something fluid, plastic, uncertain, malleable. We have not learnt to bring into it this luminous laughter that dissolves all darkness, all difficulty, all discord, all disharmony, everything that jars, that weeps and wails.

And this Sun, this Sun of divine laughter is at the centre of all things, the truth of all things: we must learn to see it, to feel it, to live it.

And for that, let us avoid people who take life seriously; they are very boring people.

As soon as the atmosphere becomes grave you can be sure that something is wrong, that there is a troubling influence, an old habit trying to reassert itself, which should not be accepted. All this regret, all this remorse, the feeling of being unworthy, of being at fault — and then one step further and you have the sense of sin. Oh! To me it all seems to belong to another age, an age of darkness.

But everything that persists, that tries to cling and endure, all these prohibitions and this habit of cutting life in two — into small things and big things, the sacred and the profane.... "What!" say the people who profess to follow a spiritual life, "how can you make such little things, such insignificant things the object of spiritual experience?" And yet this is an experience that becomes more and more concrete and real, even materially; it's not that there are "some things" where the Lord is and "some things" where He is not. The Lord is *always* there. He takes nothing seriously, everything amuses Him and He plays with you, if you know how to play. You do not know how to play, people do not know how to play. But how well He knows how to play! How well He plays! With everything, with the smallest things: you have some things to put on the table? Don't feel that you have to think and arrange, no, let's play: let's put this one here and that one there, and this one like that. And then another time it's different again.... What a good game and such fun!

So, it is agreed, we shall try to learn how to laugh with the Lord.

14 January 1963

84 – The supernatural is that the nature of which we have not attained or do not yet know, or the means of which we have not yet conquered. The common taste for miracles is the sign that man's ascent is not yet finished.

85 – It is rationality and prudence to distrust the supernatural; but to believe in it is also a sort of wisdom.

86 – Great saints have performed miracles; greater saints

have railed at them; the greatest have both railed at them and performed them.

87 – Open thy eyes and see what the world really is and what God; have done with vain and pleasant imaginations.

Why didn't you or Sri Aurobindo make a greater use of miracles as a means of overcoming resistance in the external human consciousness? Why this kind of self-effacement where outer things are concerned, this non-intervention or discretion?

As for Sri Aurobindo, I only know what he told me several times. People give the name of "miracle" only to interventions in the material or the vital world. And these interventions are always mixed with ignorant and arbitrary movements.

But the number of miracles that Sri Aurobindo performed in the mind is incalculable; but naturally you could only see it if you had a very straight, very sincere, very pure vision — a few people did see it. But he refused — this I know — he refused to perform any vital or material miracles, because of this mixture.

My experience is that in the present state of the world, a direct miracle, material or vital, must necessarily take into account a great many elements of falsehood that are unacceptable — they are necessarily miracles of falsehood. And they are unacceptable. I have seen what people call miracles; I saw many of them at one period, but this gave a right of existence to many things which to me are not acceptable.

What men call "miracles" nowadays are almost always performed by vital beings or by men who are in contact with vital beings, and this is a mixture — it accepts the reality of certain things, the truth of certain things that are not true. And this is the basis on which it works. So that is unacceptable.

I did not quite understand what you meant by saying

Jnana

that Sri Aurobindo performed miracles in the mind.

I mean that he used to introduce the supramental force into the mental consciousness. Into the mental consciousness, the mental consciousness that governs all material movements, he would introduce a supramental formation or power or force which immediately changed the organisation. This produces immediate effects which seem illogical because they do not follow the normal course of movements according to mental logic.

He himself used to say that when he was in possession of the supramental power, when he could use it at will and focus it on a specific point with a definite purpose, it was irrevocable, inevitable: the effect was absolute. That can be called a miracle.

For example, take someone who was sick or in pain; when Sri Aurobindo was in possession of this supramental power — there was a time when he said that it was completely under his control, that is, he could do what he wanted with it, he could apply it where he liked — then he would apply this Will, for example, to some disorder, either physical or vital or, of course, mental — he would apply this force of greater harmony, of greater order, this supramental force, and focus it there, and it would act immediately. And it was an order: it created an order, a harmony greater than the natural harmony. That is, if it was a case of healing, for example, the healing would be more perfect and more complete than any obtained by ordinary physical and mental methods.

There were a great many of them. But people are so blind, so embedded in their ordinary consciousness that they always give "explanations", they can always give an explanation. Only those who have faith and aspiration and something very pure in themselves, that is, who truly want to know, they were able to perceive it.

When the Power was there, he even used to say that it was effortless; all he had to do was to apply this supramental power of order and harmony and instantly the desired result was achieved.

> *What is a miracle? Because Sri Aurobindo often said that there are no miracles and, at the same time he says in* Savitri, *for example: "All's miracle here and can by miracle change."*[9]

That depends on how you look at it, from this side or that.

You give the name of miracle only to things which cannot be clearly explained or for which you have no mental explanation. From this point of view you can say that countless things that happen are miracles, because you cannot explain the how or the why of them.

> *What would be a true miracle?*

I can't see what a true miracle can be because, after all, what is a miracle? A true miracle... Only the mind has the notion of miracles; because the mind decides, by its own logic, that given this and that, another thing can or cannot be. But this represents all the limitations of the mind. Because, from the point of view of the Lord, how can there be a miracle? Everything is Himself which He objectifies.

So here we come to the great problem of the way which is being followed, the eternal way, as Sri Aurobindo explains it in *Savitri*. Of course, one can conceive that what was objectified first was something which had an inclination for objectivisation. The first thing to recognise, which seems consistent with the principle of evolution, is that the objectivisation is progressive, it is not total for all eternity.... (*Silence*) It is very difficult to tell, because we cannot get out of our habit of conceiving that there is a definite quantity unfolding indefinitely and that

---

[9] *Savitri*, Cent. Vol. 18, p. 85.

there can only be a beginning if there is a definite quantity. We always have, at least in our way of speaking, the idea of a *moment* (*laughing*) when the Lord decides to objectify Himself. Like this, the explanation becomes easy: He objectifies Himself gradually, progressively, and this results in a progressive evolution. But that is only a manner of speaking; because there is no beginning, there is no end, and yet there is a progression. The sense of succession, the sense of evolution, the sense of progress only exists with the manifestation. It is only when one speaks of the earth that one can give an explanation that is both very rational and in accord with the facts, because the earth has a beginning, not in its soul but in its material reality.

It is also likely that a material universe has a beginning.

(*Silence*)

If you look at it this way, for a universe a miracle would be the sudden intrusion of something from another universe. And for the earth, this reduces the problem to something very understandable — a miracle is the sudden intrusion of something which did not belong to the earth: it produces a radical and immediate change by introducing a principle which did not belong to this physical world of earth.

But there again, it is said that at the very centre of each element *everything exists* in principle; so even that miracle is not possible.

One could say that the sense of miracle belongs only to a finite world, a finite consciousness, a finite conception. It is the sudden entry — the intrusion, the intervention, the penetration — without preparation, of something which did not exist in this physical world. So obviously, any manifestation of a will or a consciousness which belongs to a domain that is more infinite and more eternal than earth, is necessarily a miracle on earth. But if you leave the finite world, the understanding of the finite world, miracles do not exist. The Lord can play at miracles if it so amuses Him, but there are no miracles — He plays every possible game.

You can begin to understand Him only when you *feel* in this way, that He plays every possible game, and "possible" does not mean possible according to the human conception, but possible according to His own conception!

And there, there is no room for miracles — except that it looks like a miracle.

(*Silence*)

If, instead of a slow evolution, something belonging to the supramental world appeared suddenly, man, the mental being, could call that a miracle, because it would be the intervention of something which he does not consciously carry within himself and which intervenes in his conscious life. And in fact, if you consider this taste for miracles, which is very strong — much stronger in children and in hearts that have remained childlike than in highly mentalised individuals — it is a faith in the realisation of the aspiration for the marvellous, of something higher than anything one can expect from normal life.

Indeed, in education, both tendencies should be encouraged side by side: the tendency to thirst for the marvellous, for what seems unrealisable, for something which fills you with the feeling of divinity; while at the same time encouraging exact, correct, sincere observation in the perception of the world as it is, the suppression of all imagination, a constant control, a highly practical and meticulous sense for exact details. Both should go side by side. Usually, you kill the one with the idea that this is necessary in order to foster the other — this is completely wrong. Both can be simultaneous and there comes a time when one has enough knowledge to know that they are the two aspects of the same thing: insight, a higher discernment. But instead of a narrow, limited insight and discernment, the discernment becomes entirely sincere, correct, exact, but it is vast, it includes a whole domain that does not yet belong to the concrete manifestation.

From the point of view of education, this would be very important: to see the world as it is, exactly, unadorned, in the most down-to-earth and concrete manner; and to see the world as it can be, with the freest, highest vision, the one most full of hope and aspiration and marvellous certitude — as the two poles of discernment.

The most splendid, most marvellous, most powerful, most expressive, most total things we can imagine are nothing compared to what they can be; and at the same time our meticulous exactitude in the tiniest detail is never exact enough. And both must go together. When one knows this (*downward gesture*) and when one knows that (*upward gesture*), one is able to put the two together.

And this is the best possible use of the need for miracles. The need for miracles is a gesture of ignorance: "Oh, I would like things to be like this!" It is a gesture of ignorance and impotence. And those who say, "You live in a miracle", know only the lower end — and even then they know it only imperfectly — and they have no contact with anything else.

This need for miracles must be changed into a conscious aspiration for something — which is already there, which exists — which will be manifested *by the help* of all these aspirations; all these aspirations are necessary or, if one looks at it in a truer way, they are an accompaniment — an agreeable accompaniment — in the eternal unfolding.

Of course, people with a very strict logic tell you, "Why pray? Why aspire? Why ask? The Lord does what He wants and He will do what He wants." It is quite obvious, there is no need to say it, but this impulse: "O Lord, manifest!" gives a more intense vibration to His manifestation.

Otherwise, He would never have made the world as it is. There is a special power, a special delight, a special vibration in the intensity of the world's aspiration to become once more what it is.

And that is why — partly, fragmentarily — there is an evolution.

An eternally perfect universe, eternally manifesting the eternal perfection, would lack the joy of progress.

6 March 1963

88 – This world was built by Death that he might live. Wilt thou abolish death? Then life too will perish. Thou canst not abolish death, but thou mayst transform it into a greater living.

89 – This world was built by Cruelty that she might love. Wilt thou abolish cruelty? Then love too will perish. Thou canst not abolish cruelty, but thou mayst transfigure it into its opposite, into a fierce Love and Delightfulness.

90 – This world was built by Ignorance and Error that they might know. Wilt thou abolish ignorance and error? Then knowledge too will perish. Thou canst not abolish ignorance and error, but thou mayst transmute them into the utter and effulgent exceeding of reason.

91 – If Life alone were and not death, there could be no immortality; if love were alone and not cruelty, joy would be only a tepid and ephemeral rapture; if reason were alone and not ignorance, our highest attainment would not exceed a limited rationality and worldly wisdom.

92 – Death transformed becomes Life that is Immortality; Cruelty transfigured becomes Love that is intolerable

ecstasy; Ignorance transmuted becomes Light that leaps beyond wisdom and knowledge.

It is the same idea, that is, opposition and contraries are a stimulus to progress. Because to say that without cruelty Love would be tepid... The principle of Love as it exists beyond the Manifested and the Non-Manifested has nothing to do with either tepidness or cruelty. Only, Sri Aurobindo's idea would seem to be that opposites are the quickest and most effective means of shaping Matter so that it can intensify its manifestation.

As an experience, this is absolutely certain, in the sense that, first of all, when one comes into contact with eternal Love, the supreme Love, one immediately has — how to put it? — a perception, a sensation — it is not an understanding, it is something very concrete: even the most illumined material consciousness, however much it has been moulded and prepared, is *incapable* of manifesting That. The first thing one feels is this kind of incapacity. Then comes an experience: something which manifests a form of — one cannot call it exactly "cruelty", because it is not cruelty as we know it — but within the totality of circumstances, a vibration appears and, with a certain intensity, refuses love as it is manifested here. It is precisely this: something in the material world which refuses the manifestation of love as it exists at present. I am not speaking of the ordinary world, I am speaking of the present consciousness at its highest. It is an experience, I am speaking of something that has happened. So the part of the consciousness which has been struck by this opposition makes a direct appeal to the origin of Love, *with an intensity which it would not have without the experience of this refusal.* Limits are broken and a flood pours down which *could not* have manifested before; and something is expressed which was not expressed before.

When one sees this, there is obviously a similar experience from the point of view of what we call life and death. It is this kind of constant "brooding" or presence of Death and the possibility of death, as it is said in *Savitri*: we have a constant companion throughout the journey from cradle to grave; we are constantly accompanied by this threat or presence of Death. Well, along with this, in the cells, there is a call for a Power of Eternity, with an intensity which would not be there except for this constant threat. Then one understands, one begins to feel quite concretely that all these things are only ways of intensifying the manifestation, of making it progress, of making it more perfect. And if the means are crude, it is because the manifestation itself is very crude. And as it becomes more perfect and fit to manifest that which is *eternally progressive*, the very crude means will give way to subtler ones and the world will progress without any need for such brutal oppositions. This is simply because the world is still in its infancy and human consciousness is still entirely in its infancy.

This is a very concrete experience.

It follows that when the earth no longer needs to die in order to progress, there will be no more death. When the earth no longer needs to suffer in order to progress, there will be no more suffering. And when the earth no longer needs to hate in order to love, there will be no more hatred.

(*Silence*)

This is the quickest and most effective means to bring creation out of its inertia and lead it towards its fulfilment.

(*Long silence*)

There is a certain aspect of creation — which may be a very modern one — it is the need to escape from disorder and confusion, from disharmony and confusion: a confusion, a disorder which takes every possible form, which becomes struggle, useless effort, wastage. It depends on the domain you are in, but in the material world, in action, it means useless complications,

Jnana

waste of energy and material, waste of time, incomprehension, misunderstanding, confusion, disorder. This is what used to be called *crookedness* in the Vedas — I do not know the equivalent of this word, it is something twisted, which instead of going straight to the mark makes sharp, unnecessary zigzags. This is one of the things that is most opposed to the harmony of a purely divine action which has a simplicity... that seems childlike. Direct — direct, instead of making absurd and completely useless circumvolutions. Well, it is obviously the same thing: disorder is a way of stimulating the need for the pure divine simplicity.

The body feels very strongly, very strongly that everything could be simple, so simple!

And so that the being — this kind of individual agglomerate — can be transformed, it needs precisely to become more simple, simple, simple. All these complications of Nature, which they are now beginning to understand and study, which are so intricate for the slightest thing — the smallest of our functions is the result of a system so complicated that it is almost unthinkable; certainly it would be impossible for human thought to plan and put together all these things — now science is discovering them, and one can see very clearly that if the functioning is to be divine, that is, if it is to escape this disorder and confusion, it must be simplified, simplified, simplified.

(*Long silence*)

That is to say, Nature, or rather Nature in her attempt at self-expression, was obliged to resort to an unbelievable and almost infinite complication in order to reproduce the primal Simplicity.

And we come back to the same thing. From this excess of complication arises the possibility of a simplicity which would not be empty but full — a full simplicity, a simplicity that contains everything; whereas without these complications, simplicity is empty.

Now they are making discoveries like that. In anatomy, for

example, they are discovering surgical treatments which are unbelievably complicated! It is like their classification of the elements of Matter — what frightful complexity! And all this is for the purpose of... in an effort to express Unity, the one Simplicity — the divine state.

(*Silence*)

Perhaps it will go quickly.... But the question comes to this — an aspiration that is *sufficient*, intense and effective enough, to attract That which can transform complication into Simplicity, cruelty into Love, and so on.

And it is no use complaining and saying that it is a pity, because it is like that. Why is it like that?... Probably, when it is no longer like that, we shall know. We could put it another way: if we knew, it would no longer be like that.

So, to speculate: "It would have been better if it had not been like that, etc." — all that is unpractical, it is no use at all, it is useless.

We must hurry up and do what is needed to put an end to it, that is all; it is the only practical thing.

For the body it is very interesting. But it is a mountain, a mountain of experiences that seem very small, but because of their multiplicity, they have their place.[10]

15 May 1963

93 — **Pain is the touch of our Mother teaching us how to bear and grow in rapture. She has three stages of her schooling, endurance first, next equality of soul, last ecstasy.**

---

[10] When this talk was first published, Mother remarked, "The scientists will deny it, they will say that I am talking nonsense; but it is because I do not use their terms, it is just a matter of vocabulary."

As far as moral things are concerned, this is absolutely obvious, it is indisputable — all moral suffering moulds your character and leads you straight to ecstasy, when you know how to take it. But when it comes to the body...

It is true that doctors have said that if one can teach the body to bear pain, it becomes more and more resilient and less easily disrupted — this is a concrete result. In the case of people who know how to avoid getting completely upset as soon as they have a pain somewhere, who are able to bear it quietly, to keep their balance, it seems that the body's capacity to bear the disorder without going to pieces increases. This is a great achievement. I have asked myself this question from the purely practical, external standpoint and it seems to be like this. Inwardly, I have been told this many times — told and shown by small experiences — that the body can bear much more than we think, if no fear or anxiety is added to the pain. If we eliminate the mental factor, the body, left to itself, has neither fear nor apprehension nor anxiety about what is going to happen — no anguish — and it can bear a great deal.

The second step is when the body has decided to bear it — you see, it takes the decision to bear it: immediately, the acuteness, what is acute in the pain disappears. I am speaking absolutely materially.

And if you are calm — here, another factor comes in, the need for inner calm — if you have the inner calm, then the pain changes into an almost pleasant sensation — not "pleasant" in the ordinary sense, but an almost comfortable feeling comes. Again, I am speaking purely physically, materially.

And the last stage, when the cells have faith in the divine Presence and in the sovereign divine Will, when they have this trust that all is for the good, then ecstasy comes — the cells open, like this, become luminous and ecstatic.

That makes four stages — only three are mentioned here.

The last one is probably not within everyone's reach, but the first three are quite evident — I *know* it is like that. The only thing that used to worry me was that it was not a purely psychological experience and that there was some wear in the body by the fact of enduring suffering. But I have asked doctors and I was told that if the body is taught to bear pain when it is very young, its capacity to endure increases so much that it can really resist disease; that is, the disease does not follow its normal course, it is arrested. That is precious.

10 August 1963

> 94 – All renunciation is for a greater joy yet ungrasped. Some renounce for the joy of duty done, some for the joy of peace, some for the joy of God and some for the joy of self-torture, but renounce rather as a passage to the freedom and untroubled rapture beyond.

I have rarely had this experience of renunciation — for there to be renunciation, one must be attached to things, and there was always this thirst, this need to go further, to go higher, to feel better, to do better, to have something better. And rather than having a feeling of renunciation one has the feeling that it is a good riddance — you get rid of something cumbersome that weighs you down and hinders your advance. That is what I was saying the other day: we are still everything we no longer want to be and He is everything we want to become — what we call "we" in our egoistic stupidity is precisely what we do not want to be any more, and we would be so happy to throw all that off, to get rid of all that, so as to be able to be what we want to be.

This is a very living experience.

The only process that I have known, and which has been repeated several times during my life, is the renunciation of an error: something you believe to be true — which probably was true for a time — on which you base part of your action, but which in fact was only an opinion. You thought that it was a true evaluation with all its logical consequences, and your action — part of your action — was based on that, and it all followed automatically; and suddenly, an experience, a circumstance or an intuition, warns you that your evaluation is not as true as it looked. Then there is a whole period of observation, of study — or sometimes it comes like a revelation, a massive demonstration — and not only the idea or the false knowledge, but all its consequences must be changed — perhaps a whole way of acting on some point. And at that moment there is a kind of sensation, something akin to the sensation of renunciation, which means that you must break up a whole set of things which had been built — sometimes it can be quite extensive, sometimes it is something very small, but the experience is the same: it is the movement of a force, a power that dissolves, and there is resistance from everything which has to be dissolved, from all the past habits; and it is this movement of dissolution, with its corresponding resistance, which is probably expressed in the ordinary human consciousness as a feeling of renunciation.

I saw this very recently — it is insignificant, these circumstances have no importance in themselves; they are interesting only in the context of the study. This is the only phenomenon that is familiar to me because it has been repeated several times in my life. As the being progresses, the power of dissolution increases, becomes more and more immediate and the resistance diminishes. But I have the memory of a period of maximum resistance — it was more than half a century ago — and it was nothing but that, it was always something outside myself — not outside my consciousness, but outside my will — something which resisted the will. I have never had the feeling of having to renounce anything, but I have had the feeling of having to apply pressure on things to dissolve them. Whereas now, more and more, the pressure is imperceptible, it is immediate; as soon as the force to dissolve a whole set of things manifests, there is no resistance, everything dissolves; on the contrary, there is hardly any feeling of liberation — there is something which is amused again and says: "Oh, again! How many times one limits oneself...." How many times you think that you are advancing, continuously, smoothly, uninterruptedly, and yet how many times you set a little limit in front of yourself. It is not a big limit, for it is a very small thing in an immense whole, but it is a small limit to your action. And so when the Force acts to dissolve the limit, at first you feel liberated, you are glad; but now, it is not even that, it is a smile. Because it is not a feeling of liberation, it is simply like removing a stone from your path so that you can go on.

This idea of renunciation can only arise in a self-centred consciousness. Naturally, people — the ones I call altogether primitive — are attached to things: when they have something, they do not want to let it go! It seems so childish to me!... When they have to part with something, it hurts! Because they identify themselves with the things they have. But this is childishness. The true process behind all this is the amount of resistance in things that were formed on a certain basis of knowledge — which was a knowledge at a particular time and which is no longer so at another — a partial knowledge, not fleeting but impermanent. There is a whole set of things built upon this knowledge and they resist the force that says: "No! it is not true, (*laughing*) your basis is no longer true, let's take it away!" And then, oh! it hurts — this is what people experience as renunciation.

The difficulty is not really to renounce, but to accept (Mother smiles) *when we see life as it is now.... But then, if we accept, how can we live in the midst of all this and have this "untroubled rapture"* — *not there, but here?*

This has been my problem for weeks.

I have come to this conclusion: in principle, it is the

consciousness and the union with the Divine that bring rapture — this is the principle — therefore, the consciousness and the union with the Divine, whether in the world as it is or in the construction of a future world, must be the same — in principle. That is what I repeat to myself all the time: "How is it that you do not have this rapture?"

I have it — when the whole consciousness is centralised in union; at any time, in the midst of anything, with this movement of concentration of the consciousness on union, the rapture comes. But I must say that it disappears when I am working.... It is a world — a very chaotic world of work, where I act on everything around me; and necessarily, I am obliged to receive what is around me, so as to be able to act on it. I have reached a state in which all that I receive, even the things that are considered most painful, leave me absolutely calm and indifferent — "indifferent", not an inactive indifference: without any painful reaction of any kind, absolutely neutral (*gesture turned towards the Eternal*), with perfect equality. But in this equality there is a precise knowledge of what is to be done, of what is to be said, of what is to be written, of what is to be decided, in short, everything that action entails. All that happens in a state of perfect neutrality, with the sense of Power at the same time: the Power flows, the Power acts, and the neutrality remains — but there is no rapture. I do not have the enthusiasm, the delight, the fullness of action.

And I must say that this rapturous state of consciousness would be dangerous in the present condition of the world. Because it produces reactions that are almost absolute — I see that this state of rapture has a *formidable* power. But I insist on the word formidable, in the sense that it is intolerant or intolerable — intolerable rather — to everything that is unlike it. It is the same thing or almost — not quite the same, but almost — as the supreme divine Love; the vibration of this ecstasy or rapture is a small beginning of the vibration of divine Love, and that is absolutely — yes, there is no other word for it — intolerant, in the sense that it will not permit the presence of anything that is contrary to it.

So it would have frightful consequences for the ordinary consciousness. I see it clearly, because sometimes this Power comes — this Power comes and one has the impression that everything is going to explode. For it can tolerate nothing but union, it can tolerate nothing but the response that accepts, that receives and accepts. And it is not an arbitrary will, it is by the *very fact* of its existence which is All-Power, "All-Power" not in the sense in which we understand it, but really All-Power. That is to say that it exists entirely, totally, exclusively. It contains everything, but anything that is contrary to its vibration is compelled to change, since nothing can disappear. So this immediate, almost brutal, absolute change, in the world as it is, is a catastrophe.

This is the answer that I have received to my problem.

Because it was that, I was wondering, "Why? I who am..." At any instant all I have to do is this (*gesture upwards*) and it is... there is nothing left but the Lord, everything is That — but so absolutely that everything which is not That disappears! But at the moment the proportion is such (*laughing*), that too many things would have to disappear!

I have understood that.

17 and 24 August 1963

95 – Only by perfect renunciation of desire or by perfect satisfaction of desire can the utter embrace of God be experienced, for in both ways the essential precondition is effected, — desire perishes.

It is impossible to satisfy desire perfectly — it is something impossible. And also to renounce desire. You renounce one desire and you have another. Therefore both are relatively impossible; what is possible is to enter into a state where there is no desire.

(*Long silence*)

It is a pity that I cannot note down all these experiences that come, because these last few days and during a whole period, there has been a very clear perception of the true working which is the expression of the supreme Will translated spontaneously, naturally, automatically through the individual instrument; one might even say — for the mind is quiet, it keeps quiet — through the body; and the perception of the moment when this expression of the divine Will is clouded — distorted — by the introduction of desire, the special vibration of desire, which has a quality all its own and which has many apparent causes: it is not only the thirst for something, the need for something, or the attachment to something; the same vibration can be set in motion, for example, by the fact that the will which is expressed seems to be, or at least is mistaken for, the expression of the supreme Will; but there has been a confusion between the immediate action which was obviously the expression of the supreme Will and the result which should have followed — it is a mistake we very often make. We are in the habit of thinking that when we want something it should come to us, because the vision is too shortsighted — too shortsighted and too limited; instead of having an overall vision which would show us that this particular vibration was necessary to set off a certain number of other vibrations and that it is the *totality* of all that which will have an effect, which is not the immediate effect of the vibration emitted. I do not know if this is clear, but it is a constant experience.

As a matter of fact, during this period, I have studied and observed this phenomenon: how the vibration of desire is added to the vibration of Will emitted by the Supreme — in our little everyday actions. And with the vision from above, if we take care to maintain the consciousness of this vision from above, we can see how this vibration emitted was exactly the vibration emitted by the Supreme, but instead of obtaining the immediate result expected by the surface consciousness, it was meant to set off a whole series of vibrations and to achieve another, more distant and more complete result. I am not speaking of great things or of actions on a terrestrial scale, I am speaking of the very small things in life: for example, saying to someone, "Give me this", and instead of giving it, that someone does not understand and gives something else. So if we do not take care to preserve an overall vision, a certain vibration may occur, for example a vibration of impatience or of dissatisfaction, together with the impression that the vibration from the Lord is not understood and not received. Well, this little added vibration of impatience or, in fact, of not understanding what is happening, this impression of a lack of receptivity or response, is of the same quality as desire — it cannot be called a desire, but it is the same kind of vibration — this is what comes to complicate things. If we have the complete, exact vision, we know that "Give me this" will produce something other than the immediate result and that this other thing will bring in something else which is exactly what should be. I do not know if I am making myself clear, it is rather complicated! But this gave me the key to the difference in quality between the vibration of Will and the vibration of desire, and at the same time the possibility of eliminating this vibration of desire by a wider and more total vision — wider, more total and far-seeing, that is to say, the vision of a greater whole.

I insist on this point, because this eliminates all moral factors. It eliminates this pejorative notion of desire. More and more, the vision is eliminating all notions of good and bad, right and wrong, inferior and superior, and all that. There is only what might almost be called a difference of vibratory quality — "quality" still gives the idea of superiority and inferiority; it is not quality, it is not intensity. I do not know the scientific term they use to distinguish one vibration from another, but that's what it is.

And so what is noteworthy is that the vibration, what one might call the quality of the vibration that comes from the Lord, is constructive — it builds and it is peaceful and luminous; while the other vibration of desire, or any similar vibration, complicates, destroys, confuses and twists things — confuses and distorts them, twists them. And this takes away the light; it produces a greyness, which can be intensified by violent movements into very dark shadows. But even when there is no passion, when passion does not intervene, it is like that. The physical reality has become nothing but a field of vibrations that mingle and unfortunately also clash and conflict with one another; and the clash, the conflict is a climax of this kind of turmoil and disorder and confusion created by certain vibrations which are in fact vibrations of ignorance — because we do not know. They are vibrations of ignorance and they are too small, too narrow, too limited — too short. The problem is no longer perceived from a psychological point of view at all; there are only vibrations.

If we consider it from the psychological point of view... on the mental plane, it is very easy; on the vital plane it is not very difficult; on the physical plane it is a little heavier, for it takes the form of "needs"; but here too there has been a field of experience these last few days: the study of medical and scientific conceptions of the structure of the body, its needs, what is good or bad for it; and that, reduced to its essence, comes down to the same question of vibrations. It was rather interesting: there was an appearance — for all things as they are seen by the ordinary consciousness are pure appearances — there was an appearance of food-poisoning and it became the object of a special study in order to find out whether there was anything absolute in it or whether the poisoning was relative, that is, based on ignorance and a bad reaction, and on the absence of the true vibration. The conclusion was that it is a question of proportion between the amount, the sum of vibrations that belong to the Lord, and the vibrations that still belong to obscurity; and, depending on the proportion, it takes the form of something concrete and real or of something that can be eliminated, that is, which does not resist the influence of the vibration of Truth. And it was very interesting, for as soon as the consciousness was informed of the cause of the disturbance in the functioning of the body — the consciousness saw where it came from, what it was — immediately, the observation began with the idea, "Let us see what is happening." First, put the body in a state of perfect rest with the certitude — which is always there — that nothing happens except by the will of the Lord, that the result is also the will of the Lord, and that therefore one should be completely quiet; so the body is completely quiet, untroubled, it is not restless, not vibrating, nothing — completely quiet. And then, to what extent are the effects inevitable? As a certain amount of matter containing an element unfavourable to the elements of the body and to the life of the body has been absorbed, what is the proportion of favourable and unfavourable elements, or of favourable and unfavourable vibrations? Then I saw very clearly that the proportion varies according to the number of body cells under the direct influence, which respond only to the supreme vibration, and the others which still belong to the ordinary way of vibrating. It was very clear, because one could see all the possibilities, from the ordinary mass which is completely upset by this intrusion and in which one has to fight with all the ordinary methods to get rid of the undesirable element, to the total response of the cells to the supreme Force, which means that the intrusion can have no effect. But this is still the dream of tomorrow — we are on the way. And the proportion has become quite favourable — I cannot say all-powerful, far from it — quite favourable, which means that the consequences of the disturbance did not last very long and the damage was, so to say, minimal.

But all the experiences at the moment, one after the other — all the *physical* experiences of the body — lead to the same conclusion: everything depends on the proportion of elements responding exclusively to the influence of the Supreme, the elements that are half and half, on the way to transformation, and the elements that are still in the old process of vibration of Matter. Their number seems to be diminishing; it seems to

Jnana

be diminishing greatly, but there are still enough of them to produce unpleasant effects or reactions — things that are not transformed, that still belong to ordinary life. But every problem — whether psychological or purely material or chemical — the whole problem comes down to this: they are nothing but vibrations. And there is the perception of this totality of vibrations and the perception of what one might call, very crudely and approximately, the difference between constructive and destructive vibrations. We could say — it is simply a way of putting it — that all vibrations that come from the One and express Oneness are constructive and that all the complications of the ordinary separative consciousness lead to destruction.

(Long silence)

It is always said that it is desire which creates difficulties, and indeed it is like that. Desire may simply be something added to the vibration of will. The Will — when it is the one Will, the supreme Will expressing itself — is direct, immediate, there are no possible obstacles; and so everything that delays, hinders, causes complication or even failure is *necessarily* an admixture of desire.

One can see it in everything. For example, take an external field of action, with the external world, external things — of course, to say that it is "external" is simply to put oneself in a false position — but, for example, from the higher consciousness, the Truth-consciousness, you tell someone, "Go" — I am giving one example among millions — "Go and see this person and tell him this in order to obtain that." If this person is receptive, immobile within and surrendered, then he goes, he sees the person and tells him and the thing is done — without *any* complication whatever, like that. If this person has an active mental consciousness, if he does not have total faith, if he has all the mixture of everything brought in by ego and ignorance, he sees difficulties, he sees problems to be solved, he sees all the complications — and of course, all this happens. And so according to the proportion — everything is always a question of proportion — according to the proportion, it creates complications, it takes time, the thing is delayed or even worse, it is distorted, it does not happen exactly as it should, it is changed, diminished, distorted or in the end it is not done at all — there are many, many degrees, but all that belongs to the domain of complications — mental complications — and desire. Whereas the other way is immediate. There are countless examples of these cases — of all cases — and also of the "immediate case". Then people tell you: "Oh, you have performed a miracle!" — no miracle has been performed: that is how it should always be. It is because the intermediary did not add himself to the action.

I do not know if this is clear, but anyway...

So this ranges from the smallest thing to an action on the terrestrial scale. There are examples, in terrestrial action, of things that have been done in this way — if there is a good intermediary. Nobody understood how it was done, why it was done — like that, very, very simply, everything turned out well. And in other cases, to get a visa or a permit one has to move mountains. So, from the smallest thing, the smallest physical indisposition to a worldwide action, it is all the same principle, everything comes to the same principle.

4 November 1963

> 96 – Experience in thy soul the truth of the Scripture; afterwards, if thou wilt, reason and state thy experience intellectually and even then distrust thy statement; but distrust never thy experience.

This doesn't require any explanation.

That is to say, it should be explained to children that the statement, *whatever it may be*, the Scriptures, *whatever they*

may be, are always a diminution of the experience, they are always less than the experience.
There may be people who need to know this.

> 97 – When thou affirmest thy soul-experience and deniest the different soul-experience of another, know that God is making a fool of thee. Dost thou not hear His self-delighted laughter behind thy soul's curtains?

Oh, it's delightful!
One can only smile and say, "Never doubt your experience, for your experience is the truth of your being, but do not imagine that it is a universal truth; and never on the basis of this truth deny the truth of others, because for each one, his experience is the truth of his being. And a total truth would only be the totality of all these individual truths... plus the experience of the Lord Himself!"

> 98 – Revelation is the direct sight, the direct hearing or the inspired memory of Truth, *dṛṣṭi, śruti, smṛti*; it is the highest experience and always accessible to renewed experience. Not because God spoke it, but because the soul saw it, is the word of the Scriptures our supreme authority.

I assume that this is an answer to the Biblical belief in the "Commandments of God" received by Moses, supposedly uttered by the Lord Himself and heard by Moses — it is an indirect way of saying (*Mother laughs*) that this is not possible.
"Our supreme authority" "because the soul saw it" — but it can only be a supreme authority for the soul that saw it, not for every soul. For the soul that had this experience and saw, it is the supreme authority, but not for the others.
This was one of the things which used to make me think when I was a small child: these ten "Commandments", which

are besides extraordinarily commonplace. Love thy father and thy mother.... Do not kill.... It is revoltingly commonplace. And Moses went up Mount Sinai to hear that!

Now, I do not know whether Sri Aurobindo was thinking of the Indian Scriptures.... There were also Chinese Scriptures....

(*Silence*)

More and more my experience is that revelation — it does come — revelation may be universally applicable, but it is always personal in form, always personal.

It is as if one had an *angle* of vision of the Truth. It is necessarily, necessarily an angle, from the very moment it is put into words.

You have a wordless, thoughtless experience of a kind of vibration which gives you a feeling of absolute truth and then, if you remain very still, without seeking to know anything, after some time it is as if the vibration were passing through a filter and it is translated as a kind of idea. Then this idea — it is still rather hazy, that is, very general — if you continue to keep very still, attentive and silent, this idea passes through another filter, and then a kind of condensation occurs, like drops, and it turns into words.

But then, when you have had the experience very sincerely — that is, when you are not fooling yourself — it is necessarily only one point, *one way* of saying the thing, that's all. And it cannot be more than that. Besides, it is very easy to observe that when you are in the habit of using a particular language, it comes in that language; for me it always comes either in English or in French, it does not come in Chinese or in Japanese! The words are inevitably English or French; and sometimes there is a Sanskrit word — but that is because, physically, I learnt Sanskrit. I have occasionally heard — not physically — Sanskrit pronounced by another being; but it does not crystallise, it remains nebulous; and when I come back to an entirely material consciousness, I remember a vague sound, not a precise word. Therefore, it is *always* an individual angle from the very moment it is formulated.

✦ You must have a kind of *very austere* sincerity. You are seized with enthusiasm, because the experience brings an extraordinary power: the Power is there — it is there, before the words, and it diminishes with the words — but the Power is there and with this Power you feel very universal, you have the feeling: "It is a universal revelation" — yes, it is a universal revelation, but when you put it into words, it is no longer universal; then it is relevant only for minds that are built to understand this way of speaking. The Force is behind, but you have to go beyond the words.

(*Silence*)

Things of this sort come to me more and more often and I jot them down on a piece of paper. It is always the same process, always. First of all, a kind of explosion, an explosion of truth-power — it is like a great, white fireworks display (*Mother smiles*), much more than a fireworks display! And it spins round and round (*gesture above the head*), it churns and churns; then there is the impression of an idea — but the idea is lower, it is like a covering; the idea contains its own sensation, it also brings a sensation — the sensation was there before, but without the idea, and so the sensation could not be defined. There is only one thing, it is always an explosion of luminous Power. And then, afterwards, if you look at it and remain very quiet — the head, especially, should keep quiet — everything becomes silent (*motionless, upward gesture*), then suddenly someone speaks inside the head — someone speaks. It is this explosion speaking. Then I take a pencil and paper and I write. But between what speaks and what writes there is still a little space to be crossed, so that when it is written down something up there is not satisfied. So I remain quiet a little longer — "No, not that word, this one"

— sometimes it takes two days to become quite final. But those who are satisfied with the power of the experience make short work of this, and send out into the world sensational revelations that are distortions of the Truth.

You must be very steady, very quiet, very critical — especially very quiet, silent, silent, silent, without trying to seize hold of the experience — "Oh! What is it, what is it?" — that spoils everything. But watch — watch very closely. In the words there is something left, something that remains of the original vibration — so little! But there is something, something that makes you smile, that is pleasant, like a sparkling wine, and here (*Mother indicates a word or a passage in an imaginary note*), here it is dull. Then you look with your knowledge of the language, or with your sense of word-rhythm: "Look, there's a pebble." You must remove the pebble; and then you wait and suddenly it comes, plop! it falls into place: the right word. If you are patient, after a day or two, it becomes absolutely accurate.

5 February 1964

99 – The word of Scripture is infallible; it is in the interpretation the heart and reason put upon the Scripture that error has her portion.

I am not quite sure that this is not ironical.... To people who say "The Scripture is infallible", he answers: "Yes, yes, of course the Scriptures are infallible, but beware of your own understanding!"

But here is the word of truth:

100 – Shun all lowness, narrowness and shallowness in religious thought and experience. Be wider than the widest horizons, be loftier than highest Kanchanjungha, be profounder than the deepest oceans.

5 February 1964

Jnana

101 – In God's sight there is no near or distant, no present, past or future. These things are only a convenient perspective for His world-picture.

102 – To the senses it is always true that the sun moves round the earth; this is false to the reason. To the reason it is always true that the earth moves round the sun; this is false to the supreme vision. Neither earth moves nor sun; there is only a change in the relation of sun-consciousness and earth-consciousness.

(Long silence)

Impossible, I can't say anything.

This would mean that our normal perception of the physical world is a false perception.

Yes, naturally.

But then what would the true perception be like?

Well, yes, there it is!

The true perception of the physical world — trees, people, stones — what do they look like to a supramental eye?

This is precisely what one cannot say! When you have the vision and the consciousness of the Order of Truth, of what is direct, the direct expression of the Truth, you immediately have an impression of something inexpressible, because all words belong to the other domain; all images, all comparisons, all expressions belong to the other domain.

This is precisely the great difficulty I had — it was on the 29th of February. During the whole time that I lived in this consciousness of the *direct* manifestation of the Truth, I tried to formulate what I was feeling, what I was seeing — it was impossible. There were no words. And immediately, simply the formulation would cause an instantaneous fall back into the other consciousness.

On that occasion, the memory of this aphorism about the sun and the earth came back to me... even to say a "change of consciousness" — a change of consciousness is also a movement.

I don't think one can say anything. I feel incapable of saying anything, because all the things we say are uninteresting approximations.

But when you are in this Truth-Consciousness, is it a "subjective" experience or does Matter itself change its appearance?

Yes, everything — the whole world is different! Everything is different. And the experience has convinced me of one thing, which I still feel continually, that both states — of Truth and Falsehood — are simultaneous, concomitant, and that only... yes, what he calls a "change of consciousness", that is to say that one is either in this consciousness or in that consciousness, but one does not move for all that.

We are obliged to use words that move, because for us everything moves; but this change of consciousness is not a movement — it is not a movement. So then how can we speak about it or describe it?...

Even if we say, "one state taking the place of another", with "taking the place of" we immediately introduce movement.... All our words are like that, what can we say?...

Yesterday again, the experience was absolutely concrete and powerful, that there is no need to move oneself or to move anything whatever for this Truth-Consciousness to replace the consciousness of deformation or distortion. That is to say, the capacity to live and be this true — essential and true — vibration seems to have the power to *substitute* this vibration for the vibration of falsehood and distortion, to such an extent that... for example, the natural result of distortion or of the vibration of distortion, should be an accident or a catastrophe; but if, inside these vibrations, there is a consciousness which has the power to become conscious of the vibration of Truth and therefore to manifest the vibration of Truth, it can — and must — annul the other, which would be translated in the external phenomenon by an intervention that would avert the catastrophe.

It is a growing impression that the True is the only way to change the world, that all the other processes of slow transformation are always at a tangent — one draws nearer and nearer but one never arrives — and that the last step must be this: the substitution of the true vibration.

We do have partial proofs. But since they are partial, they are not conclusive, because for the ordinary vision and understanding explanations can always be found: one can say that the accident, for example, was "intended" and "fated" to be forestalled, and that it was not forestalled by this intervention at all, but by the "determinism" that had decided it. And how to prove it? How to prove even to oneself that it is not so? It is impossible.

As soon as you express it, you enter into the mind, and as soon as you enter the mind, there is this kind of logic, which is frightful because it is all-powerful: if everything already exists, co-existing from all eternity, how can one thing be changed into another?... How can anything "change"?

You are told — Sri Aurobindo has just said it himself — that for the consciousness of the Lord there is no past, no time, no movement, nothing — everything is. To translate this, we say "from all eternity", which is nonsense, but anyway, everything is. So everything *is* (*Mother folds her arms*), and that is all there is to it, there is nothing to be done. This conception, or rather this way of speaking — for it is only a way of speaking — cancels all sense of progress, it cancels evolution, it cancels... You are told that it is part of the determinism that you should strive for progress — yes, all that is empty talk.

And note that this way of speaking is only a minute of experience, it is *not* the whole experience. There is a moment when one *feels* like that, but it is not total, it is partial. It is only *one* way of feeling, it is not everything. There is something much deeper and much more inexpressible than that in the eternal consciousness — much more. This is only the first bewilderment one feels when one leaves the ordinary consciousness, but that is not everything. It is not everything. When the memory of this aphorism came back to me recently, I had the impression that it was merely a little glimpse one suddenly has, and a feeling of opposition between the two states, but that is not everything, it is not everything. There is something else.

There is something else which is altogether different from what we understand, but *which is translated by what we understand*.

And this is what cannot be said. It cannot be said because it is inexpressible, inexpressible.

This amounts to a feeling that everything which in our ordinary consciousness becomes false, untrue, distorted, crooked, is all *essentially true* for the Truth-Consciousness. But true in what way? That is precisely something which cannot be put into words, because words belong to Falsehood.

That is to say, the materiality of the world would not be annulled by this Consciousness, it would be transfigured?... Or would it be a completely different world?

(*Silence*)

Let us be clear.... I am afraid that what we call "Matter" is in fact only the false appearance of the world.

There is something *corresponding*, but...

This aphorism would lead to an absolute subjectivity and only this absolute subjectivity would be true—well, it is *not* like that. For that is Pralaya, Nirvana. But Nirvana is not the only thing, there is an objectivity which is real, which is not false—but how to put it!... It is something I have felt several times—several times, not only in a flash—the reality of... how to express it? One is always betrayed by one's own words.... In the perfect sense of Oneness and in the consciousness of Oneness, there is room for objectiveness, objectivity—the one does not destroy the other, not at all. One can have a feeling of differentiation: not that it is not oneself, but it is a different vision. I have told you, everything one can say is nothing, it is nonsense, because words are meant to express the unreal world, but... Yes, perhaps this is what Sri Aurobindo calls the sense of multiplicity in unity, it may correspond a little; just as one feels the inner multiplicity of one's being, something like that... I no longer have the feeling of a separate self, not at all, not at all, even in the body, but that does not prevent me from having a certain sense of objective relation—yes, look—this is the same thing as his "relation of consciousness" between earth and sun, which changes (*Mother laughs*). It is true that this is perhaps the best way of saying it! It is a relation of consciousness. It is not at all a relation of self and "others" —not at all, that is completely cancelled—but it might be like a relation of consciousness between the different parts of one's being. And obviously, that gives objectivity to the different parts.

(*Long silence*)

To come back to the example, which is very easy to understand, of the accident that is forestalled, one can very well imagine that the intervention of the Truth-Consciousness was decided "from all eternity" and that there is no *new* element, but nevertheless, it was this intervention which stopped the accident — which gives an exact picture of the power of this true consciousness over the other one. And if you project your own way of being onto the Supreme, you can imagine that it amuses Him to make all kinds of experiments, to see how things play themselves out. That is another matter. Nevertheless there is an All-Consciousness that knows all things from all eternity — all this in words that are absolutely inadequate. But nevertheless, when you look at the process, it was this intervention which was able to forestall the accident: the substitution of a false consciousness by a true one arrested the process of the false consciousness.

It seems to me that this happens quite often — much more often than one might think. For example, each time an illness is cured, each time an accident is avoided, each time a catastrophe, even a terrestrial catastrophe, is averted, in all these things, it is always an intervention of the vibration of harmony in the vibration of disorder that causes the disorder to cease.

So the people, the faithful, who always say, "By the grace of God, this has happened," are not so wrong.

I am simply observing a fact, that this vibration of order and harmony intervenes — the causes of its intervention have nothing to do with it, it is merely a scientific observation — and I have experienced this quite a number of times.

Would that be the process of world transformation?

Yes.

A more and more constant incarnation of this vibration of harmony.

That's it, yes, exactly. Exactly.

And from this point of view, I have even seen... The ordinary idea that this phenomenon must necessarily occur first in the body where the Consciousness is expressed more constantly, seems absolutely useless and subordinate; on the contrary, it occurs everywhere at the same time, wherever it can do so most easily and completely, and it is not necessarily this agglomerate of cells (*Mother points to her own body*) that is most prepared for this operation. Therefore it may remain as it is in its appearance for a very long time, even if its understanding and receptivity are exceptional. I mean that the awareness, the conscious perception of this body is infinitely superior to the awareness of all the others with which it is in contact, except at those moments — the moments — when other bodies, as if by Grace, have this perception; whereas for this body, it is a natural and constant state. It is the effective result of the fact that this Truth-Consciousness is more constantly concentrated on this group of cells than on any other — more directly. But the substitution of one vibration for the other — in circumstances, in action, in objects — occurs at the point where it can have the most striking and effectual results.

It is something I have felt very, very clearly and which one cannot feel so long as the physical ego is there, because the physical ego has the sense of its own importance and that disappears entirely with the physical ego. And when it disappears one has the precise perception that the intervention or the manifestation of the true vibration does not depend on egos or individualities — human or national individualities or even those of Nature: animals, plants, etc. It depends on a certain play of the cells and Matter in which some agglomerates are particularly favourable to the transformation — not "transformation", but substitution, to be precise: the substitution of the vibration of Truth for the vibration of Falsehood. And this phenomenon can be quite independent of any groupings or individualities — it may be one piece here, one piece there, one thing here, one thing there — and it always corresponds to a certain quality of vibration that brings about an expansion — a receptive expansion. Then the phenomenon can take place.

On Thoughts and Aphorisms

Unfortunately, as I said at the beginning, all words belong to the world of appearances.

(Silence)

And this has been my experience all this time, with a vision and a conviction — the conviction of experience: the two vibrations are like that (*gesture indicating superimposition and infiltration*), all the time. All the time, all the time.

Perhaps the feeling of wonder comes when the amount of infiltration is great enough to become perceptible. But I have the impression — and a very acute impression — that this phenomenon is taking place all the time, all the time, everywhere (*gesture indicating dots of infiltration*), in a minute, infinitesimal way; and in certain circumstances, certain conditions which are visible, visible to that vision — it is a kind of luminous expansion, I cannot explain — there, the mass of infiltration is great enough to give the impression of a miracle. But otherwise it is something that occurs all the time, all the time, ceaselessly, in the world (*same gesture of dots*), like an infinitesimal quantity of Falsehood being replaced by Light, Falsehood being replaced by Light... constantly.

And this vibration — which I feel and see — gives an impression of fire. This is what the Vedic Rishis must have translated as the "Flame" — in the human consciousness, in man, in Matter they always spoke of a Flame. It is in fact a vibration which has the intensity of a higher fire.

Several times, when the work was very concentrated or condensed, the body even felt that it was the equivalent of a fever.

Two or three nights ago, something like that happened; there was this descent of Force, a descent of this Truth-Power with a special intensity.... Well, that is what is happening — happening everywhere, all the time. So, if it happens in an agglomerate that is large enough, it appears to be a miracle — but it is the miracle of *the whole earth*.

One must hold firm, because it has consequences, it brings a sensation of Power, and very few people can feel it, experience it, without their balance being more or less disturbed, because they do not have a sufficient basis of peace, of vast and very, *very* quiet peace. Many times I have said: There is only *one* answer, one single answer: one must be quiet, quiet, and even more quiet, more and more quiet, and not trying to find a solution with the head, because it cannot. One must only be quiet — quiet, quiet, immovably quiet. Calm and peace, calm and peace — that is the *only* answer.

I do not say that it is the cure, but it is the only answer: to endure in calm and peace, to endure in calm and peace....

Then something will happen.

25 March 1964

103 – Vivekananda, exalting Sannyasa,[11] has said that in all Indian history there is only one Janaka.[12] Not so, for Janaka is not the name of a single individual, but a dynasty of self-ruling kings and the triumph-cry of an ideal.

104 – In all the lakhs of ochre-clad Sannyasins,[13] how many are perfect? It is the few attainments and the many approximations that justify an ideal.

105 – There have been hundreds of perfect Sannyasins, because Sannyasa has been widely preached and numerously practised; let it be the same with the ideal freedom and we shall have hundreds of Janakas.

---

[11] Renunciation of the life and works of the world.
[12] Ancient king of Mithila, famous for having attained spiritual knowledge while leading the life of the world.
[13] Monks who have renounced the life and works of the world.

106 — Sannyasa has a formal garb and outer tokens; therefore men think they can easily recognise it; but the freedom of a Janaka does not proclaim itself and it wears the garb of the world; to its presence even Narada[14] was blinded.

107 — Hard is it to be in the world, free, yet living the life of ordinary men; but because it is hard, therefore it must be attempted and accomplished.

It seems so obvious!

It is obvious, but difficult.

To be free from all attachment does not mean running away from all occasion for attachment. All these people who assert their asceticism, not only run away but warn others not to try!

This seems so obvious to me. When you need to run away from a thing in order not to experience it, it means that you are not above it, you are still on the same level.

Anything that suppresses, diminishes or lessens cannot bring freedom. Freedom has to be experienced in the whole of life and in all sensations.

As a matter of fact I have made a whole series of studies on the subject, on the purely physical plane.... In order to be above all possible error, we tend to eliminate any occasion for error. For example, if you do not want to say any useless words, you stop speaking; people who take a vow of silence imagine that this is control of speech — it is not true! It is only eliminating the occasion for speech and therefore for saying useless things. It is the same thing with food: eating only what is necessary. In the transitional state we have reached, we no longer want to lead this entirely animal life based on material

---

[14] A famous Devarshi or divine seer.

exchange and food; but it would be foolish to believe that we have reached a state where the body can subsist entirely without food — nevertheless there is already a great difference, since they are trying to find the essential nutrients in things in order to lessen the volume. But the natural tendency is to fast — it is a mistake!

For fear of being mistaken in our actions, we stop doing anything at all; for fear of being mistaken in our speech, we stop speaking; for fear of eating for the pleasure of eating, we do not eat at all — this is not freedom, it is simply reducing the manifestation to a minimum; and the natural conclusion is Nirvana. But if the Lord wanted only Nirvana, nothing but Nirvana would exist! It is obvious that He conceives of the co-existence of all opposites, and that for Him this must be the beginning of a totality. So obviously, if one feels meant for that, one can choose only one of His manifestations, that is to say, the absence of manifestation. But it is still a limitation. And this is not the only way to find Him, far from it!

It is a very common tendency which probably originates from an ancient suggestion or perhaps from some lack, some incapacity — reduce, reduce, reduce one's needs, reduce one's activities, reduce one's words, reduce one's food, reduce one's active life — and all that becomes so narrow. In one's aspiration not to make any more mistakes, one eliminates any occasion for making them. It is not a cure.

But the other way is much, much more difficult.

(Silence)

No, the solution is to act only under the divine impulsion, to speak only under the divine impulsion, to eat only under the divine impulsion. That is the difficult thing, because naturally, you immediately confuse the divine impulsion with your personal impulses.

I suppose this was the idea of all the apostles of renunciation:

to eliminate everything coming from outside or from below so that if something from above should manifest one would be in a condition to receive it. But from the collective point of view, this process could take thousands of years. From the individual point of view, it is possible; but then one must keep intact the aspiration to receive the true impulsion — not the aspiration for "complete liberation", but the aspiration for *active* identification with the Supreme, that is to say, to will only what He wills, to do only what He wants: to exist by and in Him alone. So one can try the method of renunciation, but this is for one who wants to cut himself off from others. And in that case, can there be any integrality? It seems impossible to me.

To proclaim publicly what one wants to do is a considerable help. It may give rise to objections, scorn, conflict, but this is largely compensated for by public "expectation", so to say, by what other people expect from you. This was certainly the reason for those robes: to let people know. Of course, that may bring you the scorn, the bad will of some people, but then there are all those who feel they must not interfere or meddle with this, that it is not their concern.

I do not know why, but it always seemed to me like showing off — it may not be and in some cases it is not, but all the same it is a way of saying to people, "Look, this is what I am." And as I say, it may help, but it has its drawbacks.

It is another childishness.

All these things are means, stages, steps, but... true freedom is to be free of everything — including means.

(Silence)

It is a restriction, a constriction, whereas the True Thing is an opening, a widening, an identification with the whole.

When you reduce, reduce, reduce yourself, you do not have any feeling of losing yourself, it takes away your fear of losing yourself — you become something solid and compact. But if you

choose the method of widening — the greatest possible widening — you must not be afraid of losing yourself.
It is much more difficult.

Then how can one do this in an external world which absorbs you constantly? I am thinking of people who live in the West, for example; they are constantly swallowed up by their work, their appointments, the telephone, they don't even have a minute to purify what comes pouring in on them all the time, and recover. In such conditions, how can one do this?

Oh, you must know what to take and what to leave!
That is the other extreme.... Certainly, monasteries, retreats, escape into the forests or caves are necessary to counterbalance modern hyper-activity; and yet there is less of all that now than there was one or two thousand years ago. But to me this seems to have been a lack of understanding — it did not last.
Of course, it is this excessive activity which makes an excessive immobility necessary.

But how can one find a way to be what one should be, in normal conditions?

How can one avoid falling into one kind of excess or the other?

Yes, to live normally and to be free.

My child, that is why the Ashram was created! That was the idea. Because, in France, I was always asking myself: How can one find the time to find oneself? How can one even find the time to understand how to become free? So then I thought: a place where material needs will be sufficiently provided for, so that if one truly wants to become free, one can do so. And the

Ashram was founded on this idea, not on any other — a place where people would have enough to live on so as to have time to think of the True Thing.

(*Mother smiles*) Human nature is such that laziness has taken the place of aspiration — not for everyone, but anyway in quite a general way — and licence or libertinism has taken the place of freedom — which would tend to prove that the human race has to pass through a period of rough handling before it is ready to pull itself away more sincerely from its slavery to activity.

Indeed, the first movement is this: "Oh! To find the place where one can concentrate, find oneself, truly live without being preoccupied with material things." That is the first aspiration. It was even on this basis, at any rate in the beginning, that disciples were chosen — but it does not last! Things become easy and so one lets oneself go. There are no moral restraints and so one acts foolishly.

But one cannot even say that there was a mistake in the selection — one would be tempted to believe it, but it is not true; because the selection was made according to a very precise and clear inner indication.... It is probably the difficulty of keeping the inner attitude unmixed. This is exactly what Sri Aurobindo wanted, what he was trying for. He said: "If I could find one hundred people, that would be enough." But it did not stay one hundred for long, and I must say that even when it was a hundred, it was already mixed.

Many came, attracted by the True Thing, but... one lets oneself go. That is, it is impossible to hold firm in one's true position.

Yes, I have noticed that in the extreme difficulty of the outer conditions of the world, the aspiration was much more intense.

Yes, of course!

It is much more intense, it is almost a question of life and death.

Yes, that's it! That is to say, man is still so crude that he needs extremes. That is what Sri Aurobindo said: For love to be true, hatred was necessary; true love could be born only under the pressure of hatred.[15] That's it. Well, one must accept things as they are and try to go further. That is all.

That is probably why there are so many difficulties — difficulties accumulate here: difficulties of character, health and circumstances. It is because the consciousness awakens under the stress of difficulties. If everything is easy and peaceful, one falls asleep.

That is also how Sri Aurobindo explained the necessity of war. In peacetime, one becomes slack.

It is a pity.

I cannot say that I find it very pretty, but it seems to be like that.

This is just what Sri Aurobindo said in *The Hour of God*: If you have the Force and the Knowledge and misuse the moment, woe to you.

It is not revenge, it is not punishment, not at all, but you draw upon yourself a necessity, the necessity for a violent impulsion — to react to something violent.

(*Silence*)

This is an experience I am having more and more: for the contact with this true divine Love to be able to manifest, that is, to express itself freely, it demands an extraordinary strength in beings and things, which does not yet exist. Otherwise everything falls apart.

There are lots of very convincing details, but of course, because they are "details" or very personal things, one cannot

---

[15] See Aphorisms 88 to 92.

speak of them; but on the evidence of repeated experiences, I have to say this: when this Power of *pure* Love — which is so wonderful, which is beyond all expression — as soon as it begins to manifest abundantly, freely, it is as if quantities of things crumbled down immediately — they cannot stand. They cannot stand, they are dissolved. Then... then everything stops. And this stopping, which one might think is a disgrace, is just the opposite! It is an infinite Grace.

Simply to perceive, a little concretely and tangibly, the difference between the vibration in which one lives normally and almost continually, and that vibration — simply to observe this infirmity, which I call sickening — it really makes you feel sick — that is enough to stop everything.

Only yesterday, this morning, there are long moments when this Power manifests; then suddenly, there is a kind of wisdom, an immeasurable wisdom which causes everything to subside in perfect tranquillity: what must be shall be, it will take the time that is needed. And then everything is all right. In this way, everything is all right immediately. But the splendour fades.

One has only to be patient.

Sri Aurobindo also has written this: Aspire intensely, but without impatience.... The difference between intensity and impatience is very subtle — it is all a difference in vibration. It is subtle, but it makes all the difference.

Intensely, but without impatience. That's it. One must be in that state.

And for a very long time, a very long time, one must be satisfied with inner results, that is, results in one's personal and individual reactions, one's inner contact with the rest of the world — one must not expect or be premature in wanting things to materialise. Because our hastiness usually delays things.

If it is like that, it is like that.

We — I mean men — live harassed lives. It is a kind of half-awareness of the shortness of their lives; they do not think of it, but they feel it half-consciously. And so they are always wanting — quick, quick, quick — to rush from one thing to another, to do one thing quickly and move on to the next one, instead of letting each thing live in its own eternity. They are always wanting: forward, forward, forward.... And the work is spoilt.

That is why some people have preached: the only moment that matters is the present moment. In practice it is not true, but from the psychological point of view it ought to be true. That is to say, to live to the utmost of one's capacities at every minute, without planning or wanting, waiting or preparing for the next. Because you are always hurrying, hurrying, hurrying.... And nothing you do is good. You are in a state of inner tension which is completely false — completely false.

All those who have tried to be wise have always said it — the Chinese preached it, the Indians preached it — to live in the awareness of Eternity. In Europe also they said that one should contemplate the sky and the stars and identify oneself with their infinitude — all things that widen you and give you peace.

These are means, but they are indispensable.

And I have observed this in the cells of the body; they always seem to be in a hurry to do what they have to do, lest they have no time to do it. So they do nothing properly. Muddled people — some people turn everything upside down, their movements are jerky and confused — have this to a high degree, this kind of haste — quick, quick, quick.... Yesterday, someone was complaining of rheumatic pains and he was saying, "Oh, it is such a waste of time. I do things so slowly!" I said (*Mother smiles*), "So what!" He didn't like it. You see, for someone to complain when he is in pain means that he is soft, that is all; but to say, "I am wasting so much time, I do things so slowly!" It gave a very clear picture of the haste in which men live. You go hurtling through life... to go where?... You end with a crash!

What is the use of that?

On Thoughts and Aphorisms

(Silence)

In reality, the moral of all these aphorisms is that it is much more important to be than to seem to be — one must live and not pretend to live — and that it is much more important to realise something entirely, sincerely, perfectly than to let others know that you are realising it!

It is the same thing again: when you are compelled to say what you are doing, you spoil half your action.

And yet, at the same time, this helps you to take your bearings, to find out exactly where you are.

That was the wisdom of the Buddha who spoke of "the Middle Way": neither too much of this nor too much of that, neither falling into this nor falling into that — a little of everything and a balanced way... but *pure*. Purity and sincerity are the same thing.

16 September 1964

108 – When he watched the actions of Janaka, even Narada the divine sage thought him a luxurious worldling and libertine. Unless thou canst see the soul, how shalt thou say that a man is free or bound?

This raises all sorts of questions. For example, how is it that Narada could not see the soul?

For me, it is very simple. Narada was a demi-god, he belonged to the overmind world and he was able to materialise himself, but these beings have no psychic. The gods do not have within them the divine spark, which is the core of the psychic, because only on earth — I am not even speaking of the material universe — only on earth did this descent of divine Love take place, which was the origin of the divine Presence in the core of Matter. And naturally, since they have no psychic being, they do not know the psychic being. Some of these beings have even wanted to take a physical body so as to have the experience of the psychic being — but not many of them.

As a rule, they did it only partially, through an "emanation", not a total descent. For example, Vivekananda is said to have been an incarnation — a *Vibhūti* — of Shiva; but Shiva himself has clearly expressed his will to come down on earth only with the supramental world. When the earth is ready for the supramental life, he will come. And almost all these beings will manifest — they are waiting for that moment, they do not want any of the present struggle and the obscurity.

Certainly Narada was one of those who came here.... In fact, it was for fun! He liked to play with circumstances. But he had no knowledge of the psychic being and that must have prevented him from recognising the psychic being where it existed.

But all these things cannot be explained; they are personal ideas and experiences; this knowledge is not objective enough to be taught. One can say nothing about a phenomenon which depends on one's personal experience and which has a value only for the person who has the experience.

What Sri Aurobindo said is based on the traditional learning of India and he spoke of what agreed with his own experience.

So to see the soul, one must know one's own soul?

Yes, to be in relation with the soul, that is, the psychic being, one must have a psychic being oneself, and only men — men who belong to the evolution, who are sons of the terrestrial creation — possess a psychic being.

None of these gods has a psychic being. It is only by coming down and uniting with the psychic being of a man that they can have one, but they have none themselves.

12 January 1965

109 – All things seem hard to man that are above his attained level and they are hard to his unaided effort; but they become at once easy and simple when God in man takes up the contract.

This is perfect.

As it happens, two or three days ago I wrote something in reply to a question and I said something like this: Sri Aurobindo is the Lord, but only a part of the Lord, not the Lord in His totality, because the Lord is all — all that is manifested and all that is not manifested. Then I added: There is nothing that is not the Lord, nothing — there is nothing that is not the Lord, but few indeed are those who are *conscious* of the Lord. And it is this unconsciousness of the creation which constitutes its Falsehood.

All at once it was so obvious: "There it is! There it is!" How did Falsehood come? But that's it, it is the unconsciousness of the creation that constitutes the Falsehood of the creation. And as soon as the creation once more becomes conscious of *being* the Lord, Falsehood will cease.

And it's that, isn't it? Everything is difficult, laborious, hard, painful because everything is done outside the consciousness of the Lord. But when He takes possession of His domain once more — or rather when we allow Him to take possession of His domain once more — and when things are done in His consciousness, with His consciousness, everything will become not only easy, but wonderful, glorious — and in an inexpressible delight.

It came like something self-evident. We say, "What is it? What do we call Falsehood? Why is the creation false?" It is not an illusion in the sense of not existing: it really exists, but... it is not conscious of what it is! Not only unconscious of its origin, but unconscious of its essence, of its truth — it is not conscious of its truth. And that is why it lives in Falsehood.

This aphorism is magnificent. There is nothing to say, it says everything.

3 March 1965

110 – To see the composition of the sun or the lines of Mars is doubtless a great achievement; but when thou hast the instrument that can show thee a man's soul as thou seest a picture, then thou wilt smile at the wonders of physical Science as the playthings of babies.

This is the continuation of what we were saying before about those who want to "see". Ramakrishna is supposed to have said to Vivekananda, "You can see the Lord just as you see me and hear His voice just as you hear mine." Some people understood this as an announcement that the Lord was on earth in flesh and blood. I said (*laughing*): "No, it is not that! What he meant is that if you enter the true consciousness, you can hear Him — I say, hear much more clearly than you hear physically and see much more clearly than you see physically." — "Oh! But..." — Immediately they open their eyes wide, it becomes something unreal!

Do the wonders of physical science make you smile?

The "wonders" are all right, that is their business. But it is their overweening self-assurance that makes me smile. They imagine that they know. They imagine that they have the key, that is what makes one smile. They imagine that with everything they have learnt they are the masters of Nature — that is childishness. Something will always escape them so long as they are not in touch with the creative Force and the creative Will.

It is an experiment you can easily make. A scientist can explain all visible phenomena, he can even use physical forces and make them do what he wants — and they have achieved staggering results from the material point of view — but if you just ask them this question, this simple question, "What is death?" — in fact they know nothing about it. They can describe the phenomenon as it happens materially, but if they are sincere, they are obliged to say that it explains nothing.

There always comes a time when it no longer explains anything. Because to know... to know is to have power.

(Silence)

Ultimately, what is most accessible to materialistic thought, to scientific thought, is the fact that they cannot foresee. They can foresee many things, but the unfolding of terrestrial events is beyond their prevision. I think that this is the only thing they can admit — there is a problematical element, a field of unpredictability which eludes all their calculations.

I have never talked with a typical scientist who had the most up-to-date knowledge, so I am not quite sure, I do not know how far they admit the unpredictable or the incalculable.

What Sri Aurobindo means, I think, is that when one is in communion with the soul and has the knowledge of the soul, that knowledge is so much more wonderful than material knowledge that there is almost a smile of disdain. I do not think he means that the knowledge of the soul teaches you things about material life that one cannot learn through science.

The only point — I do not know whether science has reached it — is the unpredictability of the future. But perhaps they say it is because they have not yet reached perfection in their instruments and methods. For example, perhaps they think that when man first appeared on earth, if they had had the instruments which they have now, they would have been able to foresee the transformation of the animal into man or the appearance of man as a consequence of "something" in the animal — (*Mother smiles*). I don't know about their most modern claims. In that

Jnana

case, they ought to be able to measure or perceive the difference in the atmosphere now, after the intrusion of something which was not there before, because that still belongs to the material domain.[16] But I do not think this is what Sri Aurobindo meant; I think he meant that the world of the soul and the inner realities are so much more wonderful than physical realities, that all physical "wonders" make you smile — it is more like that.

> *But the key you mention, this key which they do not have, isn't it precisely the soul? A power of the soul over Matter, to change Matter and to work physical wonders too. Doesn't the soul have this power?*

It has that power and exercises it constantly, but the human consciousness is not aware of it; and the big difference is that it is becoming aware. But it is becoming aware of something that is *always there*, and which others deny because they cannot see it.

For example, I have had the opportunity to study this. For me, circumstances, characters, all events and all beings move according to certain "laws", so to say, which are not rigid, but which I can perceive and which enable me to see: this will lead to that and that will lead there, and since this person is like that, this will happen to him. It is more and more precise. Because of this, I could, if necessary, make predictions. But this relation of

---

[16] When the disciple asked Mother whether this "something" was in fact the supramental force, she answered: "I would rather not give it a name, because people will make a dogma out of it. That is what happened when what is called 'the first supramental manifestation' occurred in 1956. I tried my best to prevent it from being made into a dogma. But if I say, 'On such a date, such a thing happened', it will be written in big letters and if anyone says anything else he will be told, 'You are a heretic.' So I do not want that. But it is indisputable that the atmosphere has changed, there is something new in the atmosphere — we can call it the 'descent of the supramental truth', because for us these words have a meaning, but I do not want to make a declaration out of it, because I do not want that to be *the* classical or 'true' way of describing the event. That is why I leave my phrase vague, purposely."

cause and effect in that domain is quite obvious for me and it is corroborated by the facts; for them — those who do not have this vision and consciousness of the soul, as Sri Aurobindo says — circumstances unfold according to other superficial laws, which they consider as the natural consequences of things, completely superficial laws that do not stand up to deep analysis. But they do not have the inner capacity, so it does not worry them, it seems obvious to them.

I mean that this inner knowledge does not have the power to convince them. So that when in connection with any particular event I see: "Oh, but it is quite, quite obvious — for me — I have seen the Force of the Lord at work here, I have *seen* such and such a thing happen and of course that is what is going to occur" — for me, it is quite obvious, but I do not say what I know, because it does not correspond to anything in their experience; to them it would sound like rambling or pretension. That is to say, when you do not have the experience yourself, another person's experience is not convincing, it cannot convince you.

It is not so much a power of acting on Matter — that is happening constantly; but, unless hypnotic methods are used, which are worthless, which lead nowhere — it is a power to open the understanding (*gesture of piercing through the top of the head*); that is what is so difficult.... A thing one has not experienced does not exist.

Even if some kind of miracle were to happen in front of them, they would have a material explanation for it; for them it would not be a miracle in the sense of an intervention of a force or power other than the material forces and powers. They would have their material explanation. For them it would not be convincing.

You can only understand if you yourself have touched this domain in your experience.

And one can see, one can see clearly: there is a possibility of understanding only insofar as something has awakened. That is the support, the basis.

In short, perhaps it is not so much a question of "transforming Matter" as of becoming aware of the true working.

That is exactly what I mean. The transformation can take place up to a certain point without one even being aware of it.

They say that there is a great difference: when man came, the animal had no way of perceiving it. Well, I say it is exactly the same thing: in spite of everything man has realised, man has no way of perceiving it — certain things may occur and he will only know about it much later, when "something" within him has developed enough for him to perceive it.

Even scientific development carried to its extreme, to the point where one really feels that there is almost no difference, where they arrive at this unity of substance, for example, where it seems that there is only an almost indiscernible or imperceptible transition between one state and the other — the material and the spiritual — well, no, it is not like that. To perceive this kind of unity, one must already carry within oneself the experience of *the other thing*; otherwise one cannot perceive it.

And precisely because they have acquired the capacity to explain, they explain external phenomena to themselves in such a way that they remain in their denial of the reality of inner phenomena — they say that these are, as it were, extensions of what they have studied.

Only, because of his very constitution, because there hardly exists a human being who hasn't at least a reflection, or a shadow, or a beginning of a relation with his subtle being, his inner being, his soul — because of that there is always a flaw in their denial. But they consider that to be a weakness — it is their only strength.

(*Silence*)

It is really when one has the experience — the experience and

On Thoughts and Aphorisms

knowledge and identity with the higher forces — that one can see the relativity of all external knowledge; but until then, no, one cannot, one denies the other realities.

I think this is what Sri Aurobindo meant: only when the other consciousness has been developed will the scientist smile and say, "Yes, it was all very well, but..."

In reality, one cannot lead to the other — except by an act of grace; if inwardly, there is an absolute sincerity which enables the scientist to see, to sense, to perceive the point at which it eludes him, then that can lead him to the other state of consciousness, but *not* by his own procedures. Something must abdicate and accept the new methods, the new perceptions, the new vibration, the new state of soul.

So, it is an individual matter. It is not a question of class or category — the question is whether the scientist is ready to be... something else.

(Silence)

One can only state one thing: everything you know, however beautiful, is nothing compared to what you can know if you are able to use the other methods.

(Silence)

This has been the whole object of my work recently: how to touch this refusal to know? It has been there for a long time. It is the continuation of what Sri Aurobindo said in one of his letters: he says that India has done much more for spiritual life with her methods than Europe has done with all her doubts and questionings. That's exactly it. It is a kind of refusal — the refusal to accept a particular method of knowledge which is not the purely material one, and the denial of experience, of the reality of experience. How can one convince them of that?... And then, there is the method of Kali which is to give a sound thrashing. But according to me that means a lot of damage without much result. This is another big problem.

It seems that the only method which can overcome all resistances is the method of Love. But then the adverse forces have perverted love in such a way that many very sincere people, sincere seekers, have steeled themselves, so to say, against this method, because of its distortion. That is the difficulty. That is why it is taking time. However...

29 May 1965

111 – Knowledge is a child with its achievements; for when it has found out something, it runs about the streets whooping and shouting; Wisdom conceals hers for a long time in a thoughtful and mighty silence.

112 – Science talks and behaves as if it had conquered all knowledge. Wisdom, as she walks, hears her solitary tread echoing on the margin of immeasurable Oceans.

Silence... Oh! It is better to practise it than to talk about it.

It is an experience I had here, long ago: the difference between wanting to spread and make use of what one has learnt, immediately, and the contact with higher knowledge, where one remains as quiet as one can so that it can have a transforming effect. I have had the living experience of this — half a day of living experience — but now that seems old to me, old, far behind.

What is the power of this silence? When one rises above, one enters into a kind of great silence, that is frozen, that is everywhere; but what is the power of this silence? Does it do anything?

This is what people used to seek in the past when they wanted to escape from life. They would go into a trance, they would leave their body quite still and they would go within and they were perfectly happy. And with the Sannyasis who had themselves buried alive it was like that. They said, "Now, I have finished my work" — their language was very impressive — "I have finished, I am entering into Samadhi" and they had themselves buried alive. They went into a room or something, and then it was closed and that was the end of it. And that is what happened: they went into a trance, and after some time, naturally, their body was dissolved and they were in peace.

But Sri Aurobindo says that this silence is powerful.

Powerful, yes.

Well, I would like to know exactly how it is powerful? Because one has the feeling that one could stay there for an eternity...

Not an eternity — Eternity.

... without anything changing.

No, because it is not manifested, it is outside the manifestation. But Sri Aurobindo wants us to bring it down here. That is the difficulty. And one must accept infirmity and even the appearance of imbecility, everything, and not one out of fifty million has the courage for that.

There are millions of ways of fleeing. There is only one way to remain: it is truly to have courage and endurance, to accept every appearance of infirmity, helplessness, incomprehension, even an apparent denial of the Truth. But if one does not accept that, it will never change. Those who want to remain great, luminous, strong, powerful and so on and so forth, well, let them stay up there, they cannot do anything for the earth.

And this incomprehension is a very small thing—a very small thing because the consciousness is such that it is not affected in the least—but it is a total and all-embracing incomprehension! That is to say, one is insulted and held in contempt and all that, just because of what one is doing; for, according to them—all the "great minds" of the earth—one has forsaken one's divinity. They do not put it like that, they say: "What? You claim to have a divine consciousness, and then..." And one meets it in everybody, in all circumstances. From time to time, someone, for a moment, has a flash, but it is quite exceptional, whereas, "Well then, show your power"—this is everywhere.

For them, the Divine on earth ought to be all-powerful, obviously.

That's it: "Show your power, change the world. And to begin with, do what I want. I mean, the first and most important thing is to do what I want—show your power!" That is what they say constantly.

25 September 1965

113 – Hatred is the sign of a secret attraction that is eager to flee from itself and furious to deny its own existence. That too is God's play in His creature.

114 – Selfishness is the only sin, meanness the only vice, hatred the only criminality. All else can easily be turned into good, but these are obstinate resisters of deity.

This corresponds to a kind of vibration—the vibration received from people who hate. It is a vibration that is fundamentally the same, so to say, as the vibration of love. In its very depths there is the same sensation. Although on the surface it is the opposite, it is supported by the same vibration. And one could say that one is the slave of what one hates just as much as of what one loves, perhaps even more so. It is something that grips you, that haunts you, and which you cherish; a sensation you cherish, for underneath its violence there is a warmth of attraction which is just as great as the warmth you feel for what you love. And it seems that this distortion in the appearance only exists in the activity of the manifestation, that is, entirely on the surface.

One is obsessed by what one hates even more than by what one loves. And the obsession comes from this inner vibration.

All these "feelings" — what to call them? — have a mode of vibration, with something very essential at the core, and covering layers, as it were. And the most central vibration is the same, and as it expands to express itself, it becomes distorted. With love, it is quite obvious; it becomes, outwardly, in the vast majority of cases, something whose nature is quite different from the inner vibration, because it is something that withdraws into itself, shrivels up and wants to draw things towards itself in an egoistic movement of possession. You *want* to be loved. You say, "I love that person," but at the same time there is what you want; the feeling is lived as, "I want to be loved." And so this distortion is almost as great as the distortion of hatred which consists in wanting to destroy what you love in order not to be bound by it. Because you cannot obtain what you want from the object of your love, you want to destroy it in order to become free; in the other case, you shrivel up almost in an inner rage, because you cannot obtain, you cannot absorb what you love. And truly speaking (*laughing*), from the standpoint of the deeper truth, there is not much difference!

It is only when the central vibration remains pure and expresses itself in its initial purity, which is an unfolding — what to call it?... it is something that radiates, a vibration that spreads out in splendour; and it is a blossoming, yes, a radiant blossoming — then it remains true. And materially, this is translated as self-giving, self-forgetfulness, generosity of soul. And that is the only true movement. But what is usually called "love" is as far removed from the central vibration of true Love as hatred; only, one withdraws, shrivels up and hardens, and the other strikes. This is what makes all the difference.

And it is not seen with ideas, it is seen with vibrations. It is very interesting.

In fact I have had to study this a great deal recently. I have had the opportunity to see these vibrations. The external results may be deplorable, from the practical point of view they may be dreadful; that is to say, this kind of vibration encourages the urge to harm, to destroy; but from the standpoint of the deeper truth, this distortion is not much greater than the other, it is only of a more aggressive nature — and even then...

If one pursues this experience further and deeper, if one concentrates on this vibration, one realises that it is the initial vibration of creation, the vibration which has been altered, distorted in all that exists. And then there is a kind of all-embracing warmth — one cannot call it exactly a "sweetness", but it is a kind of strong sweetness — an all-embracing warmth in which there is as much smile as sadness — much more smile than sadness....

This does not justify the distortion, but it is above all a reaction to the choice that the human mentality — especially the human morality — has made between one kind of distortion and another. There is a whole series of distortions that have been labelled "bad" and there is a whole series of distortions towards which people are full of indulgence, almost compliments. And yet from the essential point of view these distortions are not much better than the others — it is a matter of choice.

In fact, one should first perceive *the* central vibration and then appreciate its *unique* and wonderful quality so much that one would automatically and spontaneously avoid all distortions, whatever they may be, the virtuous as well as the vicious.

We always come back to the same thing, there is only one

solution: to attain the truth of things and cling to it — this essential truth, the truth of essential Love — and cling to it.

25 December 1965

115 – The world is a long recurring decimal with Brahman for its integer. The period seems to begin and end, but the fraction is eternal; it will never have an end and never had any real beginning.

116 – The beginning and end of things is a conventional term of our experience; in their true existence these terms have no reality, there is no end and no beginning.

Only last week there was a whole development of this experience.
    In fact, it is the same thing for worlds as for individuals, for universes as for worlds. Only the duration is different — an individual is small, a world is a little bigger, and a universe is a little bigger still! But what has a beginning has an end.

And yet Sri Aurobindo says that "there is no end and no beginning."

We have to use words but the Thing escapes. What we know as "the eternal Principle", "the Supreme", "God", has neither beginning nor end — we are obliged to say "it is", but it is not like that, because it is beyond Non-Manifestation and Manifestation; it is something which we are unable to understand and perceive in the Manifestation — and that is what has neither beginning nor end. But constantly and eternally, That is manifested in something that begins and ends. Only there are two ways of "ending", one which appears to be a destruction, an annihilation, and another which is a transformation; and it would seem that as the Manifestation becomes more perfect, the necessity of destruction diminishes until a time comes when it will disappear and be replaced by a process of progressive transformation. But this is a very human and external way of putting it.

I am fully aware of the inadequacy of words, but through the words you must catch hold of the Thing.... The difficulty for human thought and still more for expression, is that words always carry a sense of beginning.

(*Silence*)

I have had a perception of this manifestation — a "pulsating" manifestation, one might say, which expands and contracts, expands and contracts.... And there comes a time when there is such an expansion, such a fluidity, plasticity, capacity for change that there is no longer any need for it to be reabsorbed so that it can take a new form; and there will be a progressive transformation. I used to know an occultist who said that this is the seventh universal creation, that there have already been six *pralayas*[17] and that this is the seventh creation, but that this one will be able to transform itself without being reabsorbed — which obviously has no importance whatsoever, for when one has the eternal consciousness it does not matter whether it is like this or like that. Only in the limited human consciousness is there this kind of ambition or need for something that has no end, because, within, there is what might be called the "memory of eternity" and this memory of eternity aspires for the manifestation to share in this eternity. But if this sense of eternity is active and present, we do not grieve; we do not grieve when we throw away a spoiled garment — we may be attached to it, but even so we do not grieve! It is the same thing: if a universe disappears, it means that it has fully fulfilled its function, it has come to the end of its possibilities and must be replaced by another one.

[17] Reabsorption of a world.

I have followed the whole curve. When you are very small in consciousness and development, you feel a great need that the earth should not disappear, that it should continue perpetually — it can go on transforming itself, but it should always be the earth that goes on. A little later, when you are a little more mature, you give it much less importance. And when you are in constant communion with the sense of eternity, it becomes merely a question of choice; it is no longer a need, because it is something that does not affect the active consciousness. A few days ago — I do not remember when, but very recently — I lived this Consciousness for a whole morning and I saw, in the curve of the being's development, that this kind of need, which seems to be deep-seated, for the life of the earth to be prolonged — for the life of the earth to be prolonged indefinitely — this need is objectified, so to say, it is no longer so deep-seated; it is like looking at a performance and judging whether it should be like this or like that. It was an interesting change of viewpoint.

It is like an artist, but an artist giving shape to himself, making one trial, two trials, three trials, as many as he needs, and then achieving something complete enough in itself and receptive enough to be able to adapt to new manifestations, to the needs of these new manifestations, so that it would not be necessary to draw everything back in, to mix it all up and bring it all out again. But it is nothing more than this, and as I say, a question of choice. After all, the manifestation is made for the delight of objectivisation — the delight or interest or, well... And once what has taken shape is plastic enough, receptive enough, flexible enough and vast enough to be capable of being constantly moulded by the new forces that are manifesting, there is no longer any need to unmake everything in order to remake it.

With the curve also came an adage, "What has a beginning must have an end" — this seems to be one of those human mental constructions that are not necessarily true. But subjectively, what is interesting is that the problem gradually becomes less acute as one views it from higher up, or from a more central point, to be more exact.

It seems that it is the same... not "principle", because it is not a principle — the same law for the individual as for worlds and universes.

(*Long silence*)

As soon as one tries to express it (*Mother makes a gesture of reversal*), everything becomes warped.... I was looking at this experience of the relation with the Consciousness, the All; this relation of the human being with the All; of the earth — the consciousness of the earth — with the All; of the consciousness of the manifested universe with the All; and of the consciousness that presides over the universe — over all the universes — with the All; and this inexpressible phenomenon that each point of consciousness — a point that does not occupy any space — each point of consciousness is capable of *all* experiences.... It is very difficult to express.

One could say that only limits make differences — differences in time, differences in space, differences in size, differences in power. It is only the limits. And as soon as the consciousness goes outside its limits at any point in the manifestation, whatever the dimension of this manifestation — yes, the dimension of this manifestation has absolutely no importance — at any point in the manifestation, if one goes outside the limits, it is *the* Consciousness.

From this standpoint one could say that it is the acceptance of limits that has made the manifestation possible. The possibility of manifestation came with the acceptance of the sense of limits.... It is impossible to express. Always, as soon as one begins to speak, one has the impression of something which does this (*same gesture of reversal*), a kind of tipping over, and it is finished, the essential thing has gone. Then the metaphysical sense comes along and says, "One could put it like this, one could put it like that...." To use words: every point contains the Consciousness of Infinity and Eternity — these are words, nothing but words. But the possibility of this experience is there. It is like stepping back out of space.... It might be amusing to say that even stone, even... oh, water certainly, fire certainly, has *the* power of Consciousness — the original — all the words that come are stupid — essential, primordial — all that means nothing — eternal, infinite Consciousness.... All this is meaningless, it gives me the impression of dust thrown on glass to prevent it from being transparent!... Finally, in conclusion, after having relived this experience — these last few days I have had it repeatedly, it reigned supreme, in spite of everything, work, activities, it ruled over everything — any attachment to any formula, even the ones that have stirred people through the ages, seems childish to me. And now it's only a matter of choice: you can choose whether it is like this or like that or like that; you can say this or this or that — amuse yourselves, my children... if it amuses you.

But it is certain — this is an observation for general use — it is certain that the human mind, in order to have the urge to act, needs to build a dwelling-place — more or less large, more or less complete, more or less flexible — but it needs a dwelling-place. Only (*laughing*) it is not that! That distorts everything!

And what is strange, what is strange, is that outwardly one goes on living automatically according to certain ways of life, which no longer even have the virtue of seeming necessary to you, which no longer even have the force of habit, and which are accepted and lived almost automatically, with a sense — a kind of feeling or sensation, but it is neither feeling nor sensation, it is a kind of very subtle perception — that Something, so immense that it is undefinable, wants it. I say "wants" it or I say "chooses" it, but it is "wills" it; it is a Will that does not function like the human will, but which wills it — which wills it or sees it or decides it. And in each thing there is this luminous, golden, imperative vibration... which is necessarily all-powerful. And it provides as a background the perfect well-being of certitude, which, a little lower down in the consciousness, expresses itself by a smile of benevolent amusement.

> *Further on, Sri Aurobindo speaks of worlds that have no beginning and no end, and he says that their creation and their destruction is "a play of hide-and-seek with our outward consciousness"...* [18]

It is certainly a very elegant way of saying the same thing I have just said!

> *What I wanted to ask is whether from the "other side", the material world continues to be perceived clearly or whether it all evaporates?*

This is another experience of these last few days. It came to me with an absolute certitude — although it is very difficult to express — that this so-called "error" of the material world as it is, was indispensable; that is to say, the material mode or way of perceiving, of becoming aware of things, was gained through the "error" of this creation and would not have existed without it, and it is not something that will vanish into non-existence when we gain the true consciousness — it is something that *is added* in a special way — which was perceived, lived at that moment in the essential Consciousness.

It was like a justification of the creation that has made possible a certain mode of perception — which might be described by the words "precision", "exactness" in objectivisation — which could not have existed without it. Because when this

---

[18] 117 — "Neither is it that I was not before nor thou nor these kings nor that all we shall not be hereafter." Not only Brahman, but beings and things in Brahman are eternal; their creation and destruction is a play of hide-and-seek with our outward consciousness.

On Thoughts and Aphorisms

Consciousness — the perfect Consciousness, the true Consciousness, *the* Consciousness — was there, present and lived to the exclusion of any other, there was something like a mode of vibration, so to say, a mode of vibration with objective precision and exactness, which could not have existed without this material form of creation.... You see, there was always this great "Why?" — "Why is it like this?" Why is there all this, which brought about everything that the human consciousness interprets as suffering, misery and helplessness and everything, all the horrors of ordinary consciousness — why? Why is it? And so this was the answer: in the true Consciousness there is a mode of vibration, of precision and exactness and clarity in objectivisation, which could not have existed without that, which would not have had any opportunity to manifest. That is certain. That is the answer — the all-powerful answer to the "why".

It is obvious — obvious — that what we experience as progress, as a progressive manifestation, is not simply a law of the material manifestation as we know it, but the very principle of the eternal Manifestation. To come down to the level of terrestrial thought, one might say that there is no manifestation without progress. But what *we* call progress, what is "progress" to our consciousness, up there it is... it can be anything, a necessity, whatever you like — there is a kind of absolute that we do not understand, an absolute of being: it is like that because it is like that, that is all. But for our consciousness it is more and more, better and better — and these words are stupid — it is more and more perfect, better and better perceived. That is the very principle of manifestation.

One experience came very fleetingly, but precisely enough to allow one to say, very clumsily, that — I was about to say the "flavour" of the Non-Manifest — the Non-Manifest has a special flavour because of the Manifest.

All this is just words, but that is all we have. Perhaps one day we shall have words or a language which can say these things properly; it is possible, but it will be always a translation.

There is a level here (*pointing to the chest*) where something plays with words, with images, with phrases, like this (*shimmering, undulating gesture*), that makes pretty pictures; it has a power of bringing you into contact with the Thing, which may be greater — at least as great, but perhaps greater — than here (*pointing to the forehead*), than the metaphysical expression — "metaphysical" is a manner of speaking. Images, that is to say, poetry. Here there is an almost more direct way of access to that inexpressible vibration. I see Sri Aurobindo's expression in its poetic form, it has a charm and a simplicity — a simplicity and a sweetness and a penetrating charm — which brings you into direct contact much more intimately than all the things of the head.

> *When one is in this eternal Consciousness, to have a body or not to have a body, does not make much difference; but when one is what is called "dead", does the perception of the material world remain clear and precise or does it become as vague and imprecise as the consciousness of the other worlds can be when one is on this side, in this world? Sri Aurobindo speaks of a game of hide-and-seek. But the game of hide-and-seek is interesting if one state of being does not preclude the consciousness of the other states of being.*

Yesterday or the day before, throughout the day, from morning till night, something was saying, "I am — I am or I have the consciousness of the dead on earth." I am translating it into words, but it was as if I was being told, "This is what the consciousness of a dead person is like, relative to the earth and physical things... I am a dead person living on earth." According to the position of the consciousness — for the consciousness is always changing its position — according to the position of the consciousness, it was, "This is how dead people are, relative to the earth"; then, "I am absolutely like a dead person relative to the earth"; then, "I am living as a dead person lives in the consciousness of the earth"; then, "I am exactly like a dead person living on earth..." and so on. I went on behaving, speaking, acting as usual. But it has been like this for a long time. For a long time, for more than two years, I have been seeing the world like this (*upward gesture from one level to another*) and now I see it like this (*downward gesture*). I do not know how to explain this because there is nothing mentalised about it, and non-mentalised sensations have something hazy about them which is hard to define. But the words and the thought were a certain distance away (*gesture around the head*), like something that watches and evaluates, that is to say, which says what it sees — something that is all around. And today, two or three times, it was extremely strong — I mean that this state dominated the whole consciousness — a kind of impression or sensation or perception — but it is none of these: I am a dead person living on earth.

How to explain that?

And so, for example, with regard to sight, there is no objective precision (*Mother makes a gesture of not seeing with the eyes*). I see through and by the consciousness. As regards hearing, I hear in a very different way; there is a kind of "discrimination" — it is not "discernment" — something in the perception which chooses, something which decides — decides, but not automatically — what is heard and what is not heard, what is perceived and what is not perceived. It already exists with sight but it is even stronger with hearing: for some things one can only hear a continuous hum and others are crystal-clear; others are vague, scarcely audible. With sight it is the same thing: everything is behind a luminous mist, as it were — very luminous, but still a mist, that is to say, there is no precision — and then, suddenly, there is something absolutely precise and clear, an extraordinarily precise vision of detail. Usually, the vision is the expression of the consciousness in things. That is to say, everything seems more and more subjective, less and less objective.... And they are not visions that impose themselves on the sight or sounds that impose themselves on the hearing; there is a kind of movement of consciousness which makes some things perceptible and others a kind of very vague background.

The consciousness chooses what it wants to see.

There is nothing personal — nothing personal. Of course there is a feeling of choice and decision, but there is no feeling of personal choice and decision. Besides, the "personal" becomes little more than the need to introduce this (*Mother touches her hands*). For example, eating is very queer, very queer.... It is as if someone were looking on at a body — which is not even something very precise and very definite, but a kind of conglomeration that holds together — and were looking on... at something that is happening! No, it is really a queer state. Today, it was very strong, it dominated the whole consciousness. And there are even moments when one has the feeling that the slightest thing would make you lose the contact (*gesture of disconnection, as if the link with the body were broken*) and it is only when one keeps very still and very indifferent — indifferent — that it can continue.

These experiences are always preceded by a kind of very intimate and very inward closeness to the Supreme Presence, with a kind of suggestion: "Are you ready for anything?" Naturally I reply, "Anything." And the Presence becomes so marvellously intense that there is a kind of thirst in the whole being: that it should be like that constantly. Only That exists, only That has any reason to exist. And in the midst of it comes the suggestion: "Are you ready for anything?"

I am speaking of the body, not of the inner beings, but of the body.

And the body always says yes. It does this (*gesture of surrender*): no choice, no preference, not even aspiration, a total,

total surrender. And then things like this come to me; all day yesterday, it was: "A dead person living on earth." With the perception — not yet very marked, but quite clear — of the very great difference between this way of living and that of other people — all of them. It is not yet clear-cut or distinct or very precise, but it is very clear. It is very clear, very perceptible. It is another way of living.

One might be inclined to say that it is not a gain from the point of view of consciousness, since things fade away. I do not know, is it a gain?

It can only be a transition. It is a transitional state.

From the point of view of consciousness, it is a tremendous gain! Because every bondage, every attachment to outer things, all that is finished, it has fallen away completely — fallen away completely: an absolute freedom. That is to say, only That — the Supreme Master — is master. From this point of view, it can only be a gain. It is such a radical realisation.... This seems to be an absolute of freedom, something that is considered to be impossible to realise while leading an ordinary life on earth.

This corresponds to the experience of absolute freedom one has in the higher parts of the being when one is no longer at all dependent on the body. But what is remarkable — I insist strongly on this — is that the consciousness *of the body* has these experiences and it is a body which is still visibly here!

Obviously, there is nothing left of what gives "confidence in life" to human beings. Apparently there is no longer any support from the outer world, there is nothing but... the supreme Will. To translate this into plain words, well, the body has the feeling that it lives only because the supreme Lord wants it to live, otherwise it could not live.

Yes, but it seems to me that a state of perfection ought

to embrace everything, that is to say, one could be in the supreme state without abolishing the material state.

But that does not abolish it!

But still you say that it is "far away", that it is "behind a veil", that it has lost its exactness and precision.

That is a purely human and superficial perception. I don't at all feel that I have lost anything, on the contrary! I feel it is a much higher state than the one I had before.

Even from the material point of view?

What the Lord wants is done — that is all; that is the beginning and the end of it.
If He told me... Whatever He wants the body to do, it can do it; it no longer depends on physical laws.

What He wants to see, He sees, what He wants to hear, He hears.

Beyond all question.

And when He wants to see or hear materially, He sees and hears perfectly.

Oh! Perfectly. There are moments when the sight is more precise than it has ever been. But it is fleeting, it comes and goes; because, probably, it is only like an assurance of what is to come. But for example, the perception of the inner reality of people — not what they think they are or what they pretend to be or what they seem to be: all that disappears — but the perception of their inner reality is infinitely more precise than before. I see a photograph, for example; it is no longer a matter of seeing "through" something: I see almost nothing but what the person *is*. The "through" diminishes to such an extent that sometimes it does not exist at all.

Naturally, if a human will wanted to act on this body, if a human will said, "Mother must do this or Mother must do that, or she should be able to do this, she should be able to do that..." it would be completely disappointed; it would say, "She is no longer good for anything", because the body would not obey it any more.... And human beings constantly exert their will on one another, or the human being himself receives suggestions and manifests them as his own will, without noticing that all that is the outer Falsehood.

(*Silence*)

There is a kind of certainty in the body that if even for a few seconds I were to lose contact — "I" means the body — with the Supreme, it would instantly die. Only the Supreme keeps it alive. That's how it is. So, naturally, for the ignorant and stupid consciousness of human beings this is a pitiful condition — to me it is the true condition! Because for them, instinctively, spontaneously, in an absolute way, so to say, the sign of perfection is the power of life, ordinary life.... Well, that no longer exists at all — it has completely gone.

Yes, many times, several times, the body has asked the question, "Why do I not feel Thy Power and Thy Force in me?" And the reply has always been a smiling one — one puts it into words, but it is without words — the reply is always: "Patience, patience, for that to happen you must be *ready*."

4 and 9 March 1966

117 – "Neither is it that I was not before nor thou nor these kings nor that all we shall not be hereafter." Not only Brahman, but beings and things in Brahman are eternal;

their creation and destruction is a play of hide-and-seek with our outward consciousness.

118 – The love of solitude is a sign of the disposition towards knowledge; but knowledge itself is only achieved when we have a settled perception of solitude in the crowd, in the battle and in the mart.

119 – If when thou art doing great actions and moving giant results, thou canst perceive that *thou* art doing nothing, then know that God has removed His seal from thy eyelids.

120 – If when thou sittest alone, still and voiceless on the mountain-top, thou canst perceive the revolutions thou art conducting, then hast thou the divine vision and art freed from appearances.

121 – The love of inaction is folly and the scorn of inaction is folly; there is no inaction. The stone lying inert upon the sands which is kicked away in an idle moment, has been producing its effect upon the hemispheres.

This is the experience I have had these last few days, yesterday or the day before. The feeling of an irresistible Power governing everything: the world, things, people, everything, without needing to move materially, and that this excessive material activity is only like the foam that forms when water flows very fast — the foam on the surface; but that the Force runs on underneath like an all-powerful stream.
There is nothing else to say.
One always comes back to that: to know is all right, to speak is good, to do is all very well, but to *be* is the only thing which has any power.

You see, people are restless, because things do not move quickly; so I had this vision of the formation, of the divine creation in the making, under the surface, all-powerful, irresistible, and in spite of everything, of all this outer turmoil.

But in order to express itself, this great flow of Power needs instruments, doesn't it?

A brain.

But, exactly, not only a brain. This Power can express itself, as in the past, in a mental or overmental way; it can express itself vitally through force; it can express itself through the muscles; but how can it express itself physically, purely, directly — since you often speak of "material power"? What is the difference between the Action above and the true Action here?

Each time I have been conscious of the Power, the experience has been similar. The Will from above is translated into a vibration which certainly takes on some vital force but which acts in a subtle physical domain. One perceives a certain quality of vibration which is difficult to describe, but which gives the impression of something coagulated, not fragmented, something which seems to be denser than air, but which is extremely homogeneous, with a golden luminosity, with a tremendous driving power, and which expresses a certain will — which is not of the same nature as human will, which has the nature of vision rather than of thought; it is like a vision that imposes itself in order to be realised — in a domain that is very close to material Matter, but invisible, except to the inner sight. And that vibration exerts a pressure on people, things, circumstances, to mould them according to its vision. And it is irresistible. Even people who think the opposite, who want the opposite, do what is wanted without wanting to; even the things that by their very nature are opposed to it are turned around.

For national events, relations among nations, world circumstances, it acts like that, constantly, constantly, as a tremendous Power. And so if one is oneself in a state of union with the divine Will, without any intervention of thought, or any conception or idea, one can follow it, one sees and knows.[19]

The resistances of the inertia that is in every consciousness and in Matter mean that this Action, instead of being direct and perfectly harmonious, becomes confused, full of contradictions, clashes and conflicts; instead of everything resolving itself "normally", so to say, smoothly — as it should be — all this inertia that resists and opposes, gives it a tangled movement in which things collide and there is disorder and destruction, which become necessary only because of the resistance, but which were *not indispensable*, which might not have existed — which truly speaking should not have been — because this Will, this Power is a Power of perfect harmony where each thing is in its place, and it organises things wonderfully. It comes as an absolutely luminous and perfect organisation, which one can see when one has the vision; but when it comes down and presses on Matter, everything begins to seethe and resist. Therefore, to attempt to impute the disorders and confusions and destructions to the divine Action, to the divine Power, is another human foolishness. It is the inertia — not to mention the bad will — which *causes* the catastrophe. It is not that the catastrophe was intended, nor even foreseen, it is *caused* by the resistance.

---

[19] It is interesting to note that shortly before this conversation, Mother received the following question: "Is the American presence and intervention in Vietnam justifiable?" She replied: "From what point of view are you asking this question?

"If it is from the political point of view — politics are sunk in falsehood and I have nothing to do with them.

"If it is from the moral point of view — morality is a shield which ordinary men flourish to protect themselves from the Truth.

"If it is from the spiritual point of view — the divine Will alone is justifiable and That is what men travesty and distort in all their actions."

And then, there is added the vision of the action of Grace, which comes to moderate the results wherever possible, that is to say, wherever it is accepted. And this explains why aspiration, faith, complete trust on the part of the earthly human element, have a harmonising power, because they allow the Grace to come and set right the consequences of this blind resistance.

This is a clear vision — clear, clear, even in the details.

One could, if one wanted to, make prophecies by saying what has been seen. But there is a kind of super-compassion which prevents this prophecy, because the Word of Truth has a power of manifestation and to express the result of the resistance would make that state concrete and diminish the action of the Grace. That is why even when one sees, one cannot speak, one *must not speak*.

But Sri Aurobindo certainly meant that it is this Power, this Force which does everything — which does everything. When one sees it or is one with it, one knows at the same time, one knows that *That* is really the only thing that acts and creates; everything else is the result of the domain or the world or the material or the substance in which it acts — the result of the resistance, but not the Action. And to unite with *That* means to unite with the Action; to unite with what is below means to unite with the resistance.

And so because it wriggles and tosses and turns, wants and thinks and makes plans... it imagines that it is doing something — it is resisting.

Later, a little later, I shall be able to give examples for very small things, showing how the Force acts and what interferes and mixes with it, or is moved by this Force and distorts its movement, and the result, that is to say, the physical appearance as we see it. Even the example of a very small thing with absolutely no importance for the world, gives a clear idea of the way in which everything happens and is distorted here.

And this applies to everything, everything, all the time, all the time. And so, when one is doing the yoga of the cells, one notices the same thing: there is the Force that acts, and then (*Mother laughs*) what the body does with this Action!...

(*Silence*)

Immediately there comes the how and why. But that belongs to the domain of mental curiosity, because the important thing is to stop the resistance. That is the important thing, to stop the resistance so that the universe can become what it should be: the expression of a harmonious, luminous, wonderful power, of an unparalleled beauty. Afterwards, when the resistance has stopped, if out of curiosity we want to know why it happened... it won't matter any more. But now, one cannot find the remedy by seeking the reason why, but by taking the true attitude. That is the only thing that matters.

To stop the resistance by a total surrender, a total self-giving in every cell, if one can do that.

They begin to feel the intense delight of existing only by the Lord, for the Lord, in the Lord.

When this is established everywhere, all will be well.

6 July 1966

122 – If thou wouldst not be the fool of Opinion, first see wherein thy thought is true, then study wherein its opposite and contradiction is true; last, discover the cause of these differences and the key of God's harmony.

123 – An opinion is neither true nor false, but only serviceable for life or unserviceable; for it is a creation of Time and with time it loses its effect and value. Rise thou above opinion and seek wisdom everlasting.

124 – Use opinion for life, but let her not bind thy soul in her fetters.

On Thoughts and Aphorisms

> *(After a silence)*
>
> I was trying to find out in what way opinions are serviceable.... Sri Aurobindo says that they are "serviceable" or "unserviceable" — in what way can an opinion be serviceable?

They are helpful for a moment, in action.

No, this is precisely what I deplore; people act according to their opinion, and that is worthless. I am constantly receiving letters from people who want or do not want to do something and tell me: "This is my opinion, this is true, that is not true", and always, more than ninety-nine times out of a hundred it is wrong, it is nonsense.

One feels very clearly — in fact, it is visible — that the opposite opinion has just as much value, that it is simply a question of attitude, nothing more. And naturally the ego's preferences are always involved: you like it better like that and so you have the opinion that it is like that.

But until one can act with the higher light, one needs to use opinions.

It would be better to have some wisdom rather than an opinion, that is, to consider all the possibilities, all the aspects of the question and then try to be as unegoistic as possible and to see, for example, in the case of an action, which one can be of service to the greatest number of people or is the least destructive, the most constructive. Anyway, even from a standpoint that is not spiritual, but merely utilitarian and unselfish, it is better to act according to wisdom than according to one's opinion.

Yes, but what would be the right way to proceed when

one doesn't have the light, without involving one's opinion or one's ego?

I think it is to consider all the aspects of the problem, to lay them before your consciousness as disinterestedly as possible and to see which one is the best — if this is possible — or which one is the least harmful if there are unpleasant consequences.

I wanted to ask: what is the best attitude? Is it an attitude of intervention or an attitude of non-interference? Which is better?

Ah, that's just it, to intervene you must be sure that you are right; you must be sure that your vision of things is superior, preferable or truer than the vision of the other person or people. Then it is always wiser not to intervene — people intervene without rhyme or reason, simply because they are in the habit of giving their opinion to others.

Even when you have the vision of the true thing, it is *very rarely* wise to intervene. It only becomes indispensable when someone wants to do something which will necessarily lead to a catastrophe. Even then, intervention (*smiling*) is not always very effective.

In fact, intervention is justified only when you are absolutely sure that you have the vision of truth. Not only that, but also a clear vision of the consequences. To intervene in someone else's actions, one must be a prophet — a prophet. And a prophet with total goodness and compassion. One must even have the vision of the consequences that the intervention will have in the destiny of the other person. People are always giving each other advice: "Do this, don't do that." I see it: they have no idea how much confusion they create, how they increase confusion and disorder. And sometimes they impair the normal development of the individual.

On Thoughts and Aphorisms

> I consider that opinions are always dangerous and most often absolutely worthless.

You should not meddle with other people's affairs, unless first of all you are infinitely wiser than they are — of course, one always thinks that one is wiser! — but I mean in an objective way and not according to your own opinion; unless you see further and better and are yourself above all passions, desires and blind reactions. You must be above all these things yourself to have the right to intervene in someone else's life — even when he asks you to do so. And when he does not, it is simply meddling with something which is not your business.

(Mother goes into a long contemplation, and then continues.)

I have just seen a curious image! It looked like a very steep mountain slope and someone — like the symbol of Man — was climbing. A being... It's strange, I have seen this several times: beings without clothes who are not naked! I mean, they have a kind of robe of light. But it does not look like a radiating light or anything of that kind. It is like an atmosphere, or rather the aura, the aura made visible. And this transparence does not conceal the form and at the same time the form is not naked.... And then from the sky — there was a vast sky stretching from top to bottom, like a painting, a very clear, very luminous, very pure sky — there were countless... hundreds of birdlike things flying towards him and he was beckoning them to him. The picture was mainly pale blue, white; from time to time there was something a little darker like a wing-tip or the top of a crest, but that was incidental. And they kept coming in hundreds and he summoned them together with a gesture, then he sent them down to earth — he was standing on a steep slope — he sent them down, into the valley. And there, they became... *(Mother laughs)* they were opinions! They became opinions! There were dark ones, light ones, brown ones, blue ones....

Jnana

They were like birds flying down towards earth, like that. But it was a picture — and yet it was not a picture, because it was moving. It was very amusing.

And he said: "Look, that is how opinions are formed".... They came from the sky, a vast sky — vast and luminous and clear, neither blue nor white nor pink nor... it was luminous, simply luminous; and from this sky, it was... I said they came in hundreds, but they came in thousands, and he was there, he received them, and then he gestured with his hands and sent them down to earth, and... they became opinions! I think I began to laugh, it amused me.

It is strange.

They were all going down, going down — one could not see the bottom — they were going down.

So then it may be that opinions come from a sky of light! (*Mother laughs*)

In truth, images are much more expressive than words.

14 September 1966

Jnana

(Knowledge)

Fourth Period of Commentaries

(1969)

Jnana (Knowledge)

Fourth Period of Commentaries (1969)

125 – Every law, however embracing or tyrannous, meets somewhere a contrary law by which its operation can be checked, modified, annulled or eluded.

126 – The most binding Law of Nature is only a fixed process which the Lord of Nature has framed and uses constantly; the Spirit made it and the Spirit can exceed it, but we must first open the doors of our prison-house and learn to live less in Nature than in the Spirit.

There is no law of Nature that cannot be overcome and changed, if we have the faith that all is ruled by the Lord and that it is possible for us to come into direct contact with Him, if we know how to escape from the prison-house of age-old habits and give ourselves unreservedly to His will.

In truth, nothing is fixed, everything is in perpetual change; and this ascending transformation will lead this inconscient and mortal creation back step by step to the eternal and all-powerful consciousness of the Lord.

3 August 1969

127 – Law is a process or a formula; but the soul is the user of processes and exceeds formulas.

The laws of Nature are imperative for the physical nature only so long as this nature is not under the influence of the psychic being (the soul); for the psychic being is in possession of the divine power which can, for its own ends, use all processes and formulas and transform them at will.

5 August 1969

128 – Live according to Nature, runs the maxim of the West; but according to what nature, the nature of the body or the nature which exceeds the body? This first we ought to determine.

129 – O son of Immortality, live not thou according to Nature, but according to God; and compel her also to live according to the deity within thee.

What does Sri Aurobindo mean here by "the nature which exceeds the body"?

The nature which exceeds the body is the nature which goes on living even after the disappearance of the body; it is the psychic nature which is immortal and divine in essence. The psychic can and must become conscious of the Divine at its centre and consciously unite with Him.

7 August 1969

130 – Fate is God's foreknowledge outside Space and Time of all that in Space and Time shall yet happen; what He has foreseen, Power and Necessity work out by the conflict of forces.

If everything is foreseen, what is the role of human aspiration and effort?

In each domain (physical, vital and mental) everything is foreseen; but the intrusion of a higher domain (overmental and

Jnana

beyond) introduces another determinism into events and can change the course of things. This is what aspiration can achieve. As for human effort, it is one of the things that are determined and its role is foreseen in the overall play of forces.

9 August 1969

131 – Because God has willed and foreseen everything, thou shouldst not therefore sit inactive and wait upon His providence, for thy action is one of His chief effective forces. Up then and be doing, not with egoism, but as the circumstance, instrument and apparent cause of the event that He has predetermined.

132 – When I knew nothing, then I abhorred the criminal, sinful and impure, being myself full of crime, sin and impurity; but when I was cleansed and my eyes unsealed, then I bowed down in my spirit before the thief and the murderer and adored the feet of the harlot; for I saw that these souls had accepted the terrible burden of evil and drained for all of us the greater portion of the churned poison of the world-ocean.

For one who has fully realised that the world is nothing but the One Supreme in His manifestation, all human moral notions necessarily disappear to give way to a vision of the whole in which all values are changed — oh, how greatly changed!

14 August 1969

133 – The Titans are stronger than the gods because they have agreed with God to front and bear the burden of His wrath and enmity; the gods were able to accept only the pleasant burden of His love and kindlier rapture.

On Thoughts and Aphorisms

> To understand rightly what Sri Aurobindo truly means, one must know the wonderful sense of humour in his way of thinking.
>
> *16 August 1969*

So the gods are cowards! Then where is their greatness and splendour? Why do we worship inferior beings? And the Titans must be the most lovable sons of the Divine?

What Sri Aurobindo writes here is a paradox to awaken sluggish minds. But one must understand all the irony these phrases contain and above all the intention he puts behind the words. Besides, cowardly or not, I see no need for us to worship the gods, great or small. Our worship must go to the Supreme Lord alone, one in all things and beings.

6 November 1961[1]

134 – When thou art able to see how necessary is suffering to final delight, failure to utter effectiveness and retardation to the last rapidity, then thou mayst begin to understand something, however faintly and dimly, of God's workings.

135 – All disease is a means towards some new joy of health, all evil and pain a tuning of Nature for some more intense bliss and good, all death an opening on widest immortality. Why and how this should be so, is God's secret which only the soul purified of egoism can penetrate.

136 – Why is thy mind or thy body in pain? Because thy soul behind the veil wishes for the pain or takes delight in

---

[1] This question was asked on an earlier occasion.

it; but if thou wilt — and perseverest in thy will — thou canst impose the spirit's law of unmixed delight on thy lower members.

One has only to attempt the experience and to persevere in one's effort, then one will find that what is stated here is perfectly true.

19 August 1969

137 – There is no iron or ineffugable law that a given contact shall create pain or pleasure; it is the way the soul meets the rush or pressure of Brahman upon the members from outside them that determines either reaction.

It is obvious that the same event or the same contact causes pleasure in one and pain in another, depending on the inner attitude taken by each one.

And this observation leads towards a great realisation; for once one has not only understood but also felt that the Supreme Lord is the originator of all things and one remains constantly in contact with Him, all becomes the action of His Grace and is changed into calm and luminous bliss.

21 August 1969

138 – The force of soul in thee meeting the same force from outside cannot harmonise the measures of the contact in values of mind-experience and body-experience; therefore thou hast pain, grief or uneasiness. If thou canst learn to adjust the replies of the force in thyself to the questions of world-force, thou shalt find pain becoming pleasurable or turning into pure delightfulness. Right relation is the condition of blissfulness, Ritam[2] the key of Ananda.[3]

[2] Right; Truth of knowledge and action.
[3] Delight of existence.

On Thoughts and Aphorisms

Human beings are in the habit of basing their relationships with others on physical, vital and mental contacts; that is why there is almost always discord and suffering. If, on the contrary, they based their relationships on psychic contacts (between soul and soul), they would find that behind the troubled appearances there is a profound and lasting harmony which can express itself in all the activities of life and cause disorder and suffering to be replaced by peace and bliss.

28 August 1969

139 – Who is the superman? He who can rise above this matter-regarding broken mental human unit and possess himself universalised and deified in a divine force, a divine love and joy and a divine knowledge.

The superman is now in the making and a new consciousness has very recently manifested on earth to bring this process to perfection.

But it is unlikely that any human being has yet arrived at this fulfilment, especially since it must be accompanied by a transformation of the physical body, and this has not yet been accomplished.

30 August 1969

140 – If thou keepest this limited human ego and thinkest thyself the superman, thou art but the fool of thy own pride, the plaything of thy own force and the instrument of thy own illusions.

This naturally implies that all the ambitious people who now declare themselves to be supermen can only be impostors or people full of pride who deceive themselves and try to deceive others.

30 August 1969

141 – Nietzsche saw the superman as the lion-soul passing out of camel-hood, but the true heraldic device and token of the superman is the lion seated upon the camel which stands upon the cow of plenty. If thou canst not be the slave of all mankind, thou art not fit to be its master and if thou canst not make thy nature as Vasishtha's cow of plenty with all mankind to draw its wish from her udders, what avails thy leonine supermanhood?

To be the slave of all mankind means to be ready to serve mankind; and to make oneself as the cow of plenty means to be able to pour forth abundantly all the force, the light, the power that mankind needs in order to emerge from its ignorance and incapacity; for if this were not so, a superhuman being would be a burden rather than a help to earth.

31 August 1969

142 – Be to the world as the lion in fearlessness and lordship, as the camel in patience and service, as the cow in quiet, forbearing and maternal beneficence. Raven in all the joys of God as a lion over its prey, but bring also all humanity into that infinite field of luxurious ecstasy to wallow there and to pasture.

These are the qualities needed for the growth of the being until its divinisation; it is also a reminder that no transformation can be complete without the ascent of humanity.

1 September 1969

On Thoughts and Aphorisms

> 143 – If Art's service is but to imitate Nature, then burn all the picture galleries and let us have instead photographic studios. It is because Art reveals what Nature hides that a small picture is worth more than all the jewels of the millionaires and the treasures of the princes.

> 144 – If you only imitate visible Nature, you will perpetrate either a corpse, a dead sketch or a monstrosity; Truth lives in that which goes behind and beyond the visible and sensible.

Photography is said to be a medium of modern art. What is your opinion about this?

It all depends on the way in which photography is used. Its natural purpose and common use is documentary; the more exact and precise it is, the more useful it is.

But undeniably, there are artists who use photography as a medium of expression. But then what they do is no longer an exact copy of Nature, it is an arrangement of forms and colours intended to express something else which is usually hidden by physical appearances.

4 September 1969

> 145 – O Poet, O Artist, if thou but holdest up the mirror to Nature, thinkest thou Nature will rejoice in thy work? Rather she will turn away her face. For what dost thou hold up to her there? Herself? No, but a lifeless outline and reflection, a shadowy mimicry. It is the secret soul of Nature thou hast to seize, thou hast to hunt eternally after the truth in the external symbol, and that no mirror will hold for thee, nor for her whom thou seekest.

What is this "eternal symbol"[4] *which Sri Aurobindo speaks of here?*

The eternal symbol is the secret soul of Nature and it is the Truth of this soul that the poet and the artist must seek and express.

7 September 1969

146 – I find in Shakespeare a far greater and more consistent universalist than the Greeks. All his creatures are universal types from Lancelot Gobbo and his dog up to Lear and Hamlet.

147 – The Greeks sought universality by omitting all finer individual touches; Shakespeare sought it more successfully by universalising the rarest individual details of character. That which Nature uses for concealing from us the Infinite, Shakespeare used for revealing the Ananta-guna in man to the eye of humanity.

148 – Shakespeare, who invented the figure of holding up the mirror to Nature, was the one poet who never condescended to a copy, a photograph or a shadow. The reader who sees in Falstaff, Macbeth, Lear or Hamlet imitations of Nature, has either no inner eye of the soul or has been hypnotised by a formula.

149 – Where in material Nature wilt thou find Falstaff, Macbeth or Lear? Shadows and hints of them she possesses, but they themselves tower over her.

---

[4] The translation used was based on a text which read "eternal symbol" instead of "external symbol".

150 – There are two for whom there is hope, the man who has felt God's touch and been drawn to it and the sceptical seeker and self-convinced atheist; but for the formularists of all the religions and the parrots of free thought, they are dead souls who follow a death that they call living.

Don't the "formularists" of the religions help the ordinary masses by giving them an image of God? Don't you think that religion helps ordinary people?

Everything that happens, happens by the will of the Supreme Lord in order to lead the whole creation to the knowledge of the Supreme.

But by far the greatest part of this action works by contrast and negation. This is how religions work for most so-called believers, who follow their religion with no faith and even less experience.

14 September 1969

151 – A man came to a scientist and wished to be instructed; his instructor showed him the revelations of the microscope and telescope, but the man laughed and said, "These are obviously hallucinations inflicted on the eye by the glass which you use as a medium; I will not believe till you show these wonders to my naked seeing." Then the scientist proved to him by many collateral facts and experiments the reliability of his knowledge but the man laughed again and said, "What you term proofs, I term coincidences, the number of coincidences does not constitute proof; as for your experiments, they are obviously effected under abnormal conditions and constitute a sort of insanity of Nature." When confronted with the results of mathematics, he

was angry and cried out, "This is obviously imposture, gibberish and superstition; will you try to make me believe that these absurd cabalistic figures have any real force and meaning?" Then the scientist drove him out as a hopeless imbecile; for he did not recognise his own system of denials and his own method of negative reasoning. If we wish to refuse an impartial and open-minded enquiry, we can always find the most respectable polysyllables to cover our refusal or impose tests and conditions which stultify the inquiry.

Scientists, who are mostly materialists, use the same procedures to refute occult and spiritual knowledge as ignorant imbeciles use to refute science.

What is clear proof to a man of goodwill is imposture to one who refuses to learn.

17 September 1969

152 – When our minds are involved in matter, they think matter the only reality; when we draw back into immaterial consciousness, then we see matter a mask and feel existence in consciousness alone as having the touch of reality. Which then of these two is the truth? Nay, God knoweth; but he who has had both experiences, can easily tell which condition is the more fertile in knowledge, the mightier and more blissful.

153 – I believe immaterial consciousness to be truer than material consciousness, because I know in the first what in the second is hidden from me and also can command what the mind knows in matter.

How can one always remain in an immaterial consciousness?

One cannot and it would not be good.

Sri Aurobindo does not mention here the consciousness that is higher than either of the two consciousnesses in question (material and immaterial), that is, the supramental consciousness which contains all the other consciousnesses in itself and can thus know everything on all planes of being. This is the consciousness we should aspire for, this is the consciousness which can teach us the total Truth.

18 September 1969

154 – Hell and Heaven exist only in the soul's consciousness. Ay, but so does the earth and its lands and seas and fields and deserts and mountains and rivers. All world is nothing but arrangement of the Soul's seeing.

155 – There is only one soul and one existence; therefore we all see one objectivity only; but there are many knots of mind and ego in the one soul-existence, therefore we all see the one Object in different lights and shadows.

156 – The Idealist errs; it is not Mind which created the worlds, but that which created mind has created them. Mind only mis-sees, because it sees partially and by details, what is created.

How can idealism help us in our life here?

Sri Aurobindo seems to be referring here to a school of philosophy which holds that the Idea has created the worlds. Naturally, this is wrong.

Idealists who refuse to be the slaves of Matter need not be proponents of this philosophy and can, by their idealism, help men to be no more the slaves of material desires.

22 September 1969

157 – Thus said Ramakrishna and thus said Vivekananda. Yes, but let me know also the truths which the Avatar cast not forth into speech and the prophet has omitted from his teachings. There will always be more in God than the thought of man has ever conceived or the tongue of man has ever uttered.

158 – What was Ramakrishna? God manifest in a human being; but behind there is God in His infinite impersonality and His universal Personality. And what was Vivekananda? A radiant glance from the eye of Shiva; but behind him is the divine gaze from which he came and Shiva himself and Brahma and Vishnu and OM all-exceeding.

Will the Avatars still need to take birth on earth once the supramental consciousness is firmly established?

This question will be easier to answer when the supermind is manifested in living beings on earth.

I had always heard that Sri Aurobindo was "the last Avatar"; but he is probably the last Avatar in a human body — afterwards, we do not know....

23 September 1969

159 – He who recognises not Krishna, the God in man, knows not God entirely; he who knows Krishna only, knows not even Krishna. Yet is the opposite truth also wholly true that if thou canst see all God in a little pale

unsightly and scentless flower, then hast thou hold of His supreme reality.

Once one has taken the path of Sri Aurobindo's yoga, should not one stop worshipping all other gods and goddesses?

One who truly follows the path given by Sri Aurobindo, as soon as he begins to have the experience of this path, will find it impossible to confine his consciousness to the worship of any god or goddess or even of all of them together.

26 September 1969

160 – Shun the barren snare of an empty metaphysics and the dry dust of an unfertile intellectuality. Only that knowledge is worth having which can be made use of for a living delight and put out into temperament, action, creation and being.

161 – Become and live the knowledge thou hast; then is thy knowledge the living God within thee.

How far can "intellectual culture" help us on our path?

If intellectual culture is carried to its furthest limit, it leads the mind to the unsatisfactory acknowledgement that it is incapable of knowing the Truth and, in those who aspire sincerely, to the necessity of being quiet and opening in silence to the higher regions which can give you knowledge.

27 September 1969

162 – Evolution is not finished; reason is not the last word nor the reasoning animal the supreme figure of Nature.

Jnana

As man emerged out of the animal, so out of man the superman emerges.

I would like to see the English to know which tense Sri Aurobindo used for the verb *émerge* — whether it is present or future? If it is in the future, it is a promise we all know and for whose realisation we are working. If it is in the present... I have nothing to add.

29 September 1969

163 – The power to observe law rigidly is the basis of freedom; therefore in most disciplines the soul has to endure and fulfil the law in its lower members before it can rise to the perfect freedom of its divine being. Those disciplines which begin with freedom are only for the mighty ones who are naturally free or in former lives have founded their freedom.

164 – Those who are deficient in the free, full and intelligent observation of a self-imposed law, must be placed in subjection to the will of others. This is one principal cause of the subjection of nations. After their disturbing egoism has been trampled under the feet of a master, they are given or, if they have force in them, attain a fresh chance of deserving liberty by liberty.

What are these disciplines which "begin with freedom" that Sri Aurobindo speaks of here?

I suppose that Sri Aurobindo is referring to the various disciplines of initiation practised in the various initiatory schools in the days when they had some importance and authority.
Our age has become very materialistic and no longer gives

the same importance and authority to these schools.

30 September 1969

165 – To observe the law we have imposed on ourselves rather than the law of others is what is meant by liberty in our unregenerate condition. Only in God and by the supremacy of the spirit can we enjoy a perfect freedom.

True liberty is to be in constant union with the Divine and to do only what the Divine wants us to do.

But until then, it is better to impose on ourselves a higher law of action and conduct and to observe it scrupulously rather than to obey the law of other men or of moral and social conventions.

1 October 1969

When one lives in a community, does it not often become necessary to obey laws imposed by others instead of following the disciplines one would wish for oneself?

It is obvious that if you have chosen or accepted to live in a community, you must observe the laws of that community, otherwise you become an element of disorder and confusion.

But a discipline willingly accepted cannot be harmful to the inner development and the growth of the higher consciousness.

3 October 1969

166 – The double law of sin and virtue is imposed on us because we have not that ideal life and knowledge within which guides the soul spontaneously and infallibly to its self-fulfilment. The law of sin and virtue ceases for us when the sun of God shines upon the soul in truth

and love with its unveiled splendour. Moses is replaced by Christ, the Shastra by the Veda.[5]

Do you think this idea of sin and virtue has done humanity any good?

As Sri Aurobindo says, the law of sin and virtue was certainly necessary for the progress of humanity when it was given several thousand years ago. But today it no longer has any meaning or usefulness and should no longer be heeded.

It belongs to a past which should no longer have any authority.

But for this to be possible, it must be replaced by a more luminous and truer law and not by disorder and corruption.

4 October 1969

And what is this more luminous law?[6]

Perfect and spontaneous obedience to the divine order that must replace all law.

26 September 1970

Is it good to break all moral and social conventions as the new generation is doing? Don't these things have any value?

What has value at one period no longer has any at another as human consciousness goes on progressing. But one must take great care to replace a law one no longer obeys by a higher and truer law that fosters progress towards the future realisation.

[5] Shastra: Scriptures; Veda: Knowledge.
[6] This question was asked when these commentaries were first published in 1970.

One has no right to abandon a law until one is capable of knowing and following a higher and better law.

P.S. Read again what I wrote yesterday, I had already explained this to you.

5 October 1969

How can one follow this higher law?[7]

At every moment, do what God wants.

26 September 1970

167 – God within is leading us always aright even when we are in the bonds of the ignorance; but then, though the goal is sure, it is attained by circlings and deviations.

The goal foreseen by the Divine is always attained, but only those whose consciousness is united with the Divine Consciousness attain it directly and knowingly; the others — the vast majority of those who are conscious only of their external being — attain this goal only after having made many detours, which often seemed to be going in the opposite direction.

6 October 1969

168 – The Cross is in Yoga the symbol of the soul and nature in their strong and perfect union, but because of our fall into the impurities of ignorance it has become the symbol of suffering and purification.

---

[7] This question was asked when these commentaries were first published in 1970.

169 – Christ came into the world to purify, not to fulfil. He himself foreknew the failure of his mission and the necessity of his return with the sword of God into a world that had rejected him.

In this aphorism what does "the sword of God" represent?

The sword of God is the power that nothing can resist.

7 October 1969

170 – Mahomed's mission was necessary, else we might have ended by thinking, in the exaggeration of our efforts at self-purification, that earth was meant only for the monk and the city created as a vestibule for the desert.

171 – When all is said, Love and Force together can save the world eventually, but not Love only or Force only. Therefore Christ had to look forward to a second advent and Mahomed's religion, where it is not stagnant, looks forward through the Imams to a Mahdi.

Love alone as preached by Christ failed to transform man. Force alone as preached by Mahomed did not transform man, far from it.

That is why the consciousness which is at work to transform mankind, unites Force with Love, and the One who must realise this transformation will come on earth with the Power of Divine Love.

10 October 1969

172 – Law cannot save the world, therefore Moses' ordinances are dead for humanity and the Shastra of the

Brahmins is corrupt and dying. Law released into freedom is the liberator. Not the Pundit, but the Yogin; not monasticism, but the inner renunciation of desire and ignorance and egoism.

This is irrefutably clear and it is exactly what we are trying to do. But human nature is rebellious and finds it difficult to win freedom at the price of renouncing desire and ignorance and egoism.

Most human beings prefer the slavery of desire and ignorance and egoism to freedom without them.

13 October 1969

173 – Even Vivekananda once in the stress of emotion admitted the fallacy that a personal God would be too immoral to be suffered and it would be the duty of all good men to resist Him. But if an omnipotent supra-moral Will and Intelligence governs the world, it is surely impossible to resist Him; our resistance would only serve His ends and really be dictated by Him. Is it not better then, instead of condemning or denying, to study and understand Him?

174 – If we would understand God, we must renounce our egoistic and ignorant human standards or else ennoble and universalise them.

To the human way of understanding, the world is terribly immoral, full of suffering and ugliness, especially since the appearance of the human race. So it is difficult for the human consciousness to accept that this world could be the work of a personal God, because for man it seems to be the work of an omnipotent monster.

Jnana

But Sri Aurobindo adds that it is better to try to understand instead of condemning.

And surely the best way to understand is to unite with this Supreme Consciousness so as to see as It sees and understand as It understands. This is certainly the only true wisdom. And Yoga is the true way of uniting with the Supreme.

15 October 1969

175 – Because a good man dies or fails and the evil live and triumph, is God therefore evil? I do not see the logic of the consequence. I must first be convinced that death and failure are evil; I sometimes think that when they come, they are our supreme momentary good. But we are the fools of our hearts and nerves and argue that what they do not like or desire, must of course be an evil!

But what about those who are unlucky and always fail in everything they do?

First, once and for all, you should know that luck, good or bad, does not exist.

What to our ignorance looks like luck is simply the result of causes we know nothing about.

It is certain that for someone who has desires, when his desires are not satisfied, it is a sign that the Divine Grace is with him and wants, through experience, to make him progress rapidly, by teaching him that a willing and spontaneous surrender to the Divine Will is a much surer way to be happy in peace and light than the satisfaction of any desire.

17 October 1969

176 – When I look back on my past life, I see that if I had not

failed and suffered, I would have lost my life's supreme blessings; yet at the time of the suffering and failure, I was vexed with the sense of calamity. Because we cannot see anything but the one fact under our noses, therefore we indulge in all these snifflings and clamours. Be silent, ye foolish hearts! Slay the ego, learn to see and feel vastly and universally.

177 – The perfect cosmic vision and cosmic sentiment is the cure of all error and suffering; but most men succeed only in enlarging the range of their ego.

What is "the cosmic vision and cosmic sentiment" and how can they be attained?

This simply means the vision of the whole earth at the same time and the sentiment which is the result of this vision of the whole. This whole contains all things *at the same time*, light and darkness, suffering and pleasure, happiness and unhappiness, and all together makes a vibration of adoration turned towards the Divine, just as all sounds heard together make the supreme invocation to the Divine: OM.

18 October 1969

178 – Men say and think "For my country!", "For humanity!", "For the world!", but they really mean "For myself seen in my country!", "For myself seen in humanity!", "For myself imaged to my fancy as the world!". That may be an enlargement, but it is not liberation. To be at large and to be in a large prison are not one condition of freedom.

To be free, one must come out of the prison. The prison is the ego, the sense of separate personality. To be free, one must unite consciously and totally with the Supreme and through this identification break the limits of the ego and eradicate the very existence of the ego by universalising oneself, even though the individualisation of the consciousness is preserved.

19 October 1969

179 – Live for God in thy neighbour, God in thyself, God in thy country and the country of thy foeman, God in humanity, God in tree and stone and animal, God in the world and outside the world, then art thou on the straight path to liberation.

There is nothing to add. It is true — very obviously true — and to be sure, you must experience it, for only experience is absolutely convincing.

21 October 1969

180 – There are lesser and larger eternities; for eternity is a term of the soul and can exist in Time as well as exceeding it. When the Scriptures say "*śāśvatīḥ samāḥ*", they mean for a long space and permanence of time or a hardly measurable aeon; only God Absolute has the absolute eternity. Yet when one goes within, one sees that all things are secretly eternal; there is no end, neither was there ever a beginning.

How can one experience eternity?

By uniting with the Eternal, that is to say, with the Divine.

23 October 1969

On Thoughts and Aphorisms

181 – When thou callest another a fool, as thou must, sometimes, yet do not forget that thou thyself hast been the supreme fool in humanity.

182 – God loves to play the fool in season; man does it in season and out of season. It is the only difference.

For some years, almost all our children, big or small, have been in the habit of always using vulgar words in their everyday speech. For example, they punctuate every sentence with words like "idiot", "fool", etc... and other similar Indian terms, without any bad intention. How can we help them to get rid of this bad habit which has become so common?

The only remedy is to learn to think before you speak and to say only the words that are absolutely indispensable to express your thought.
The less you speak the better. And if it is indispensable to communicate something to anyone else, it would be wise to speak only the words that are indispensable, no more.

24 October 1969

183 – In the Buddhists' view to have saved an ant from drowning is a greater work than to have founded an empire. There is a truth in the idea, but a truth that can easily be exaggerated.

184 – To exalt one virtue, — compassion even, — unduly above all others is to cover up with one's hand the eyes of wisdom. God moves always towards a harmony.

Any exaggeration, any exclusiveness, is a lack of balance and a breach of harmony, and therefore an error in one who seeks perfection. For perfection can only exist in supreme harmony.

28 October 1969

185 – Pity may be reserved, so long as thy soul makes distinctions, for the suffering animals; but humanity deserves from thee something nobler, it asks for love, for understanding, for comradeship, for the help of the equal and brother.

186 – The contributions of evil to the good of the world and the harm sometimes done by the virtuous are distressing to the soul enamoured of good. Nevertheless be not distressed nor confounded, but study rather and calmly understand God's ways with humanity.

Sri Aurobindo means that there is a height in the consciousness where the ordinary notions of good and bad lose all their value.[8]
And he advises us, instead of being affected by the way things happen on earth, to rise in consciousness to communion with the Divine; then we shall understand why things are as they are.

29 October 1969

187 – In God's providence there is no evil, but only good or its preparation.

188 – Virtue and vice were made for thy soul's struggle and progress; but for results they belong to God, who fulfils himself beyond vice and virtue.

---

[8] This sentence was in English in the original.

On Thoughts and Aphorisms

Vice and virtue are inventions of human thought for the needs of evolution and progress — but in the Divine Consciousness, vice and virtue do not exist.
 The whole universe is in a slow ascending evolution towards That which it must manifest.

30 October 1969

189 – Live within; be not shaken by outward happenings.

190 – Fling not thy alms abroad everywhere in an ostentation of charity; understand and love where thou helpest. Let thy soul grow within thee.

191 – Help the poor while the poor are with thee; but study also and strive that there may be no poor for thy assistance.

To live within in a constant aspiration for the Divine enables us to look at life with a smile and to remain peaceful whatever the outer circumstances may be.
 As for the poor, Sri Aurobindo says that to come to their help is good, provided that it is not a vain ostentation of charity, but that it is far nobler to seek a remedy for poverty so that there may be no poor left on earth.

31 October 1969

192 – The old Indian social ideal demanded of the priest voluntary simplicity of life, purity, learning and the gratuitous instruction of the community, of the prince, war, government, protection of the weak and the giving up of his life in the battle-field, of the merchant, trade, gain and the return of his gains to the community by free giving, of the serf, labour for the rest and material havings.

Jnana

In atonement for his serfhood, it spared him the tax of self-denial, the tax of blood and the tax of his riches.

In the beginning, about six thousand years ago, this was absolutely true, and each individual was classed *according to his nature*. Afterwards it became a rigid and more and more arbitrary social convenience (according to birth), which completely ignored the true nature of the individual. It became a false conception and had to disappear.

But gradually, with human progress, human activities are being classified more and more in a similar, less rigid but much truer way (according to each one's nature and capacity).

7 November 1969

193 – The existence of poverty is the proof of an unjust and ill-organised society, and our public charities are but the first tardy awakening in the conscience of a robber.

194 – Valmikie, our ancient epic poet, includes among the signs of a just and enlightened state of society not only universal education, morality and spirituality but this also that there shall be "none who is compelled to eat coarse food, none uncrowned and unanointed, or who lives a mean and petty slave of luxuries."

195 – The acceptance of poverty is noble and beneficial in a class or an individual, but it becomes fatal and pauperises life of its richness and expansion if it is perversely organised into a general or national ideal.

196 – Poverty is no more a necessity of social life than disease of the natural body; false habits of life and an ignorance of our true organisation are in both cases the peccant causes of an avoidable disorder.

On Thoughts and Aphorisms

> *Will a day come when there will be no more poor people and no more suffering in the world?*

That is absolutely certain for all those who understand Sri Aurobindo's teaching and have faith in him.

It is with the intention of creating a place where this can come about that we want to establish Auroville.

But for this realisation to be possible, each one of us must make an effort to transform himself, for most of the sufferings of men are the result of their own mistakes, both physical and moral.

8 November 1969

> *How can you believe that in Auroville there will be no more suffering so long as people who come to live there are men of the same world, born with the same weaknesses and faults?*

I have never thought that there would no more be suffering in Auroville, because men, as they are, love suffering and call it to them even while they curse it.

But we shall try to teach them to truly love peace and to try to practise equality.

What I meant was involuntary poverty and begging.

Life in Auroville will be organised in such a way that this does not exist — and if beggars come from outside, either they will have to go away or they will be given shelter and taught the joy of work.

9 November 1969

> *What is the fundamental difference between the ideal of the Ashram and the ideal of Auroville?*

There is no fundamental difference in the attitude towards the future and the service of the Divine.

But the people in the Ashram are considered to have consecrated their lives to Yoga (except, of course, the students who are here only for their studies and who are not expected to have made their choice in life).

Whereas in Auroville simply the goodwill to make a collective experiment for the progress of humanity is sufficient to gain admittance.

10 November 1969

197 – Athens, not Sparta, is the progressive type for mankind. Ancient India with its ideal of vast riches and vast spending was the greatest of nations. Modern India with its trend towards national asceticism has fully become poor in life and sunk into weakness and degradation.

198 – Do not dream that when thou hast got rid of material poverty, men will even so be happy or satisfied or society freed from ills, troubles and problems. This is only the first and lowest necessity. While the soul within remains defectively organised, there will always be outward unrest, disorder and revolution.

This is quite obvious and this is what we are trying to make people understand. A safe and quiet life is not enough to make people happy. Inner development is necessary, and the peace that comes from a conscious contact with the Divine.

13 November 1969

199 – Disease will always return to the body if the soul is flawed; for the sins of the mind are the secret cause of the sins of the body. So too poverty and trouble will

always return on man in society, so long as the mind of the race is subjected to egoism.

200 – Religion and philosophy seek to rescue man from his ego; then the kingdom of heaven within will be spontaneously reflected in an external divine city.

Sri Aurobindo used the words philosophy and religion so that everyone could understand. But he knew very well that the effective remedy for human egoism lies beyond philosophy and religion, in a true spiritual life accepted and lived on earth by the physical consciousness itself — this makes it truly capable of getting rid of the ego once and for all.

15 November 1969

201 – Mediaeval Christianity said to the race, "Man, thou art in thy earthly life an evil thing and a worm before God; renounce then egoism, live for a future state and submit thyself to God and His priest." The results were not over-good for humanity. Modern knowledge says to the race, "Man, thou art an ephemeral animal and no more to Nature than the ant and the earthworm, a transitory speck only in the universe. Live then for the State and submit thyself antlike to the trained administrator and the scientific expert." Will this gospel succeed any better than the other?

202 – Vedanta says rather, "Man, thou art of one nature and substance with God, one soul with thy fellowmen. Awake and progress then to thy utter divinity, live for God in thyself and in others." This gospel which was given only to the few, must now be offered to all mankind for its deliverance.

Jnana

There is nothing to add. Sri Aurobindo has clearly and masterfully stated first the evil and then its remedy. All we have to do is to put into practice what he has taught us.

16 November 1969

203 – The human race always progresses most when most it asserts its importance to Nature, its freedom and its universality.

204 – Animal man is the obscure starting-point, the present natural man the varied and tangled mid-road, but supernatural man the luminous and transcendent goal of our human journey.

Man finds his full power for progress when he no longer feels bound to Nature or limited by her laws.

Nature is only a limited expression of the Divine, whereas man was created to become the conscious expression of the Divine, with all the possibilities of power and light which that implies.

18 November 1969

205 – Life and action culminate and are eternally crowned for thee when thou hast attained the power of symbolising and manifesting in every thought and act, in art, literature and life, in wealth-getting, wealth-having or wealth-spending, in home, government and society, the One Immortal in His lower mortal being.

No doubt, this is the description of man when he reaches the summit of his being. But it is only the first step of the superman.

24 November 1969

Karma

(Works)

Fourth Period of Commentaries

(1969–1970)

Karma (Works)

Self-development and spiritual aspiration enable one to master one's karma.

To learn is good. To become is better.

The Mother

206 – God leads man while man is misleading himself; the higher nature watches over the stumblings of his lower mortality; this is the tangle and contradiction out of which we have to escape into the self-unity to which alone is possible a clear knowledge and a faultless action.

The only safety in life, the only way to escape from the consequences of past errors, is an inner development leading to conscious union with the Divine Presence; the only effective guide, the Truth of our being and of all beings.

25 November 1969

207 – That thou shouldst have pity on creatures is well, but not well, if thou art a slave to thy pity. Be a slave to nothing except to God, not even to His most luminous angels.

For those who want to live according to Truth, the only way is to become conscious of the Divine Presence and to live exclusively according to Its Will.

This is the only way to escape from evil and suffering, the only way to be always in peace, light and joy.

26 November 1969

208 – Beatitude is God's aim for humanity; get this supreme good for thyself first that thou mayst distribute it entirely to thy fellow-beings.

209 – He who acquires for himself alone, acquires ill though he may call it heaven and virtue.

Man has a right to beatitude since that is what he was created for. But any egocentric movement is the very opposite of this beatitude; so that if you seek it for yourself alone, you repel it instead of attracting it. By self-forgetfulness, by self-giving, without asking anything in return, by merging, so to say, into this beatitude so that it may shine upon all, you find the inner peace and joy which never leave you.

29 November 1969

What is the difference between "self-forgetfulness" and "self-giving"?

Self-forgetfulness may simply be a passive state resulting from a total lack of egoism. Self-giving, which takes its full value when it is directed towards the Divine, is an active movement which includes love in its purest and highest form.

A total self-giving to the Divine is the true purpose of existence.

30 November 1969

210 – In my ignorance I thought anger could be noble and vengeance grandiose; but now when I watch Achilles in his epic fury, I see a very fine baby in a very fine rage and I am pleased and amused.

211 – Power is noble, when it overtops anger; destruction is grandiose, but it loses caste when it proceeds from

vengeance. Leave these things, for they belong to a lower humanity.

Anger and vengeance belong to a lower humanity, the humanity of yesterday and not of tomorrow.

1 December 1969

212 – Poets make much of death and external afflictions; but the only tragedies are the soul's failures and the only epic man's triumphant ascent towards godhead.

Usually man is not afflicted with the only thing truly tragic, the failure to find one's soul and to live according to its law.[1]

In truth, the only thing that is truly tragic is not to become conscious of one's soul, the psychic being, and not to be entirely guided by it in one's life.

To die before having found one's soul and lived according to its law, that is the true failure.

And the true epic, the true glory is to find the Divine in oneself and to live according to His law.

3 December 1969

213 – The tragedies of the heart and the body are the weeping of children over their little griefs and their broken toys. Smile within thyself, but comfort the children; join also, if thou canst, in their play.

It is the narrowness of the human consciousness that makes tragedies out of events which for the Divine Consciousness are only movements in the general evolution. But even when one

---

[1] This sentence was in English in the original.

sees that, one can and must keep a profound sympathy for those who are still living in the throes of ignorance.

4 December 1969

214 – "There is always something abnormal and eccentric about men of genius." And why not? For genius itself is an abnormal birth and out of man's ordinary centre.

215 – Genius is Nature's first attempt to liberate the imprisoned god out of her human mould; the mould has to suffer in the process. It is astonishing that the cracks are so few and unimportant.

Once a man becomes conscious of the Divine and unites with Him, he certainly becomes abnormal to ordinary eyes, for he no longer has the weaknesses that make up ordinary human nature.

But fortunately for him, by the very fact of his inner realisation, he loses man's habit of boasting and is thus able to avoid the ill will of others.

5 December 1969

216 – Nature sometimes gets into a fury with her own resistance, then she damages the brain in order to free the inspiration; for in this effort the equilibrium of the average material brain is her chief opponent. Pass over the madness of such and profit by their inspiration.

It is indeed wise to look at everything with the calm smile of perfect trust. For, with his present consciousness, man can hardly understand the aims of the Supreme Lord.

7 December 1969

217 – Who can bear Kali rushing into the system in her fierce force and burning godhead? Only the man whom Krishna already possesses.

This is a charming and most expressive way of saying that only the conscious Divine Presence is capable of mastering and conquering all violence.

8 December 1969

218 – Hate not the oppressor, for, if he is strong, thy hate increases his force of resistance; if he is weak, thy hate was needless.

219 – Hatred is a sword of power, but its edge is always double. It is like the Kritya[2] of the ancient magicians which, if baulked of its prey, returned in fury to devour its sender.

220 – Love God in thy opponent, even while thou strikest him; so shall neither have hell for his portion.

221 – Men talk of enemies, but where are they? I only see wrestlers of one party or the other in the great arena of the universe.

All this is written to awaken mankind to the sense of its own unity. When one has become conscious of this Unity and when one sees the Divine in all beings, it is easy to feel as Sri Aurobindo recommends.

9 December 1969

---

[2] Magic process.

222 – The saint and the angel are not the only divinities; admire also the Titan and the Giant.

223 – The old writings call the Titans the elder gods. So they still are; nor is any god entirely divine unless there is hidden in him also a Titan.

224 – If I cannot be Rama, then I would be Ravana; for he is the dark side of Vishnu.[3]

This means that sweetness without strength and goodness without power are incomplete and cannot totally express the Divine.

I could say in keeping with the kind of image used by Sri Aurobindo, that the charity and generosity of a converted Asura are infinitely more effective than those of an innocent angel.

11 December 1969

225 – Sacrifice, sacrifice, sacrifice always, but for the sake of God and humanity, not for the sake of sacrifice.

226 – Selfishness kills the soul; destroy it. But take care that your altruism does not kill the souls of others.

227 – Very usually, altruism is only the sublimest form of selfishness.

How can altruism kill the soul of others?

By helping others materially (altruism), if at the same time you want to impose your own viewpoint on them, you will kill their

---

[3] Rama was an avatar or incarnation of Vishnu; Ravana was a Titan (Asura), mortal enemy of Rama.

soul, because moral and social rules can be no substitute for the inner law which each one must receive from his soul.

13 December 1969

228 – He who will not slay when God bids him, works in the world an incalculable havoc.

229 – Respect human life as long as you can; but respect more the life of humanity.

230 – Men slay out of uncontrollable anger, hatred or vengeance; they shall suffer the rebound now or hereafter; or they slay to serve a selfish end, coldly; God shall not pardon them. If thou slay, first let thy soul have known death for a reality and seen God in the smitten, the stroke and the striker.

In what kind of circumstances does God give the command to slay?

This is a question I cannot answer, because God has never asked me to slay.

14 December 1969

231 – Courage and love are the only indispensable virtues; even if all the others are eclipsed or fall asleep, these two will save the soul alive.

232 – Meanness and selfishness are the only sins that I find it difficult to pardon; yet they alone are almost universal. Therefore these also must not be hated in others, but in ourselves annihilated.

233 — Nobleness and generosity are the soul's ethereal firmament; without them, one looks at an insect in a dungeon.

234 — Let not thy virtues be such as men praise or reward, but such as make for thy perfection and God in thy nature demands of thee.

Could you give me your definitions of the following words?
1. Courage and love
2. Meanness and selfishness
3. Nobleness and generosity.

1. Courage is the total absence of fear in any form.
2. Love is self-giving without asking anything in return.
3. Meanness is a weakness that calculates and demands from others the virtues one does not possess oneself.
4. Selfishness is to put oneself at the centre of the universe and to want everything to exist for one's own satisfaction.
5. Nobleness is to refuse all personal calculation.
6. Generosity is to find one's own satisfaction in the satisfaction of others.

15 December 1969

235 — Altruism, duty, family, country, humanity are the prisons of the soul when they are not its instruments.

236 — Our country is God the Mother; speak not evil of her unless thou canst do it with love and tenderness.

237 — Men are false to their country for their own profit; yet they go on thinking they have a right to turn in horror from the matricide.

How can "altruism, duty, family, country, humanity" become true instruments of the soul?

The soul belongs to the Divine, and owes obedience and service to the Divine alone. If the Divine commands it to work for family, country or humanity, then it is all right and it can do so without being imprisoned.

If the command does not come from the Divine, to serve these things is only to obey social and moral conventions.

17 December 1969

238 – Break the moulds of the past, but keep safe its gains and its spirit, or else thou hast no future.

239 – Revolutions hew the past to pieces and cast it into a cauldron, but what has emerged is the old Aeson with a new visage.

240 – The world has had only half a dozen successful revolutions and most even of these were very like failures; yet it is by great and noble failures that humanity advances.

What does Sri Aurobindo mean by "great and noble failures"?

The greatness and nobleness of an event do not depend on material success, but on the feelings which inspire it and the goal which men have pursued.

It is not success that confers greatness but the motive of action and the nobleness of the feelings which inspire it.

18 December 1969

241 – Atheism is a necessary protest against the wickedness of

the Churches and the narrowness of creeds. God uses it as a stone to smash these soiled card-houses.

242 – How much hatred and stupidity men succeed in packing up decorously and labelling "Religion"!

Which is better: religion or atheism?

So long as religions exist, atheism will be indispensable to counter-balance them. Both must disappear to make way for a sincere and disinterested search for Truth and a total consecration to the object of this search.

21 December 1969

243 – God guides best when He tempts worst, loves entirely when He punishes cruelly, helps perfectly when violently He opposes.

244 – If God did not take upon Himself the burden of tempting men, the world would very soon go to perdition.

245 – Suffer yourself to be tempted within so that you may exhaust in the struggle your downward propensities.

246 – If you leave it to God to purify, He will exhaust the evil in you subjectively; but if you insist on guiding yourself, you will fall into much outward sin and suffering.

247 – Call not everything evil which men call evil, but only that reject which God has rejected; call not everything good which men call good, but accept only what God has accepted.

If one gives oneself completely to the Divine, is it necessary to develop one's personal will, one's power of choice, etc.? Will these things not become obstacles?

Personal will and power of choice are necessary qualities for those who live in the ordinary ignorance and illusion.

True self-giving to the Divine of course means their surrender. But unfortunately, many people live in the illusion that they have entirely given themselves to the Divine, and yet preserve in themselves a very active "ego" which prevents them from clearly perceiving the Divine Will; if these people abandon their personal will and discernment, they are in danger of becoming incoherent and erratic.

You must first acquire a perfect sincerity in order to be sure of not deceiving yourself, and you must have clear evidence that it is truly the Divine Will which moves and guides you.

22 December 1969

248 – Men in the world have two lights, duty and principle; but he who has passed over to God, has done with both and replaced them by God's will. If men abuse thee for this, care not, O divine instrument, but go on thy way like the wind or the sun fostering and destroying.

249 – Not to cull the praises of men has God made thee His own, but to do fearlessly His bidding.

250 – Accept the world as God's theatre; be thou the mask of the Actor and let Him act through thee. If men praise or hiss thee, know that they too are masks; and take God within for thy only critic and audience.

The first thing needed is to become conscious of the Divine Will, and in order to do that one must no longer have any desires or personal will.

The best way to achieve this is to direct one's whole aspiration towards the Divine Perfection, to give oneself to it without reserve and to rely on That alone for all satisfaction.

All the rest will follow as a result.

23 December 1969

251 – If Krishna be alone on one side and the armed and organised world with its hosts and its shrapnel and its maxims on the other, yet prefer thy divine solitude. Care not if the world passes over thy body and its shrapnel tear thee to pieces and its cavalry trample thy limbs into shapeless mire by the wayside; for the mind was always a simulacrum and the body a carcass. The spirit liberated from its casings ranges and triumphs.

This is to tell us that the only choice to be made is to unite with the Divine in spite of everything, even the opposition of the whole world, because the world only has an apparent strength in the mental and the physical, whereas the Divine possesses the eternal power of Truth.

26 December 1969

252 – If thou think defeat is the end of thee, then go not forth to fight, even though thou be the stronger. For Fate is not purchased by any man nor is Power bound over to her possessors. But defeat is not the end, it is only a gate or a beginning.

253 – I have failed, thou sayest. Say rather that God is circling about towards His object.

254 – Foiled by the world, thou turnest to seize upon God. If the world is stronger than thou, thinkest thou God is weaker? Turn to Him rather for His bidding and for strength to fulfil it.

Why does God need to "circle about towards His object"? He can easily reach it immediately if He wants to, and make everybody's work easier and more effective.

Surely Sri Aurobindo did not say that "God" *needs* to circle about, because he is all-powerful; but his power is not an arbitrary one as men understand it.

To begin to understand anything about this, one must know and feel that in the whole universe *there is nothing* which is not an expression of his omnipotent and omnipresent will; and only by consciously uniting with Him can one begin to understand this, not mentally, but through an experience of consciousness and vision.

In his ordinary consciousness, even with the widest intelligence, man can only grasp an infinitesimal part of creation and so he cannot understand it and still less judge it.

And if we want to hasten the transformation of the world, the best we can do is to give ourselves without reserve or calculation to That which knows.

28 December 1969

255 – So long as a cause has on its side one soul that is intangible in faith, it cannot perish.

256 – Reason gives me no basis for this faith, thou murmurest. Fool! if it did, faith would not be needed or demanded of thee.

257 – Faith in the heart is the obscure and often distorted reflection of a hidden knowledge. The believer is often more plagued by doubt than the most inveterate sceptic. He persists because there is something subconscient in him which knows. That tolerates both his blind faith and twilit doubts and drives towards the revelation of that which it knows.

Is it good to have a "blind faith" which neither questions nor reasons?

What men usually call blind faith is in fact what the Divine Grace sometimes gives to those whose intelligence is not developed enough to have true knowledge. So blind faith can be something very respectable, although it is of course clear that one who has *true* knowledge is in a far superior position.

29 December 1969

To which plane does faith belong — mental or psychic?

Faith is an exclusively psychic phenomenon.

30 December 1969

258 – The world thinks that it moves by the light of reason, but it is really impelled by its faiths and instincts.

259 – Reason adapts itself to the faith or argues out a justification of the instincts; but it receives the impulse subconsciously, therefore men think that they act rationally.

260 – The only business of reason is to arrange and criticise the perceptions. It has neither in itself any means of

positive conclusion nor any command to action. When it pretends to originate or impel, it is masking other agencies.

261 – Until Wisdom comes to thee, use the reason for its God-given purposes and faith and instinct for theirs. Why shouldst thou set thy members to war upon each other?

What are the highest aims of reason, faith and instinct in ordinary life and in spiritual life?

Each one has his own aims according to his nature and the goal he wants to attain in ordinary life.

As for spiritual life, it has only one goal: to know the Divine and to unite with Him, by every possible means and with the help of faith, which is certainly the most powerful motive-force for beginners.

31 December 1969

262 – Perceive always and act in the light of thy increasing perceptions, but not those of the reasoning brain only. God speaks to the heart when the brain cannot understand him.

263 – If thy heart tell thee, Thus and by such means and at such a time it will happen, believe it not. But if it gives thee the purity and wideness of God's command, hearken to it.

264 – When thou hast the command, care only to fulfil it. The rest is God's will and arrangement which men call chance and luck and fortune.

It is obviously in the silence of the mind that it is possible to perceive the Divine Command. The true way of knowing is above words and thoughts.

When this phenomenon occurs, it becomes very clear, because one knows the Divine Command *first*, and the words to describe it come later.

1 January 1970

265 – If thy aim be great and thy means small, still act; for by action alone these can increase to thee.

266 – Care not for time and success. Act out thy part, whether it be to fail or to prosper.

267 – There are three forms in which the command may come, the will and faith in thy nature, thy ideal on which heart and brain are agreed and the voice of Himself or His angels.

268 – There are times when action is unwise or impossible; then go into Tapasya[4] in some physical solitude or in the retreats of thy soul and await whatever divine word or manifestation.

269 – Leap not too quickly at all voices, for there are lying spirits ready to deceive thee; but let thy heart be pure and afterwards listen.

It is indeed of utmost importance not to accept each and every voice as coming from the Divine, because one is liable to obey the command of an imposter. There is only one guarantee which is a complete absence of all personal desire, even the desire of

---

[4] Austerity, spiritual discipline.

serving the Divine, and the fact of being immersed in a total peace. Only then can one be sure of one's discernment.

3 January 1970

270 – There are times when God seems to be sternly on the side of the past; then what has been and is, sits firm as on a throne and clothes itself with an irrevocable "I shall be." Then persevere, though thou seem to be fighting the Master of all; for this is His sharpest trial.

271 – All is not settled when a cause is humanly lost and hopeless; all is settled, only when the soul renounces its effort.

This is to encourage us not to allow ourselves to be influenced by appearances and to persist in our effort even if it seems to have no result.

In life, we must do what is revealed to us as the true thing to be done, even if others mock and criticise; for the opinion of men has no value, the Divine Will alone is true and will triumph.

4 January 1970

272 – He who would win high spiritual degrees, must pass endless tests and examinations. But most are anxious only to bribe the examiner.

273 – Fight, while thy hands are free, with thy hands and thy voice and thy brain and all manner of weapons. Art thou chained in the enemy's dungeons and have his gags silenced thee? Fight with thy silent all-besieging soul and thy wide-ranging will-power and when thou art dead, fight still with the world-encompassing force that went out from God within thee.

Truth is a difficult and strenuous conquest. One must be a true warrior to make this conquest, a warrior who fears nothing, neither enemies nor death, for, against the whole world, with or without a body, the struggle continues and will end in Victory.

6 January 1970

274 – Thou thinkest the ascetic in his cave or on his mountain-top a stone and a do-nothing. What dost thou know? He may be filling the world with the mighty currents of his will and changing it by the pressure of his soul-state.

275 – That which the liberated sees in his soul on its mountain-tops, heroes and prophets spring up in the material world to proclaim and accomplish.

276 – The Theosophists are wrong in their circumstances but right in the essential. If the French Revolution took place, it was because a soul on the Indian snows dreamed of God as freedom, brotherhood and equality.

This is simply to show us that the power of the spirit is far greater than all material powers. But both are indispensable for the realisation.

7 January 1970

277 – All speech and action comes prepared out of the eternal Silence.

278 – There is no disturbance in the depths of the Ocean, but above there is the joyous thunder of its shouting and its racing shoreward; so is it with the liberated soul in the midst of violent action. The soul does not act; it only breathes out from itself overwhelming action.

This tells us again that That which causes action, the Consciousness and Power which are manifested in action, are quite different from the individuals who carry it out materially and who think in their ignorance that they are the originators of action.

8 January 1970

279 – O soldier and hero of God, where for thee is sorrow or shame or suffering? For thy life is a glory, thy deeds a consecration, victory thy apotheosis, defeat thy triumph.

For one who is totally consecrated to the Divine, there can be neither shame nor suffering, for the Divine is always with him and the Divine Presence changes all things into glory.

9 January 1970

280 – Do thy lower members still suffer the shock of sin and sorrow? But above, seen of thee or unseen, thy soul sits royal, calm, free and triumphant. Believe that the Mother will ere the end have done her work and made the very earth of thy being a joy and a purity.

281 – If thy heart is troubled within thee, if for long seasons thou makest no progress, if thy strength faint and repine, remember always the eternal word of our Lover and Master, "I will free thee from all sin and evil; do not grieve."

Here, what Sri Aurobindo calls the soul is the Divine Presence in each one of us; and the certitude of this constant Presence within us will alleviate all our sorrow by convincing us of the ultimate victory which is certain.

10 January 1970

282 – Purity is in thy soul; but for actions, where is their purity or impurity?

Sri Aurobindo does not use the word purity in the ordinary moral sense. For him, "purity" means "exclusively under the influence of the Divine", expressing only the Divine.
At present, no action on earth can be like this.

12 January 1970

283 – O Death, our masked friend and maker of opportunities, when thou wouldst open the gate, hesitate not to tell us beforehand; for we are not of those who are shaken by its iron jarring.

284 – Death is sometimes a rude valet; but when he changes this robe of earth for that brighter raiment, his horse-play and impertinences can be pardoned.

285 – Who shall slay thee, O soul immortal? Who shall torture thee, O God ever-joyous?

Why has death been associated with sorrow ever since the beginning?

Human ignorance and egoism are the cause of sorrow. But this sorrow has also played its part in the evolution of humanity.

13 January 1970

What part has sorrow played in the evolution of humanity?

Sorrow, desire, suffering, ambition and every other similar reaction in the feelings and sensations have all contributed to make consciousness emerge from the inconscience and to awaken this consciousness to the will for progress.

14 January 1970

286 – Think this when thy members would fain make love with depression and weakness, "I am Bacchus and Ares and Apollo; I am Agni pure and invincible; I am Surya ever burning mightily."

287 – Shrink not from the Dionysian cry and rapture within thee, but see that thou be not a straw upon those billows.

288 – Thou hast to learn to bear all the gods within thee and never stagger with their inrush or break under their burden.

This is to teach man not to be dominated or frightened by the gods of the various religions; for, as a human being, man carries within himself the possibility of uniting with the Supreme Lord and becoming conscious of Him.

15 January 1970

289 – Mankind have wearied of strength and joy and called sorrow and weakness virtue, wearied of knowledge and called ignorance holiness, wearied of love and called heartlessness enlightenment and wisdom.

290 – There are many kinds of forbearance. I saw a coward hold out his cheek to the smiter; I saw a physical weakling struck by a strong and self-approving bully look quietly and intently at the aggressor; I saw God incarnate smile lovingly on those who stoned him. The

first was ridiculous, the second terrible, the third divine and holy.

Sri Aurobindo tells us that to radiate love in all circumstances is a sign of the Divine who has equal love for the one who strikes him and the one who worships him — what a lesson for humanity!

17 January 1970

291 – It is noble to pardon thine own injurers, but not so noble to pardon wrongs done to others. Nevertheless pardon these too, but when needful, calmly avenge.

292 – When Asiatics massacre, it is an atrocity; when Europeans, it is a military exigency. Appreciate the distinction and ponder over this world's virtues.

All this makes us feel very deeply the foolishness of human judgments based on self-interest and the reactions of the ego.
So long as men remain in their present state of ignorance, their judgments and opinions are worthless in the face of Truth and should be considered as such.

20 January 1970

293 – Watch the too indignantly righteous. Before long you will find them committing or condoning the very offence which they have so fiercely censured.

294 – "There is very little real hypocrisy among men." True, but there is a great deal of diplomacy and still more of self-deceit. The last is of three varieties, conscious, subconscious and half-conscious; but the third is the most dangerous.

It seems to me that conscious self-deceit is the worst, isn't it?

Conscious self-deceit is rare because it implies a great development of consciousness together with a perverted will to deceive, which leads to the most dangerous kind of falsehood; but it is perhaps also the easiest to cure, for the consciousness is already awakened and it only has to be made aware of its mistake and to take the decision to correct it in order to have the power to do so.

Others must first become conscious of what they are doing and this usually takes a long time.

21 January 1970

295 – Be not deceived by men's shows of virtue, neither disgusted by their open or secret vices. These things are the necessary shufflings in a long transition-period of humanity.

296 – Be not repelled by the world's crookednesses; the world is a wounded and venomous snake wriggling towards a destined off-sloughing and perfection. Wait, for it is a divine wager; and out of this baseness, God will emerge brilliant and triumphant.

Sri Aurobindo tells us that man is a transitional being and that from all the sufferings of the world will emerge a being of light capable of manifesting the Divine.

Thus, all those who are not satisfied with the world as it is, know that their aspiration does not rise in vain and that the world is changing.

If consecration and effort are associated with the aspiration, things will move faster.

22 January 1970

On Thoughts and Aphorisms

> 297 – Why dost thou recoil from a mask? Behind its odious, grotesque or terrible seemings Krishna laughs at thy foolish anger, thy more foolish scorn or loathing and thy most foolish terror.
>
> 298 – When thou findest thyself scorning another, look then at thy own heart and laugh at thy folly.

Is it only our mental conception that sees grotesque and odious things, or are they really as we see them? And the same applies to beauty, doesn't it?

It is certain that in the present state of the physical world, appearances are still very deceptive; physical beauty is not always the sign of a beautiful soul, and an ugly or grotesque body may conceal a genius or a resplendent soul.

But for one who has more inner sensitivity, appearances are no longer deceptive and he can perceive the ugliness hidden beneath a pretty face and the beauty concealed beneath a mask of ugliness.

There are also cases, and these are becoming more and more numerous, where the appearance reveals the inner reality which then becomes discernible to all.

23 January 1970

> 299 – Avoid vain disputing; but exchange views freely. If dispute thou must, learn from thy adversary; for even from a fool, if thou listen not with the ear and the reasoning mind but the soul's light, thou canst gather much wisdom.
>
> 300 – Turn all things to honey; this is the law of divine living.
>
> 301 – Private dispute should always be avoided; but shrink

not from the public battle; yet even there appropriate[5] the strength of thy adversary.

302 – When thou hearest an opinion that displeases thee, study and find out the truth in it.

If you sincerely want to live according to the Truth, you must know that you can learn from everything and that you have the possibility of making progress at every moment. A great stupidity can often reveal a great light to you, if you know how to see it.

24 January 1970

303 – The mediaeval ascetics hated women and thought they were created by God for the temptation of monks. One may be allowed to think more nobly both of God and of woman.

304 – If a woman has tempted thee, is it her fault or thine? Be not a fool and a self-deceiver.

305 – There are two ways of avoiding the snare of woman; one is to shun all women and the other to love all beings.

What should be the ideal of a modern woman in ordinary life?

In ordinary life, women can have all the ideas they like, it is not very important.[6]

---

[5] Possible alternative reading: appreciate.
[6] Later, Mother added, "For women, in ordinary life, the ideal is good health and harmony."

On Thoughts and Aphorisms

From the spiritual point of view, men and women are equal in their capacity to realise the Divine. Each one must do so in his (or her) own way and according to his (or her) own possibilities.

25 January 1970

306 – Asceticism is no doubt very healing, a cave very peaceful and the hill-tops wonderfully pleasant; nevertheless do thou act in the world as God intended thee.

Sri Aurobindo shows us that one can be an ascetic by preference and not out of abnegation; and so he makes us understand that to be a servant of the Lord and to act only according to His will is a far higher state than any personal choice, no matter how saintly it may seem.

26 January 1970

307 – Three times God laughed at Shankara, first, when he returned to burn the corpse of his mother, again, when he commented on the Isha Upanishad and the third time when he stormed about India preaching inaction.

The Lord laughed when this man, who thought himself so wise, complied with conventions, wrote useless words and gave an example of overactivity in order to preach inaction.

27 January 1970

308 – Men labour only after success and if they are fortunate enough to fail, it is because the wisdom and force of Nature overbear their intellectual cleverness. God alone knows when and how to blunder wisely and fail effectively.

Karma

309 – Distrust the man who has never failed and suffered; follow not his fortunes, fight not under his banner.

310 – There are two who are unfit for greatness and freedom, the man who has never been a slave to another and the nation that has never been under the yoke of foreigners.

Certain essential qualities can only develop through suffering and difficulties. Men run away from them in their ignorance, but the Supreme Lord imposes them on those He has chosen to represent Him on earth in order to hasten their development — for he is the Supreme Wisdom.

28 January 1970

311 – Fix not the time and the way in which the ideal shall be fulfilled. Work and leave time and way to God all-knowing.

312 – Work as if the ideal had to be fulfilled swiftly and in thy lifetime; persevere as if thou knewest it not to be unless purchased by a thousand years yet of labour. That which thou darest not expect till the fifth millennium, may bloom out with tomorrow's dawning and that which thou hopest and lustest after now, may have been fixed for thee in thy hundredth advent.

This is exactly the attitude we should all have towards transformation: as much energy and ardour as if we were certain of achieving it in our present life, as much patience and endurance as if we needed centuries to realise it.

29 January 1970

313 – Each man of us has a million lives yet to fulfil upon earth. Why then this haste and clamour and impatience?

On Thoughts and Aphorisms

> 314 – Stride swiftly, for the goal is far; rest not unduly, for thy Master is waiting for thee at the end of thy journey.

Here again, as always, Sri Aurobindo sees every aspect of the question and while preaching calm and patience to the restless, he rouses and preaches energy to the indolent. In the union of opposites lies true wisdom and total effectiveness.

30 January 1970

> 315 – I am weary of the childish impatience which cries and blasphemes and denies the ideal because the Golden Mountains cannot be reached in our little day or in a few momentary centuries.

> 316 – Fix thy soul without desire upon the end and insist on it by the divine force within thee; then shall the end itself create its means, nay, it shall become its own means. For the end is Brahman and already accomplished; see it always as Brahman, see it always in thy soul as already accomplished.

Certainly, we all carry in our souls the divine end of the eternal journey, and our personal incapacity is the only thing that prevents us from being immediately aware of it.

Total and unconditional surrender to the Supreme Lord (Brahman) is the sole and wonderful way to cure this incapacity.

1 February 1970

> 317 – Plan not with the intellect, but let thy divine sight arrange thy plans for thee. When a means comes to thee as the thing to be done, make that thy aim; as for the end, it is, in the world, accomplishing itself and, in thy soul, already accomplished.

318 – Men see events as unaccomplished, to be striven for and effected. This is false seeing; events are not effected, they develop. The event is Brahman, already accomplished from of old, it is now manifesting.

One could say it in this way: everything exists from all eternity, and we become conscious of it progressively in what we call the material world.
This way of seeing and speaking is a complete reversal of the ordinary human consciousness.

2 February 1970

319 – As the light of a star reaches the earth hundreds of years after the star has ceased to exist, so the event already accomplished in Brahman at the beginning manifests itself now in our material experience.

Yes, but the will of Brahman that we should take part in this event dates back to the same moment and their relation remains the same. So the only thing that matters is not to act on personal impulse, but on the order received from Brahman.

4 February 1970

320 – Governments, societies, kings, police, judges, institutions, churches, laws, customs, armies are temporary necessities imposed on us for a few groups of centuries because God has concealed His face from us. When it appears to us again in its truth and beauty, then in that light they will vanish.

321 – The anarchic is the true divine state of man in the end as in the beginning; but in between it would lead us straight to the devil and his kingdom.

On Thoughts and Aphorisms

The Anarchic state is the self-government of each individual. And it will be the perfect government only when each one becomes conscious of the inner Divine and obeys Him and Him alone.

5 February 1970

322 – The communistic principle of society is intrinsically as superior to the individualistic as is brotherhood to jealousy and mutual slaughter; but all the practical schemes of Socialism invented in Europe are a yoke, a tyranny and a prison.

323 – If communism ever re-establishes itself successfully upon earth, it must be on a foundation of soul's brotherhood and the death of egoism. A forced association and a mechanical comradeship would end in a world-wide fiasco.

324 – Vedanta realised is the only practicable basis for a communistic society. It is the kingdom of the saints dreamed of by Christianity, Islam and Puranic Hinduism.

As Sri Aurobindo tells us so well, individualism is a kind of self-justified jealousy, the reign of each one for himself.

But the only true remedy is the exclusive and universal reign of the Supreme Lord, present and conscious in all beings, with a transitional government by those who are truly conscious of Him and entirely surrendered to His will.

7 February 1970

325 – "Freedom, equality, brotherhood," cried the French revolutionists, but in truth freedom only has been practised with a dose of equality; as for brotherhood,

only a brotherhood of Cain was founded — and of Barabbas. Sometimes it calls itself a Trust or Combine and sometimes the Concert of Europe.

326 – "Since liberty has failed," cries the advanced thought of Europe, "let us try liberty *cum* equality or, since the two are a little hard to pair, equality instead of liberty. For brotherhood, it is impossible; therefore we will replace it by industrial association." But this time also, I think, God will not be deceived.

As yet liberty, equality, fraternity are only words loudly proclaimed but never yet put into practice, and they cannot be put into practice so long as men remain what they are, ruled by their ego and all its desires instead of being ruled only by the One Supreme and supremely Divine.

8 February 1970

327 – India had three fortresses of a communal life, the village community, the larger joint family and the orders of the Sannyasins; all these are broken or breaking with the stride of egoistic conceptions of social life; but is not this after all only the breaking of these imperfect moulds on the way to a larger and diviner communism?

328 – The individual cannot be perfect until he has surrendered all he now calls himself to the divine Being. So also, until mankind gives all it has to God, never shall there be a perfected society.

Sri Aurobindo writes here in a clear and definite way what I tried to express before: no perfection can be attained so long as the government of the Supreme Lord is not recognised and admitted everywhere and in all things.

Liberty can only be manifested when all men know the liberty of the Supreme Lord.

Equality can only be manifested when all men become conscious of the Supreme Lord.

Fraternity can only be manifested when men feel that they are equally born of the Supreme Lord and one in His Oneness.

9 February 1970

329 – There is nothing small in God's eyes; let there be nothing small in thine. He bestows as much labour of divine energy on the formation of a shell as on the building of an empire. For thyself it is greater to be a good shoemaker than a luxurious and incompetent king.

330 – Imperfect capacity and effect in the work that is meant for thee is better than an artificial competency and a borrowed perfection.

331 – Not result is the purpose of action, but God's eternal delight in becoming, seeing and doing.

It is obvious that the greatness of an action does not depend on its scope, and its perfection does not depend on circumstances or on external conditions, but on the sincerity of the consecration with which it is done.

To do what the Divine wants you to do, in a total consecration of the being: this is the only thing that matters; the outer scope of the action is of no account.

10 February 1970

332 – God's world advances step by step fulfilling the lesser unit before it seriously attempts the larger. Affirm free nationality first, if thou wouldst ever bring the world to be one nation.

333 – A nation is not made by a common blood, a common tongue or a common religion; these are only important helps and powerful conveniences. But wherever communities of men not bound by family ties are united in one sentiment and aspiration to defend a common inheritance from their ancestors or assure a common future for their posterity, there a nation is already in existence.

334 – Nationality is a stride of the progressive God passing beyond the stage of the family; therefore the attachment to clan and tribe must weaken or perish before a nation can be born.

Thus Sri Aurobindo reveals to us the great political secret whose realisation can lead us to the union of all nations and finally to human unity.

11 February 1970

335 – Family, nationality, humanity are Vishnu's three strides from an isolated to a collective unity. The first has been fulfilled, we yet strive for the perfection of the second, towards the third we are reaching out our hands and the pioneer work is already attempted.

336 – With the present morality of the human race a sound and durable human unity is not yet possible; but there is no reason why a temporary approximation to it should

not be the reward of strenuous aspiration and untiring effort. By constant approximations and by partial realisations and temporary successes Nature advances.

As Sri Aurobindo has predicted, things are moving fast, and the situation of humanity has changed much since Sri Aurobindo began to work in the subtle physical: the idea of human unity has made great headway and is more widely understood.

12 February 1970

337 – Imitation is sometimes a good training-ship; but it will never fly the flag of the admiral.

338 – Rather hang thyself than belong to the horde of successful imitators.

This applies to artists and writers — nearly all are imitators and copyists. And yet only creators, those who have something new to say or show, should create.

13 February 1970

339 – Tangled is the way of works in the world. When Rama the Avatar murdered Vali,[7] or Krishna, who was God himself, assassinated, to liberate his nation, his tyrant uncle Kansa, who shall say whether they did good or did evil? But this we can feel, that they acted divinely.

This is a supremely elegant way of saying that all notions of good and evil are exclusively human and are worthless in the eyes of the Divine.

16 February 1970

---

[7] King of the monkeys.

340 – Reaction perfects and hastens progress by increasing and purifying the force within it. This is what the multitude of the weak cannot see who despair of their port when the ship is fleeing helplessly before the storm-wind, but it flees, hidden by the rain and the Ocean furrow, towards God's intended haven.

This is to teach us never to despair. Because, for those who are pure of heart and have an unshakable faith, the worst apparent defeat is only a veiled path leading to final victory.

17 February 1970

341 – Democracy was the protest of the human soul against the allied despotisms of autocrat, priest and noble; Socialism is the protest of the human soul against the despotism of a plutocratic democracy; Anarchism is likely to be the protest of the human soul against the tyranny of a bureaucratic Socialism. A turbulent and eager march from illusion to illusion and from failure to failure is the image of European progress.

342 – Democracy in Europe is the rule of the Cabinet minister, the corrupt deputy or the self-seeking capitalist masqued by the occasional sovereignty of a wavering populace; Socialism in Europe is likely to be the rule of the official and policeman masqued by the theoretic sovereignty of an abstract State. It is chimerical to enquire which is the better system; it would be difficult to decide which is the worse.

343 – The gain of democracy is the security of the individual's life, liberty and goods from the caprices of the tyrant one or the selfish few; its evil is the decline of greatness in humanity.

All human governments are a falsehood or a chimera. One can hope that one day the earth will be governed by the Truth only if the Supreme Lord makes this Truth evident to all.

18 February 1970

344 – This erring race of human beings dreams always of perfecting their environment by the machinery of government and society; but it is only by the perfection of the soul within that the outer environment can be perfected. What thou art within, that outside thee thou shalt enjoy; no machinery can rescue thee from the law of thy being.

345 – Be always vigilant against thy human proneness to persecute or ignore the reality even while thou art worshipping its semblance or token. Not human wickedness but human fallibility is the opportunity of Evil.

No law or government can save us from meeting in life the consequences of what we are.

Submit exclusively to the Divine Truth and It will govern life outside all human laws and governments.

19 February 1970

346 – Honour the garb of the ascetic, but look also at the wearer, lest hypocrisy occupy the holy places and inward saintliness become a legend.

347 – The many strive after competence or riches, the few embrace poverty as a bride; but, for thyself, strive after and embrace God only. Let Him choose for thee a king's palace or the bowl of the beggar.

348 – What is vice but an enslaving habit and virtue but a human opinion? See God and do His will; walk in whatever path He shall trace for thy goings.

This is perfect! True saintliness is to want and realise what the Divine wants for you, and true wisdom is to unite with Him so that you can clearly know what He wants of you and for you. All the rest is nothing but human convention and theory.

20 February 1970

349 – In the world's conflicts espouse not the party of the rich for their riches, nor of the poor for their poverty, of the king for his power and majesty nor of the people for their hope and fervour, but be on God's side always. Unless indeed He has commanded thee to war against Him! then do that with thy whole heart and strength and rapture.

350 – How shall I know God's will with me? I have to put egoism out of me, hunting it from every lair and burrow, and bathe my purified and naked soul in His infinite workings; then He himself will reveal it to me.

351 – Only the soul that is naked and unashamed can be pure and innocent, even as Adam was in the primal garden of humanity.

What is meant by "the soul that is naked and unashamed"? Isn't the soul always pure?

Yes, that is what Sri Aurobindo says. The soul does not wear any disguise, it shows itself as it is and cares nothing for men's judgments, because it is the faithful servant of the Divine whose abode it is.

23 February 1970

352 – Boast not thy riches, neither seek men's praise for thy poverty and self-denial; both these things are the coarse or the fine food of egoism.

353 – Altruism is good for man, but less good when it is a form of supreme self-indulgence and lives by pampering the selfishness of others.

354 – By altruism thou canst save thy soul, but see that thou save it not by indulging in his perdition thy brother.

355 – Self-denial is a mighty instrument for purification; it is not an end in itself nor a final law of living. Not to mortify thyself but to satisfy God in the world must be thy object.

356 – It is easy to distinguish the evil worked by sin and vice, but the trained eye sees also the evil done by self-righteous or self-regarding virtue.

Step by step and from every angle, Sri Aurobindo shows us how the Truth is above and beyond all contraries and opposites, beyond divisions — in a radiant and total Unity.

25 February 1970

357 – The Brahmin first ruled by the book and the ritual, the Kshatriya next by the sword and the buckler; now the Vaishya governs us by machinery and the dollar, and the Sudra, the liberated serf, presses in with his doctrine of

the kingdom of associated labour. But neither priest, king, merchant nor labourer is the true governor of humanity; the despotism of the tool and the mattock will fail like all the preceding despotisms. Only when egoism dies and God in man governs his own human universality, can this earth support a happy and contented race of beings.

There is nothing to say. Everything is clearly explained — only the divine government can be a true government.

26 February 1970

358 – Men run after pleasure and clasp feverishly that burning bride to their tormented bosoms; meanwhile a divine and faultless bliss stands behind them waiting to be seen and claimed and captured.

359 – Men hunt after petty successes and trivial masteries from which they fall back into exhaustion and weakness; meanwhile all the infinite force of God in the universe waits vainly to place itself at their disposal.

360 – Men burrow after little details of knowledge and group them into bounded and ephemeral thought-systems; meanwhile all infinite wisdom laughs above their heads and shakes wide the glory of her iridescent pinions.

361 – Men seek laboriously to satisfy and complement the little bounded being made of the mental impressions they have grouped about a mean and grovelling ego; meanwhile the spaceless and timeless Soul is denied its joyous and splendid manifestation.

On Thoughts and Aphorisms

This state of things must change for the supramental consciousness to reign on earth. But although the supramental consciousness has been at work on earth for more than a year,[8] has anything changed in this miserable condition?

28 February 1970

Since the supramental consciousness is at work on earth, won't these miserable conditions change in spite of everything?

Naturally, the first effect will be a change of consciousness, first among the most receptive, and then in a greater number of people.

A change in the general conditions of collective life can only come later, perhaps long after individual reactions have been transformed. The first noticeable result is a heightening of the general confusion, because the old principles have lost their authority, and men (except for a very few) are not ready to obey the Divine Command, because they are incapable of perceiving it.

1 March 1970

362 – O soul of India, hide thyself no longer with the darkened Pandits[9] of the Kaliyuga in the kitchen and the chapel, veil not thyself with the soulless rite, the obsolete law and the unblessed money of the Dakshina;[10] but seek in thy soul, ask of God and recover thy true Brahminhood and Kshatriyahood with the eternal Veda; restore the hidden truth of the Vedic sacrifice, return to the fulfilment of an older and mightier Vedanta.

---

[8] Mother is referring to the "New Consciousness" (or Superman Consciousness) which manifested on 1 January 1969.
[9] Scholars and interpreters of sacred texts.
[10] Offering made by the devotee to the brahmin priest.

This is to free us from so-called religious conventions which tell us what to do and what not to do. We must recover the true wisdom and receive directly from the Divine the precise indications for living in and for the Truth.

2 March 1970

363 – Limit not sacrifice to the giving up of earthly goods or the denial of some desires and yearnings, but let every thought and every work and every enjoyment be an offering to God within thee. Let thy steps walk in thy Lord, let thy sleep and waking be a sacrifice to Krishna.

364 – This is not according to my Shastra[11] or my Science, say the men of rule, formalists. Fool! is God then only a book that there should be nothing true and good except what is written?

365 – By which standard shall I walk, the word that God speaks to me, saying, "This is My will, O my servant," or the rules that men who are dead, have written? Nay, if I have to fear and obey any, I will fear and obey God rather and not the pages of a book or the frown of a Pandit.

366 – Thou mayst be deceived, wilt thou say, it may not be God's voice leading thee? Yet do I know that He abandons not those who have trusted Him even ignorantly, yet have I found that He leads wisely and lovingly even when He seems to deceive utterly, yet would I rather fall into the snare of the living God than be saved by trust in a dead formulary.

---

[11] Scriptures; prescribed law.

367 – Act according to the Shastra rather than thy self-will and desire; so shalt thou grow stronger to control the ravener in thee; but act according to God rather than the Shastra; so shalt thou reach to His highest which is far above rule and limit.

368 – The Law is for the bound and those whose eyes are sealed; if they walk not by it, they will stumble; but thou who art free in Krishna or hast seen his living light, walk holding the hand of thy Friend and by the lamp of eternal Veda.

369 – The Vedanta is God's lamp to lead thee out of this night of bondage and egoism; but when the light of Veda has dawned in thy soul, then even that divine lamp thou needest not, for now thou canst walk freely and surely in a high and eternal sunlight.

Strive exclusively to hear the command of the Supreme Lord, and if you are perfectly sincere, He will find a way to make you hear and recognise this command with certainty.

Such is the assurance given to all those who want to live according to the supreme Truth.

3 March 1970

370 – What is the use of only knowing? I say to thee, Act and be, for therefore God sent thee into this human body.

371 – What is the use of only being? I say to thee, Become, for therefore wast thou established as a man in this world of matter.

372 – The path of works is in a way the most difficult side

of God's triune causeway; yet is it not also, in this material world at least, the easiest, widest and most delightful? For at every moment we clash against God the worker and grow into His being by a thousand divine touches.

373 – This is the wonder of the way of works that even enmity to God can be made an agency of salvation. Sometimes God draws and attaches us most swiftly to Him by wrestling with us as our fierce, invincible and irreconcilable enemy.

In short, the divine grace is so marvellous that, whatever you do, it will lead you more or less quickly towards the Divine Goal.

5 March 1970

374 – Shall I accept death or shall I turn and wrestle with him and conquer? That shall be as God in me chooses. For whether I live or die, I am always.

375 – What is this then thou callest death? Can God die? O thou who fearest death, it is Life that has come to thee sporting with a death-head and wearing a mask of terror.

376 – There is a means to attain physical immortality and death is by our choice, not by Nature's compulsion. But who would care to wear one coat for a hundred years or be confined in one narrow and changeless lodging unto a long eternity?

If a person feels that his work is over in this life and that he has nothing more to offer, wouldn't it be better for him to die and be born again instead of dragging out an aimless existence?

This is what the unsatisfied ego asks itself when it finds that things are not going as it desires.
But someone who belongs to the Divine and wants to live in the truth knows that the Divine will keep him on earth as long as He perceives his usefulness on earth and will make him leave the earth when he has nothing more to do there. So the question cannot arise, and he will live quietly in the certitude of the Divine's supreme wisdom.

6 March 1970

You wrote yesterday: "But someone who belongs to the Divine...." Doesn't everyone, whoever he is, belong to the Divine?

When I say, "someone who belongs to the Divine", I mean a being who has abolished the ego within himself, who is constantly conscious of the Divine, who no longer has any personal will, who acts only under the divine impulsion and who has no other aim than to do what the Divine wants him to do.
I do not think there are many people in this state. And certainly these people will never worry whether their life is useful or not, since they exist only for and by the Divine and no longer have any personal life.

7 March 1970

377 – Fear and anxiety are perverse forms of will. What thou fearest and ponderest over, striking that note repeatedly in thy mind, thou helpest to bring about; for, if thy will above the surface of waking repels it, it is yet what thy

mind underneath is all along willing, and the subconscious mind is mightier, wider, better equipped to fulfil than thy waking force and intellect. But the spirit is stronger than both together; from fear and hope take refuge in the grandiose calm and careless mastery of the spirit.

378 – God made the infinite world by Self-knowledge which in its works is Will-Force self-fulfilling. He used ignorance to limit His infinity; but fear, weariness, depression, self-distrust and assent to weakness are the instruments by which He destroys what He created. When these things are turned on what is evil or harmful and ill-regulated within thee, then it is well; but if they attack thy very sources of life and strength, then seize and expel them or thou diest.

When these forces of destruction attack us, it proves that we are ready to be liberated from the ego and to emerge consciously into the Divine Presence which is at the centre of our being, in full light, in peace and joy, free at last from the sufferings imposed upon us by the ego. It is the ego which changes all the contacts of life into suffering, it is the ego which prevents us from being conscious of the Divine Presence within us and from becoming His calm, strong and happy instruments.

Let us make a complete offering of this ego with all its desires to the Divine, let us be confident and wait for the liberation that is sure to come.

9 March 1970

379 – Mankind has used two powerful weapons to destroy its own powers and enjoyment, wrong indulgence and wrong abstinence.

380 – Our mistake has been and is always to flee from the ills of Paganism to asceticism as a remedy and from the ills of asceticism back to Paganism. We swing for ever between two false opposites.

381 – It is well not to be too loosely playful in one's games or too grimly serious in one's life and works. We seek in both a playful freedom and a serious order.

Excess in any direction is a violence; and only in peace, poise and harmony can the truth be discovered and lived.

10 March 1970

382 – For nearly forty years behind the wholly good I was weakly in constitution; I suffered constantly from the smaller and the greater ailments and mistook this curse for a burden that Nature had laid upon me. When I renounced the aid of medicines, then they began to depart from me like disappointed parasites. Then only I understood what a mighty force was the natural health within me and how much mightier yet the Will and Faith exceeding mind which God meant to be the divine support of our life in this body.

All the circumstances of life are arranged to teach us that, beyond mind, faith in the Divine Grace gives us the strength to go through all trials, to overcome all weaknesses and find the contact with the Divine Consciousness which gives us not only peace and joy but also physical balance and good health.

11 March 1970

383 – Machinery is necessary to modern humanity because of our incurable barbarism. If we must encase ourselves

in a bewildering multitude of comforts and trappings, we must needs do without Art and its methods; for to dispense with simplicity and freedom is to dispense with beauty. The luxury of our ancestors was rich and even gorgeous, but never encumbered.

384 – I cannot give to the barbarous comfort and encumbered ostentation of European life the name of civilisation. Men who are not free in their souls and nobly rhythmical in their appointments are not civilised.

385 – Art in modern times and under European influence has become an excrescence upon life or an unnecessary menial; it should have been its chief steward and indispensable arranger.

So long as the mind governs life with the presumptuous certitude that it knows, how can the reign of the Divine be established?

12 March 1970

DISEASE AND MEDICAL SCIENCE

To be cured is good, but to avoid being ill is better.
The Mother

386 – Disease is needlessly prolonged and ends in death oftener than is inevitable, because the mind of the patient supports and dwells upon the disease of his body.

How absolutely true!

387 – Medical Science has been more a curse to mankind than a blessing. It has broken the force of epidemics and unveiled a marvellous surgery; but, also, it has weakened the natural health of man and multiplied individual diseases; it has implanted fear and dependence in the mind and body; it has taught our health to repose not on natural soundness but a rickety and distasteful crutch compact from the mineral and vegetable kingdoms.

388 – The doctor aims a drug at a disease; sometimes it hits, sometimes misses. The misses are left out of account, the hits treasured up, reckoned and systematised into a science.

Wonderful!

389 – We laugh at the savage for his faith in the medicine man; but how are the civilised less superstitious who have faith in the doctors? The savage finds that when a certain incantation is repeated, he often recovers from a certain disease; he believes. The civilised patient finds that when he doses himself according to a certain prescription, he often recovers from a certain disease; he believes. Where is the difference?

One could say in conclusion that it is the faith of the patient which gives the remedy its power to heal.
If men had an absolute faith in the healing power of Grace, they would perhaps avoid many illnesses.

13 March 1970

390 – The north-country Indian herdsman, attacked by fever, sits in the chill stream of a river for an hour or more and rises up free and healthy. If the educated man did the

same, he would perish, not because the same remedy in its nature kills one and cures another, but because our bodies have been fatally indoctrinated by the mind into false habits.

391 – It is not the medicine that cures so much as the patient's faith in the doctor and the medicine. Both are a clumsy substitute for the natural faith in one's own self-power which they have themselves destroyed.

392 – The healthiest ages of mankind were those in which there were the fewest material remedies.

393 – The most robust and healthy race left on earth were the African savages; but how long can they so remain after their physical consciousness has been contaminated by the mental aberrations of the civilised?

As always Sri Aurobindo's words are prophetic. For only when humanity is cured of its mental aberrations will it be able to manifest the supramental consciousness and recover the natural health which the mind has lost for it.

14 March 1970

394 – We ought to use the divine health in us to cure and prevent diseases; but Galen and Hippocrates and their tribe have given us instead an armoury of drugs and a barbarous Latin hocus-pocus as our physical gospel.

395 – Medical Science is well-meaning and its practitioners often benevolent and not seldom self-sacrificing; but when did the well-meaning of the ignorant save them from harm-doing?

396 – If all remedies were really and in themselves efficacious and all medical theories sound, how would that console us for our lost natural health and vitality? The upas-tree is sound in all its parts, but it is still an upas-tree.

397 – The spirit within us is the only all-efficient doctor and submission of the body to it the one true panacea.

398 – God within is infinite and self-fulfilling Will. Unappalled by the fear of death canst thou leave to Him, not as an experiment, with a calm and entire faith thy ailments? Thou shalt find that in the end He exceeds the skill of a million doctors.

399 – Health protected by twenty thousand precautions is the gospel of the doctor; but it is not God's evangel for the body, nor Nature's.

The sovereignty of mind has made humanity the slave of doctors and their remedies. And the result is that illnesses are increasing in number and seriousness.

The only true salvation for men is to escape from mental domination by opening to the Divine Influence which they will obtain through a total surrender.

15 March 1970

400 – Man was once naturally healthy and could revert to that primal condition if he were suffered; but Medical Science pursues our body with an innumerable pack of drugs and assails the imagination with ravening hordes of microbes.

401 – I would rather die and have done with it than spend life in defending myself against a phantasmal siege of

microbes. If that is to be barbarous, unenlightened, I embrace gladly my Cimmerian darkness.

402 – Surgeons save and cure by cutting and maiming. Why not rather seek to discover Nature's direct all-powerful remedies?

403 – It should take long for self-cure to replace medicine, because of the fear, self-distrust and unnatural physical reliance on drugs which Medical Science has taught to our minds and bodies and made our second nature.

We cannot counteract the harm done by mental faith in the need for drugs by any external measures. Only by escaping from the mental prison and emerging consciously into the light of the spirit, by a conscious union with the Divine, can we enable Him to give back to us the balance and health we have lost.

The supramental transformation is the only true remedy.

17 March 1970

404 – Medicine is necessary for our bodies in disease only because our bodies have learned the art of not getting well without medicines. Even so, one sees often that the moment Nature chooses for recovery is that in which the life is abandoned as hopeless by the doctors.

405 – Distrust of the curative power within us was our physical fall from Paradise. Medical Science and a bad heredity are the two angels of God who stand at the gates to forbid our return and re-entry.

406 – Medical Science to the human body is like a great Power which enfeebles a smaller State by its protection or like a benevolent robber who knocks his victim flat and

riddles him with wounds in order that he may devote his life to healing and serving the shattered body.

407 – Drugs often cure the body when they do not merely trouble or poison it, but only if their physical attack on the disease is supported by the force of the spirit; if that force can be made to work freely, drugs are superfluous.

Sri Aurobindo gives us a striking description of the nightmare in which we live, in order to awaken within us an unwearying aspiration towards the salvation that comes from the true consciousness and an exclusive faith in the Divine's omnipotence.

18 March 1970

Bhakti

(Devotion)

Fourth Period of Commentaries

(1969–1970)

Bhakti (Devotion)

Devotion is the key which opens the door to liberation.

The Mother

408 – I am not a Bhakta, for I have not renounced the world for God. How can I renounce what He took from me by force and gave back to me against my will? These things are too hard for me.

409 – I am not a Bhakta, I am not a Jnani, I am not a worker for the Lord. What am I then? A tool in the hands of my Master, a flute blown upon by the divine Herd-Boy, a leaf driven by the breath of the Lord.

410 – Devotion is not utterly fulfilled till it becomes action and knowledge. If thou pursuest after God and canst overtake Him, let Him not go till thou hast His reality. If thou hast hold of His reality, insist on having also His totality. The first will give thee divine knowledge, the second will give thee divine works and a free and perfect joy in the universe.

411 – Others boast of their love for God. My boast is that I did not love God; it was He who loved me and sought me out and forced me to belong to Him.

412 – After I knew that God was a woman, I learned something from far-off about love; but it was only when I became a woman and served my Master and Paramour that I knew love utterly.

On Thoughts and Aphorisms

> Sri Aurobindo had a genius for humour and all we can do is admire and remain silent.

20 March 1970

> *What does Sri Aurobindo mean by: "How can I renounce what He took from me by force and gave back to me against my will?"*
> *And also when he says: "After I knew that God was a woman..."?*

I cannot answer because, while he was in his body, he never told me anything about this.

If anyone knows the exact date on which he wrote this, it might be an indication.

Perhaps N could tell you when this was written, or whether Sri Aurobindo told him anything about it.[1]

413 – To commit adultery with God is the perfect experience for which the world was created.

I do not understand this aphorism.

This is the most perfect way in which Sri Aurobindo, with his marvellous sense of humour, could ridicule human morality. This sentence is a whole satire in itself.

21 March 1970

414 – To fear God really is to remove oneself to a distance from Him, but to fear Him in play gives an edge to utter delightfulness.

---

[1] According to the information given to Mother, these Aphorisms were written shortly after Sri Aurobindo's arrival in Pondicherry.

415 – The Jew invented the God-fearing man; India the God-knower and God-lover.

416 – The servant of God was born in Judaea, but he came to maturity among the Arabs. India's joy is in the servant-lover.

417 – Perfect love casts out fear; but still keep thou some tender shadow and memory of the exile and it will make the perfection more perfect.

418 – Thy soul has not tasted God's entire delight, if it has never had the joy of being His enemy, opposing His designs and engaging with Him in mortal combat.

419 – If you cannot make God love you, make Him fight you. If He will not give you the embrace of the lover, compel Him to give you the embrace of the wrestler.

420 – My soul is the captive of God, taken by Him in battle; it still remembers the war, though so far from it, with delight and alarm and wonder.

What does Sri Aurobindo mean by "the joy of being His enemy"?

Here too I have to say that I do not know exactly, because he never told me.

But I can tell you about my own experience. Until the age of about twenty-five, all I knew was the God of religions, God as men have created him, and I did not want him at any price. I denied his existence but with the certitude that if such a God did exist, I detested him.

When I was about twenty-five I discovered the inner God

and at the same time I learned that the God described by most Western religions is none other than the Great Adversary.

When I came to India, in 1914, and became acquainted with Sri Aurobindo's teaching, everything became very clear.

24 March 1970

421 – Most of all things on earth I hated pain till God hurt and tortured me; then it was revealed to me that pain is only a perverse and recalcitrant shape of excessive delight.

422 – There are four stages in the pain God gives to us; when it is only pain; when it is pain that causes pleasure; when it is pain that is pleasure; and when it is purely a fiercer form of delight.

423 – Even when one has climbed up into those levels of bliss where pain vanishes, it still survives disguised as intolerable ecstasy.

424 – When I was mounting upon ever higher crests of His joy, I asked myself whether there was no limit to the increase of bliss and almost I grew afraid of God's embraces.

I would like You to explain to me "the four stages of pain" which Sri Aurobindo speaks of here.

If Sri Aurobindo is speaking of moral pain, of any kind, I can say from experience that the four stages he mentions correspond to four states of consciousness which are the result of inner development and the degree of union with the divine consciousness which the individual consciousness has achieved. When the union is perfect, there only remains "a fiercer form of delight".

If it is the physical pain endured by the body, the experience does not follow such a clearly defined order; especially because union with the Divine most often causes the pain to disappear.

25 March 1970

425 – The next greatest rapture to the love of God, is the love of God in men; there, too, one has the joy of multiplicity.

426 – For monogamy may be the best for the body, but the soul that loves God in men dwells here always as the boundless and ecstatic polygamist; yet all the time — that is the secret — it is in love with only one being.

427 – The whole world is my seraglio and every living being and inanimate existence in it is the instrument of my rapture.

Someone who has experienced love for the Divine can no longer love anything but the Divine, and it is the Divine he loves in all those for whom he feels affection; besides, this is the best way to love, because in this way one can be a powerful help for others to become conscious of the Divine who manifests in them.

27 March 1970

428 – I did not know for some time whether I loved Krishna best or Kali; when I loved Kali, it was loving myself, but when I loved Krishna, I loved another, and still it was myself with whom I was in love. Therefore I came to love Krishna better even than Kali.

Sri Aurobindo always had his own way of saying things, always original and always unexpected.

29 March 1970

429 – What is the use of admiring Nature or worshipping her as a Power, a Presence and a goddess? What is the use, either, of appreciating her aesthetically or artistically? The secret is to enjoy her with the soul as one enjoys a woman with the body.

430 – When one has the vision in the heart, everything, Nature and Thought and Action, ideas and occupations and tastes and objects become the Beloved and are a source of ecstasy.

Nothing to say.

30 March 1970

431 – The philosophers who reject the world as Maya, are very wise and austere and holy; but I cannot help thinking sometimes that they are also just a little stupid and allow God to cheat them too easily.

432 – For my part, I think I have a right to insist on God giving Himself to me in the world as well as out of it. Why did He make it at all, if He wanted to escape that obligation?

433 – The Mayavadin talks of my Personal God as a dream and prefers to dream of Impersonal Being; the Buddhist puts that aside too as a fiction and prefers to dream of Nirvana and the bliss of nothingness. Thus all the dreamers are busy reviling each other's visions and parading their own as the panacea. What the soul utterly rejoices in, is for thought the ultimate reality.

Bhakti

434 – Beyond Personality the Mayavadin sees indefinable Existence; I followed him there and found my Krishna beyond in indefinable Personality.

As always, this is Sri Aurobindo's wonderful way of making clear to us the inanity of human assertions by which each one arrogantly denies anything that is not his own discovery or his own personal experience. Wisdom begins with the capacity to admit all theories, even the most contradictory.

1 April 1970

435 – When I first met Krishna, I loved Him as a friend and playmate till He deceived me; then I was indignant and could not forgive Him. Afterwards I loved Him as a lover and He still deceived me; I was again and much more indignant, but this time I had to pardon.

436 – After offending, He forced me to pardon Him not by reparation, but by committing fresh offences.

437 – So long as God tried to repair His offences against me, we went on periodically quarrelling; but when He found out His mistake, the quarrelling stopped, for I had to submit to Him entirely.

438 – When I saw others than Krishna and myself in the world, I kept secret God's doings with me; but since I began to see Him and myself everywhere, I have become shameless and garrulous.

In his writings, Sri Aurobindo had a genius for expressing the most extraordinary experiences in the most ordinary words,

On Thoughts and Aphorisms

thus giving the impression that his experiences are simple and obvious.

2 April 1970

439 — All that my Lover has, belongs to me. Why do you abuse me for showing off the ornaments He has given to me?

440 — My Lover took His crown and royal necklace from His head and neck and clothed me with them; but the disciples of the saints and the prophets abused me and said, "He is hunting after Siddhis."[2]

441 — I did my Lover's commands in the world and the will of my Captor; but they cried, "Who is this corruptor of youth, this disturber of morals?"

442 — If I cared even for your praise, O ye saints, if I cherished my reputation, O ye prophets, my Lover would never have taken me into His bosom and given me the freedom of His secret chambers.

443 — I was intoxicated with the rapture of my Lover and I threw the robe of the world from me even in the world's highways. Why should I care that the worldlings mock and the Pharisees turn their faces?

444 — To thy lover, O Lord, the railing of the world is wild honey and the pelting of stones by the mob is summer rain on the body. For is it not Thou that railest and peltest, and is it not Thou in the stones that strikest and hurtest me?

---

[2] Occult powers.

Bhakti

There is nothing to say. One can only bow before the perfection of the experience.

3 April 1970

445 – There are two things in God which men call evil, that which they cannot understand at all and that which they misunderstand and, possessing, misuse; it is only what they grope after half-vainly and dimly understand that they call good and holy. But to me all things in Him are lovable.

446 – They say, O my God, that I am mad because I see no fault in Thee; but if I am indeed mad with Thy love, I do not wish to recover my sanity.

447 – "Errors, falsehoods, stumblings!" they cry. How bright and beautiful are Thy errors, O Lord! Thy falsehoods save Truth alive; by Thy stumblings the world is perfected.

448 – Life, Life, Life, I hear the passions cry; God, God, God, is the soul's answer. Unless thou seest and lovest Life as God only, then is Life itself a sealed joy to thee.

449 – "He loves her," the senses say; but the soul says, "God, God, God." That is the all-embracing formula of existence.

In this way Sri Aurobindo reveals and formulates the secret of existence. All that remains is to understand and live it.

4 April 1970

On Thoughts and Aphorisms

450 – If thou canst not love the vilest worm and the foulest of criminals, how canst thou believe that thou hast accepted God in thy spirit?

451 – To love God, excluding the world, is to give Him an intense but imperfect adoration.

452 – Is love only a daughter or handmaid of jealousy? If Krishna loves Chandrabali,[3] why should I not love her also?

453 – Because thou lovest God only, thou art apt to claim that He should love thee rather than others; but this is a false claim contrary to right and the nature of things. For He is the One, but thou art of the many. Rather become one in heart and soul with all beings, then there will be none in the world but thou alone for Him to love.

454 – My quarrel is with those who are foolish enough not to love my Lover, not with those who share His love with me.

455 – In those whom God loves, have delight; on those whom He pretends not to love, take pity.

This is the most charming criticism one can make of jealousy and also the best way to cure it by overcoming the limits of the ego and by uniting with the Divine Love which is eternal and universal.

6 April 1970

---

[3] Sri Krishna loved Radha best among the *gopis*, but he loved Chandrabali and the other *gopis* also.

456 – Dost thou hate the atheist because he does not love God? Then shouldst thou be disliked because thou dost not love God perfectly.

457 – There is one thing especially in which creeds and churches surrender themselves to the devil, and that is in their anathemas. When the priest chants Anathema Maranatha, then I see a devil praying.[4]

458 – No doubt, when the priest curses, he is crying to God; but it is the God of anger and darkness to whom he devotes himself along with his enemy; for as he approaches God, so shall God receive him.

459 – I was much plagued by Satan, until I found that it was God who was tempting me; then the anguish of him passed out of my soul for ever.

460 – I hated the devil and was sick with his temptations and tortures; and I could not tell why the voice in his departing words was so sweet that when he returned often and offered himself to me, it was with sorrow I refused him. Then I discovered it was Krishna at His tricks and my hate was changed into laughter.

461 – They explained the evil in the world by saying that Satan had prevailed against God; but I think more proudly of my Beloved. I believe that nothing is done but by His will in heaven or hell, on earth or on the waters.

In the Supreme, opposites are reconciled and complement each other. It is division in the manifestation which has made them

---

[4] Alternative reading: devil worshipper.

into opposites; but once one's consciousness is united to the Divine Consciousness, opposition disappears.

7 April 1970

462 – In our ignorance we are like children proud of our success in walking erect and unaided and too eager to be aware of the mother's steadying touch on the shoulder. When we wake, we look back and see that God was leading and upholding us always.

463 – At first whenever I fell back into sin, I used to weep and rage against myself and against God for having suffered it. Afterwards it was as much as I could dare to ask, "Why hast thou rolled me again in the mud, O my playfellow?" Then even that came to my mind to seem too bold and presumptuous; I could only get up in silence, look at him out of the corner of my eyes — and clean myself.

So long as man prides himself on his virtue, the Supreme Lord will make him fall into sin to teach him the necessity of modesty.

8 April 1970

464 – God has so arranged life that the world is the soul's husband; Krishna its divine paramour. We owe a debt of service to the world and are bound to it by a law, a compelling opinion, and a common experience of pain and pleasure, but our heart's worship and our free and secret joy are for our Lover.

465 – The joy of God is secret and wonderful; it is a mystery and a rapture at which common sense makes mouths of mockery; but the soul that has once tasted it, can

Bhakti

never renounce, whatever worldly disrepute, torture and affliction it may bring us.

For the moment, the world still seems to be in contradiction with the pure and luminous divine joy; but a day will come when the world too will manifest this joy. This is what we must prepare it for.

9 April 1970

466 – God, the world Guru, is wiser than thy mind; trust Him and not that eternal self-seeker and arrogant sceptic.

467 – The sceptic mind doubts always because it cannot understand, but the faith of the God-lover persists in knowing although it cannot understand. Both are necessary to our darkness, but there can be no doubt which is the mightier. What I cannot understand now, I shall some day master, but if I lose faith and love, I fall utterly from the goal which God has set before me.

468 – I may question God, my guide and teacher, and ask Him, "Am I right or hast Thou in thy love and wisdom suffered my mind to deceive me?" Doubt thy mind, if thou wilt, but doubt not that God leads thee.

Life is given to us to find the Divine and unite with Him.
The mind tries to persuade us that it is not so. Shall we believe this liar?

10 April 1970

469 – Because thou wert given at first imperfect conceptions about God, now thou ragest and deniest Him. Man, dost thou doubt thy teacher because he gave not thee

the whole of knowledge at the beginning? Study rather that imperfect truth and put it in its place, so that thou mayst pass on safely to the wider knowledge that is now opening before thee.

470 – This is how God in His love teaches the child soul and the weakling, taking them step by step and withholding the vision of His ultimate and yet unattainable mountain-tops. And have we not all some weakness? Are we not all in His sight but as little children?

471 – This I have seen that whatever God has withheld from me, He withheld in His love and wisdom. Had I grasped it then, I would have turned some great good into a great poison. Yet sometimes when we insist, He gives us poison to drink that we may learn to turn from it and taste with knowledge His ambrosia and His nectar.

When man becomes a little wiser, he will not complain about anything and will take the things the Divine sends him as a manifestation of His all-compassionate Grace.
The more surrendered we are, the more we shall understand.
The more grateful we are, the happier we shall be.
11 April 1970

472 – Even the atheist ought now to be able to see that creation marches towards some infinite and mighty purpose which evolution in its very nature supposes. But infinite purpose and fulfilment presupposes an infinite wisdom that prepares, guides, shapes, protects and justifies. Revere then that Wisdom and worship it with thoughts in thy soul if not with incense in a temple, and even though thou deny it the heart of infinite Love and the mind of infinite self-effulgence. Then though thou

know it not, it is still Krishna whom thou reverest and worshippest.

Beyond words, beyond thoughts, the Supreme Presence makes itself felt and compels our wonder.
Let us beware of all mental constructions that limit and distort. Let us strive to keep the contact pure.

12 April 1970

473 – The Lord of Love has said, "They who follow after the Unknowable and Indefinable, follow after Me and I accept them." He has justified by His word the Illusionist and the Agnostic. Why then, O devotee, dost thou rail at him whom thy Master has accepted?

To the Divine Vision, all sincere human aspirations are acceptable, whatever diversity or even apparent contradiction there may be in their forms.
And all of them together are not enough to express the Divine Reality.

13 April 1970

474 – Calvin, who justified eternal Hell, knew not God but made one terrible mask of Him His eternal reality. If there were an unending Hell, it could only be a seat of unending rapture; for God is Ananda and than the eternity of His bliss there is no other eternity.

475 – Dante, when he said that God's perfect love created eternal Hell, wrote perhaps wiselier than he knew; for from stray glimpses I have sometimes thought there is a Hell where our souls suffer aeons of intolerable ecstasy and wallow as if for ever in the utter embrace of Rudra, the sweet and terrible.

On Thoughts and Aphorisms

The divine splendours are too marvellous for human littleness, which finds it hard to bear them, and an eternity of delight may well be intolerable for a human being.

14 April 1970

476 – Discipleship to God the Teacher, sonship to God the Father, tenderness of God the Mother, clasp of the hand of the divine Friend, laughter and sport with our Comrade and boy Playfellow, blissful servitude to God the Master, rapturous love of our divine Paramour, these are the seven beatitudes of life in the human body. Canst thou unite all these in a single supreme and rainbow-hued relation? Then hast thou no need of any heaven and thou exceedest the emancipation of the Adwaitin.

There is nothing to add. It is a perfect programme. It only remains for us to realise it.

15 April 1970

477 – When will the world change into the model of heaven? When all mankind becomes boys and girls together with God revealed as Krishna and Kali, the happiest boy and strongest girl of the crowd, playing together in the gardens of Paradise. The Semitic Eden was well enough, but Adam and Eve were too grown up and its God Himself too old and stern and solemn for the offer of the Serpent to be resisted.

478 – The Semites have afflicted mankind with the conception of a God who is a stern and dignified king and solemn judge and knows not mirth. But we who have seen Krishna, know Him for a boy fond of play and a child full of mischief and happy laughter.

Bhakti

479 – A God who cannot smile could not have created this humorous universe.

Ridicule is the strongest weapon against the powers of falsehood. With a single sentence, Sri Aurobindo annihilates the power of one of these man-made gods.

17 April 1970

480 – God took a child to fondle him in His bosom of delight; but the mother wept and would not be consoled because her child no longer existed.

481 – When I suffer from pain or grief or mischance, I say, "So, my old Playfellow, thou hast taken again to bullying me," and I sit down to possess the pleasure of the pain, the joy of the grief, the good fortune of the mischance; then He sees He is found out and takes His ghosts and bugbears away from me.

With sparkling humour Sri Aurobindo endeavours to make us understand the falsehood of the ordinary human consciousness and the luminous and all-powerful joy of the Divine Consciousness we must acquire.

18 April 1970

482 – The seeker after divine knowledge finds in the description of Krishna stealing the robes of the Gopis one of the deepest parables of God's ways with the soul, the devotee a perfect rendering in divine act of his heart's mystic experiences, the prurient and the Puritan (two faces of one temperament) only a lustful story. Men bring what they have in themselves and see it reflected in the Scripture.

483 – My lover took away my robe of sin and I let it fall, rejoicing; then he plucked at my robe of virtue, but I was ashamed and alarmed and prevented him. It was not till he wrested it from me by force that I saw how my soul had been hidden from me.

Let us drop our robe of virtue so that we may be ready for the Truth.[5]

22 April 1970

484 – Sin is a trick and a disguise of Krishna to conceal Himself from the gaze of the virtuous. Behold, O Pharisee, God in the sinner, sin in thyself purifying thy heart; clasp thy brother.

As always, in his striking and humorous way, Sri Aurobindo tells us that the Divine truth is above both virtue and sin.

19 April 1970

485 – Love of God, charity towards men is the first step towards perfect wisdom.

486 – He who condemns failure and imperfection, is condemning God; he limits his own soul and cheats his own vision. Condemn not, but observe Nature, help and heal thy brothers and strengthen by sympathy their capacities and their courage.

487 – Love of man, love of woman, love of things, love of thy neighbour, love of thy country, love of animals, love of humanity are all the love of God reflected in these living

---

[5] Oral reply.

images. So love and grow mighty to enjoy all, to help all and to love for ever.

488 – If there are things that absolutely refuse to be transformed or remedied into God's more perfect image, they may be destroyed with tenderness in the heart, but ruthlessness in the smiting. But make sure first that God has given thee thy sword and thy mission.

489 – I should love my neighbour not because he is neighbourhood, — for what is there in neighbourhood and distance? nor because the religions tell me he is my brother, — for where is the root of that brotherhood? but because he is myself. Neighbourhood and distance affect the body, the heart goes beyond them. Brotherhood is of blood or country or religion or humanity, but when self-interest clamours what becomes of this brotherhood? It is only by living in God and turning mind and heart and body into the image of his universal unity that that deep, disinterested and unassailable love becomes possible.

All the human reasons that are given for solidarity and mutual love are of little value and also of little effect. Only by becoming conscious of the Divine and uniting with Him can one attain and realise true Unity.

20 April 1970

490 – When I live in Krishna, then ego and self-interest vanish and only God himself can qualify my love bottomless and illimitable.

491 – Living in Krishna, even enmity becomes a play of love and the wrestling of brothers.

492 – To the soul that has hold of the highest beatitude, life cannot be an evil or a sorrowful illusion; rather all life becomes the rippling love and laughter of a divine Lover and Playfellow.

To know how to keep the Divine contact in all circumstances is the secret of beatitude.

21 April 1970

493 – Canst thou see God as the bodiless Infinite and yet love Him as a man loves his mistress? Then has the highest truth of the Infinite been revealed to thee. Canst thou also clothe the Infinite in one secret embraceable body and see Him seated in each and all of these bodies that are visible and sensible? Then has its widest and profoundest truth come also into thy possession.

494 – Divine Love has simultaneously a double play, an universal movement, deep, calm and bottomless like the nether Ocean, which broods upon the whole world and each thing that is in it as upon a level bed with an equal pressure, and a personal movement, forceful, intense and ecstatic like the dancing surface of the same Ocean, which varies the height and force of its billows and chooses the objects it shall fall upon with the kiss of its foam and spray and the clasp of its engulfing waters.

To make himself understood, Sri Aurobindo uses images that are accessible to everyone; but the marvels of Union infinitely exceed these human images.

22 April 1970

495 – I used to hate and avoid pain and resent its infliction; but now I find that had I not so suffered, I would not now possess, trained and perfected, this infinitely and multitudinously sensible capacity of delight in my mind, heart and body. God justifies Himself in the end even when He has masked Himself as a bully and a tyrant.

496 – I swore that I would not suffer from the world's grief and the world's stupidity and cruelty and injustice and I made my heart as hard in endurance as the nether millstone and my mind as a polished surface of steel. I no longer suffered, but enjoyment had passed away from me. Then God broke my heart and ploughed up my mind. I rose through cruel and incessant anguish to a blissful painlessness and through sorrow and indignation and revolt to an infinite knowledge and a settled peace.

It is the same lesson that the Supreme Lord wants to teach the body which He is transforming.

23 April 1970

497 – When I found that pain was the reverse side and the training of delight, I sought to heap blows on myself and multiply suffering in all my members; for even God's tortures seemed to me slow and slight and inefficient. Then my Lover had to stay my hand and cry, "Cease; for my stripes are enough for thee."

498 – The self-torture of the old monks and penitents was perverse and stupid; yet was there a secret soul of knowledge behind their perversities.

499 – God is our wise and perfect Friend; because He knows when to smite as well as when to fondle, when to slay us no less than when to save and to succour.

There is only one true wisdom, the wisdom of the Supreme Lord. Thus, to surrender all personal will and to want only what the Divine wants, is the only way to be truly wise.

24 April 1970

500 – The divine Friend of all creatures conceals His friendliness in the mask of an enemy till He has made us ready for the highest heavens; then, as in Kurukshetra, the terrible form of the Master of strife, suffering and destruction is withdrawn and the sweet face, the tenderness, the oft-clasped body of Krishna shine out on the shaken soul and purified eyes of his eternal comrade and playmate.

501 – Suffering makes us capable of the full force of the Master of Delight; it makes us capable also to bear the other play of the Master of Power. Pain is the key that opens the gates of strength; it is the high-road that leads to the city of beatitude.

502 – Yet, O soul of man, seek not after pain, for that is not His will, seek after His joy only; as for suffering, it will come to thee surely in His providence as often and as much as is needed for thee. Then bear it that thou mayst find out at last its heart of rapture.

503 – Neither do thou inflict pain, O man, on thy fellow; God alone has the right to inflict pain; or those have it whom He has commissioned. But deem not fanatically, as did Torquemada, that thou art one of these.

Bhakti

Never forget that so long as you are capable of preference in your relations with life and men, you cannot be a pure and perfect instrument of the Divine.

28 April 1970

504 – In former times there was a noble form of asseveration for souls compact merely of force and action, "As surely as God liveth." But for our modern needs another asseveration would suit better, "As surely as God loveth."

In our sorrowful age, almost withered by the excessive domination of the intellect, nothing can be at once more necessary and more precious than Divine Love.

29 April 1970

505 – Science is chiefly useful to the God-lover and the God-knower because it enables him to understand in detail and admire the curious wonders of His material workmanship. The one learns and cries, "Behold how the Spirit has manifested itself in matter"; the other, "Behold, the touch of my Lover and Master, the perfect Artist, the hand omnipotent."

How can one be of service[6] to the Divine since we exist by Him alone — all we can do is to clumsily return to Him a little of all that He has given us.

30 April 1970

506 – O Aristophanes of the universe, thou who watchest thy world and laughest sweetly to thyself, wilt thou not let

---

[6] The translation used was based on a text which read "Service" instead of "Science".

me too see with divine eyes and share in thy worldwide laughters?

No doubt one must have a vision as total as the Divine Vision to be able to laugh at this world as it is.

1 May 1970

507 – Kalidasa says in a daring image that the snowrocks of Kailasa are Shiva's loud world-laughters piled up in utter whiteness and pureness on the mountain-tops. It is true; and when their image falls on the heart, then the world's cares melt away like the clouds below into their real nothingness.

Human science makes very exact observations; but the field is open to imagine the true causes — why not occult causes?

2 May 1970

508 – The strangest of the soul's experiences is this, that it finds, when it ceases to care for the image and threat of troubles, then the troubles themselves are nowhere to be found in one's neighbourhood. It is then that we hear from behind those unreal clouds God laughing at us.

Lord, and when You want the image to change into your likeness, what do You do?

4 May 1970

I did not understand what You wrote yesterday.

What Sri Aurobindo calls "the image" is the physical body. So I asked the Lord what He does when He wants to transform the physical body, and last night He gave me two visions in answer.

One concerned the liberation of the body consciousness from all the conventions regarding death; and in the other He showed me what the supramental body will be. You see that I did well to ask Him!

9 May 1970

509 – Has thy effort succeeded, O thou Titan? Dost thou sit, like Ravana and Hiranyakashipou,[7] served by the gods and the world's master? But that which thy soul was really hunting after, has escaped from thee.

510 – Ravana's mind thought it was hungering after universal sovereignty and victory over Rama; but the aim his soul kept its vision fixed upon all the time was to get back to its heaven as soon as possible and be again God's menial. Therefore, as the shortest way, it hurled itself against God in a furious clasp of enmity.

511 – The greatest of joys is to be, like Narada, the slave of God; the worst of Hells being abandoned of God, to be the world's master. That which seems nearest to the ignorant conception of God, is the farthest from him.

512 – God's servant is something; God's slave is greater.

Sri Aurobindo gives us the true way to understand the Scriptures, which thus become universal symbols.

12 May 1970

513 – To be master of the world would indeed be supreme felicity, if one were universally loved; but for that one

---

[7] Two demon kings.

would have to be at the same time the slave of all humanity.

514 – After all, when thou countest up thy long service to God, thou wilt find thy supreme work was the flawed and little good thou didst in love for humanity.

That is why, rather than to serve, it is better to belong totally, absolutely to the Divine.

13 May 1970

In order to belong absolutely and totally to the Divine, isn't it necessary to begin by serving the Divine?

Certainly, to place all one's work at the service of the Divine is a very good way of approach, but it doesn't go much further than what Sri Aurobindo describes, and for some it is not satisfying.

14 May 1970

515 – There are two works that are perfectly pleasing to God in his servant; to sweep in silent adoration His temple-floors and to fight in the world's battlefield for His divine consummation in humanity.

516 – He who has done even a little good to human beings, though he be the worst of sinners, is accepted by God in the ranks of His lovers and servants. He shall look upon the face of the Eternal.

Sri Aurobindo's effort was always directed towards liberating his disciples or even his readers from all preconceptions, all conventional morality.

15 May 1970

517 – O fool of thy weakness, cover not God's face from thyself by a veil of awe, approach Him not with a suppliant weakness. Look! thou wilt see on His face not the solemnity of the King and Judge, but the smile of the Lover.

518 – Until thou canst learn to grapple with God as a wrestler with his comrade, thy soul's strength shall always be hid from thee.

Wouldn't it be good, once and for all, to get rid of all our limitations and weaknesses, if we truly want to draw close to the Divine?

16 May 1970

519 – Sumbha[8] first loved Kali with his heart and body, then was furious with her and fought her, at last prevailed against her, seized her by the hair and whirled her thrice round him in the heavens; the next moment he was slain by her. These are the Titan's four strides to immortality and of them all the last is the longest and mightiest.

I do not understand the meaning of "the Titan's four strides to immortality".

Whatever the nature of an individual may be, ultimately, in one way or another, whether he fights him or loves him, the End is always the Divine.

17 May 1970

---

[8] A demon king.

520 – Kali is Krishna revealed as dreadful Power and wrathful Love. She slays with her furious blows the self in body, life and mind in order to liberate it as spirit eternal.

Shall we complain when we see this helpless little "ego" disappearing and giving way to a luminous spark capable of understanding the universe?

21 May 1970

521 – Our parents fell, in the deep Semitic apologue, because they tasted the fruit of the tree of good and evil. Had they taken at once of the tree of eternal life, they would have escaped the immediate consequence; but God's purpose in humanity would have been defeated. His wrath is our eternal advantage.

Sri Aurobindo is trying to make us understand how the limitations of our vision prevent us from perceiving the Divine Wisdom.

22 May 1970

522 – If Hell were possible, it would be the shortest cut to the highest heaven. For verily God loveth.

523 – God drives us out every Eden that we may be forced to travel through the desert to a diviner Paradise. If thou wonder why should that parched and fierce transit be necessary, then art thou befooled by thy mind and hast not studied thy soul behind and its dim desires and secret raptures.

When we no longer have any affinity with suffering and are

cured of all perverse attachment to it, the Divine will help us to discover that it conceals the supreme bliss.

23 May 1970

524 – A healthy mind hates pain; for the desire of pain that men sometimes develop in their minds is morbid and contrary to Nature. But the soul cares not for the mind and its sufferings any more than the iron-master for the pain of the ore in the furnace; it follows its own necessities and its own hunger.

The Supreme Lord alone should be the Master and it is He, as a rule, whom the psychic being obeys.

24 May 1970

525 – Indiscriminate compassion is the noblest gift of temperament, not to do even the least hurt to one living thing is the highest of all human virtues; but God practises neither. Is man therefore nobler and better than the All-loving?

526 – To find that saving a man's body or mind from suffering is not always for the good of either soul, mind or body, is one of the bitterest of experiences for the humanly compassionate.

To be conscious of the Divine Consciousness is the supreme fulfilment offered to human realisation; all the rest are only inessentials.

25 May 1970

527 – Human pity is born of ignorance and weakness; it is the slave of emotional impressions. Divine compassion understands, discerns and saves.

528 – Pity is sometimes a good substitute for love; but it is always no more than a substitute.

To understand the divine intention and to work for its fulfilment — isn't this the surest way to help humanity?

28 May 1970

529 – Self-pity is always born of self-love; but pity for others is not always born of love for its object. It is sometimes a self-regarding shrinking from the sight of pain; sometimes the rich man's contemptuous dole to the pauper. Develop rather God's divine compassion than human pity.

530 – Not pity that bites the heart and weakens the inner members, but a divine masterful and untroubled compassion and helpfulness is the virtue that we should encourage.

Can there be any greater misfortune than to live without knowing the Supreme Lord? And yet this almost universal ill rarely excites any pity. Because one who knows that he is suffering from it also knows that the cure depends on him alone — for the Lord's compassion is infinite.

1 June 1970

531 – Love and serve men, but beware lest thou desire their approbation. Obey rather God within thee.

532 – Not to have heard the voice of God and His angels is the world's idea of sanity.

533 – See God everywhere and be not frightened by masks. Believe that all falsehood is truth in the making or truth in the breaking, all failure an effectuality concealed, all weakness strength hiding itself from its own vision, all pain a secret and violent ecstasy. If thou believest firmly and unweariedly, in the end thou wilt see and experience the All-true, Almighty and All-blissful.

By tireless constancy in effort and faith, we can unite with the Divine Consciousness which is constant and perfect beatitude.

2 June 1970

534 – Human love fails by its own ecstasy, human strength is exhausted by its own effort, human knowledge throws a shadow that conceals half the globe of truth from its own sunlight; but divine knowledge embraces opposite truths and reconciles them, divine strength grows by the prodigality of its self-expenditure, divine love can squander itself utterly, yet never waste or diminish.

Can human love change into divine love, human strength into divine strength and human knowledge into divine knowledge?

There is only one love.

Human love is nothing but divine love perverted and distorted by the instrument through which it is expressed. The same holds true for strength and knowledge. In their essence they are eternal and unlimited. It is the limitations and deficiencies of human nature which distort them and alter them beyond recognition.

3 June 1970

535 – The rejection of falsehood by the mind seeking after truth is one of the chief causes why mind cannot attain to the settled, rounded and perfect truth; not to escape falsehood is the effort of divine mind, but to seize the truth which lies masked behind even the most grotesque or far-wandering error.

What is the "divine mind"?

What Sri Aurobindo calls the divine mind is the prototype of the mental function which is totally and perfectly surrendered to the Divine and works only under divine inspiration.
When a human being exists only by and for the Divine, his mind necessarily becomes a divine mind.

4 June 1970

536 – The whole truth about any object is a rounded and all-embracing globe which for ever circles around but never touches the one and only subject and object of knowledge, God.

537 – There are many profound truths which are like weapons dangerous to the unpractised wielder. Rightly handled, they are the most precious and potent in God's armoury.

One drop of true knowledge can create a revolution if it falls into a world of ignorance.

5 June 1970

538 – The obstinate pertinacity with which we cling to our meagre, fragmentary, night-besieged and grief-besieged individual existence even while the unbroken bliss of our universal life calls to us, is one of the most amazing of God's mysteries. It is only equalled by the infinite blindness with which we cast a shadow of our ego over the whole world and call that the universal being. These two darknesses are the very essence and potency of Maya.

Until, tired of the ignorance and stupidity of the ego, we lay ourselves at the feet of the Lord and ask Him to become the sole master.

6 June 1970

539 – Atheism is the shadow or dark side of the highest perception of God. Every formula we frame about God, though always true as a symbol, becomes false when we accept it as a sufficient formula. The Atheist and Agnostic come to remind us of our error.

540 – God's negations are as useful to us as His affirmations. It is He who as the Atheist denies His own existence for the better perfecting of human knowledge. It is not enough to see God in Christ and Ramakrishna and hear His words, we must see Him and hear Him also in Huxley and Haeckel.

All mental ways of knowing the Divine are incomplete and insufficient, even if we accept them all. Only a knowledge that is lived can give us a glimpse of the truth.

7 June 1970

On Thoughts and Aphorisms

541 – Canst thou see God in thy torturer and slayer even in thy moment of death or thy hours of torture? Canst thou see Him in that which thou art slaying, see and love even while thou slayest? Thou hast thy hand on the supreme knowledge. How shall he attain to Krishna who has never worshipped Kali?

All is the Divine and the Divine alone exists.

8 June 1970